Published by Abbeydale Press
An imprint of
Bookmart Ltd
Registered Number 2372865
Trading as Bookmart Ltd
Desford Road
Enderby
Leicester
LE19 4AD

ISBN 1-86147-057-6

Reprinted 2000, 2001, 2002

Editor: Philip de Ste. Croix

Production by Omnipress
Printed in China

Photographic credits

All illustrations courtesy of the author's collection except:
H.C. Casserley/R.M. Casserley collection: *pages 20, 31, 34, 35 left, 42,
43 lower, 45 lower, 57 upper, 67, 68 lower, 143 centre*
Paul Chancellor collection: *pages 23 upper, 44, 70*
Alec Ford/John Stretton collection: *page 36*
Tom Heavyside: *pages 12 right, 13, 15 upper*
Keith Lawrence: *pages 136, 164*
Michael Mensing: *pages 71 inset right, 85 upper, 170 right, 171*
Gavin Morrison: *pages 51 lower, 84, 152, 170 upper and lower left*
Museum of Science and Industry in Manchester: *page 6 upper*
L.A. Nixon: *pages 14, 15 lower, 21 upper, 22, 30 lower left
56, 71 main picture*
Robin Stewart-Smith: *page 21 lower*
John Stretton: *page 85 lower*
Jim Winkley: *pages 6 lower, 37, 69*

Contents

Introduction

The steam locomotive was pioneered in Britain and played a crucial role in creating today's world. As the predominant form of railway motive power for more than a century, it helped revolutionize commerce and society. Paradoxically, throughout this period, its basic form and the way it functioned remained unchanged. The locomotives built in China during the 1980s differed from *Rocket* of 1829 only in size, power and complexity. The same is true of the British locomotives built between 1825 and 1960 that constitute the heart of this book. Yet each one demonstrates how, out of that basic form, has come an extraordinary diversity.

After some experimentation, the fundamental principles of the steam locomotive were settled by the 1830s. The world over, less than 100 engines had been built when its final form was established. However, there were some very different ideas about how that form should evolve. For example, by 1850, American and British practice had significantly diverged, never to be reunited.

Additionally, with the expansion of the railway network came the need for specialized types of locomotive. To take an extreme instance, a 60ft-long express locomotive with 7ft-diameter driving wheels was clearly unsuitable for shunting wagons on a tightly curved track in a dockyard. Each, though, performed a valuable role, which is why, in these pages, the dock tanks and the humble industrial shunting engines have been given equal billing with the glamorous 'Kings', 'Coronations' and 'Britannias'.

Whatever criticisms are levelled at the steam locomotive, that it was inefficient, dirty and plain hard work, it was seldom other than an influence for good. It could also, as Victorian designers especially demonstrated, have style and nobility. Those who have worked with steam will tell you that each locomotive, not just each class, had its own character. That has undeniably contributed to its enduring appeal, forging loyalties that are still robustly championed by enthusiasts. So it is the locomotives – the standard gauge ones – with which today's steam lovers are most likely to be familiar that predominate here (The world of narrow-gauge steam merits a volume to itself!).

We are fortunate in Britain that, with some much-lamented exceptions, examples of our principal locomotive designs have been preserved. In a few cases, replicas have been constructed, so it is possible to compare Richard Trevithick's Coalbrookdale engine of 1803 with the last, and best of the modern era, the 9F 2-10-0 from 1954. Some of the more famous locomotives were saved by official bodies, but many more owe their survival to the

Above: The Albert Hall is one of the enduring symbols of the Victorian age, an age that also saw the building of Britain's great railway routes, among them Brunel's broad-gauge Great Western. GW replica Iron Duke *reminded Londoners of that age with demonstration runs in April 1985.*

tenacity of private groups or individuals. It is worth recalling that over 200 of the surviving standard-gauge engines in Britain were rescued from a South Wales scrapyard.

The steam locomotive has survived all such attempts to finish it off. After 1968, it was supposed to be confined to museums but, over 30 years later, it is possible to travel behind steam somewhere in Britain most days of the year. Most amazingly, two new main-line steam locomotives are being built. Appropriately enough, the most advanced project – the construction of Peppercorn A1 Pacific No60163 *Tornado* – is centred on that cradle of the steam age, Darlington, in County Durham. It is taking shape within sight of George Stephenson's *Locomotion No1*, the engine that in 1825 inaugurated the railway age.

Right: The last main-line steam locomotives designed in Britain were fittingly among the finest: British Railways' 251 9F 2-10-0s of 1954–60. Their primary role was heavy freight, as demonstrated by Crewe-built No92240.

Raising Steam

1800–1885

S&DR 'Locomotion' • L&MR 'Rocket'

L&MR No57 'Lion' • GWR 'Iron Duke'

L&NWR No3020 'Cornwall' • MR 156 class

GNR G class '8-foot Single'

LB&SCR A1/A1X class 'Terrier'

Black Hawthorn '12-inch Standard'

Haydock Foundries NoC 'Bellerophon'

L&NWR 'Precedent' • NER 1001 class 'Long Boiler'

NER 901 class 2-4-0 • MR 1377 class 'Half-Cab'

L&NWR 'Coal Tank' • Dock Tanks

LB&SCR B1 class 'Gladstone'

L&SWR 415 (0415) 'Radial Tank'

Wigan Coal & Iron Company 'Lindsay'

1800–1885

Raising Steam

Steam has been known as a source of power for over 2,000 years. A device using steam to rotate a sphere was made in Egypt during the 1st century BC. Centuries later, the growth of mining supplied a fresh stimulus to explore its potential. During the 18th century, stationary steam engines pumped water from flooded mineshafts. Two engineers, Thomas Savery and Thomas Newcomen, led the way, and one of Newcomen's engines, built in 1712, was the first practical application of the power derived from expanding steam within a cylinder.

The drawback of the Newcomen engine was its lack of efficiency, but this was transformed by a Scottish engineer, James Watt. Furthermore, in the mid-1770s, Watt demonstrated how to convert, through a system of gears, the up-and-down movement of the beam engine to rotary motion capable of turning wheels. However, Watt left it to others to pursue his work to its logical conclusion – the mobile steam engine, or locomotive.

Some claim the first steam-driven vehicle was built by a Jesuit missionary, Ferdinand Verbiest, and demonstrated in China during the 1680s. What is certain is that, in 1769, Nicholas-Joseph Cugnot, a French military engineer, unveiled a steam-powered wagon designed to pull field guns. The following year, Cugnot drove a second such wagon through the streets of Paris and achieved a speed of 9mph. Unfortunately, it not only ran out of steam at regular intervals, but the heavy front-mounted boiler made steering difficult. When the three-wheeler overturned negotiating a corner, Cugnot was arrested and his invention impounded. Like the steam-powered road coaches seen in both Britain and France during the second half of the 18th

Above: The Liverpool & Manchester Railway was promoted as a freight carrier to break the monopoly of the Lancashire canal companies. However, as this lithograph shows, the line was soon shared by passenger trains. By 1840, it had carried 5 million people.

century, Cugnot's wagon used steam at low pressure. This was their fundamental limitation. Sustained power was generated only by high-pressure steam and this, in turn, required a steam-raising vessel – a boiler – capable of withstanding such pressures.

On Christmas Eve, 1801, a strange vehicle travelled the hilly roads of Camborne, in Cornwall. At the helm was a local engineer who was usually employed maintaining steam pumping engines, Richard Trevithick. The significance of Trevithick's road carriage was its use of steam at high pressure, and that, in doing so, it did not – contrary to many predictions – explode! Trevithick continued his experiments and, in 1803, demonstrated a second steam carriage in London. However, Trevithick built another, far more significant, steam-powered machine that year. One feature distinguished it from its predecessors: it ran on rails.

Coalbrookdale, on the River Severn in Shropshire, was the heart of Britain's burgeoning iron-and-steel industry, and Trevithick used its facilities to manufacture this first railway locomotive. Fitted with flangeless wheels and a single cylinder mounted inside the boiler, the engine was intended to work at Coalbrookdale, but there is no record of it ever operating. It may simply have been too heavy for the 3ft 0in gauge plateway.

Trevithick's next locomotive, however, did show its potential. Arguably, 22 February 1804 was the day the railway age began. For the first time, a steam locomotive pulled a train along iron rails. This momentous event took place at the Penydarren ironworks, near Merthyr Tydfil, in South Wales, where Trevithick was employed as an engineer. The train consisted of wagons loaded with ten

Above: Timothy Hackworth's design of 0-6-0, with inclined cylinders driving on to the front coupled wheels, appeared in 1838. This survivor, Derwent, was built by Kitching & Co in Darlington in 1845 and is now displayed in the town's railway museum.

tons of iron, a further five empty wagons and an unknown number of trucks filled with 70 men. Trevithick's locomotive hauled its load nine-and-a-half miles at a steady speed of between 4mph and 5mph.

Both in working with high-pressure steam and using the blast of its exhaust to create a draught for the fire, the Penydarren engine laid down a template for future development. However, if Trevithick was anticipating a rush to adopt his invention, he was to be disappointed. In 1805, another locomotive employing Trevithick's ideas was notable in two respects: it was the first engine to have flanged wheels, and it introduced steam traction to north-east England. The machine was ordered by Wylam colliery in Northumberland and built across the Tyne, in Gateshead. Although, at five tons, it proved too heavy for the colliery's wagonway, Trevithick's engine inspired engineers working for mining companies in northern England, among them the Wylam-born George Stephenson.

Richard Trevithick's final attempt to interest a broader public in the steam locomotive came in 1808. His *Catch Me Who Can* pulled passengers around a circular track laid in Euston Square in London. Sadly, it was seen as little more than a curiosity and any serious interest evaporated when a rail broke and the engine overturned. Disillusioned, Trevithick abandoned his work on locomotives.

Further development was largely confined to collieries, but there was no eagerness to adopt this new form of traction while horses were both cheaper and more reliable. However, the world at large was changing. Britain's growth as an industrial and commercial power was hampered by inadequate transport links. Roads were poor, rivers slow, and canal owners used their monopoly to exploit their customers. Then came a change in transport economics that transformed the viability of the steam locomotive. One consequence of the Napoleonic Wars was a dramatic increase in the price of horse fodder. Colliery managers were forced to re-evaluate steam power, among them John Blenkinsop of the Middleton Colliery in Leeds. Coal from his pit travelled on a 3.2-mile-long wagonway to be loaded into barges, work which occupied 50 horses.

Mines had employed wagonways for centuries and, from around 1790, the use of iron wheels and iron rails was becoming commonplace. With this combination, an increase in adhesive force was accompanied by a reduction in resistance. Moreover, iron was stronger and more durable than wood. In 1811, the Middleton's Blenkinsop patented a rail that employed a toothed wheel and rack system, similar to those still employed on mountain railways. To work the line, Blenkinsop collaborated with the engineer Matthew Murray in designing a 2-2-2 locomotive whose centre pair of driving wheels was toothed. These engaged on the rack that was attached to the edge of the running rail.

The first run took place on 24 June 1812, with a load of eight wagons containing 25 tons of coal and 50 passengers. Thousands saw loads of up to 100 tons pulled along at around 3mph. A crucial advantage of Murray's locomotive was that, unlike its predecessors, it was not so heavy that it fractured the iron-plate rails. However, it was still capable of hauling heavy loads. Blenkinsop and Murray's achievement resulted in a further three engines being built, the first *commercially* successful locomotives.

Murray's Middleton colliery engines were among some 28 locomotives built in Britain between 1803 and 1823. Other significant machines included William Hedley's *Puffing Billy* and *Wylam Dilly* of 1813. Again Wylam colliery was the test-bed as Hedley demonstrated beyond doubt that simple wheel-on-rail adhesion was adequate for all normal loads and gradients. At nearby Killingworth colliery, in 1814, George Stephenson assembled his first locomotive, *Blücher*. Over the ensuing eight years, Stephenson built further engines, notably for Hetton colliery in County Durham.

The growth of these colliery railways, and the improving reliability of their locomotives, came to wider attention. Some years before, a commercial traveller from Nottingham, Thomas Gray, observed: 'Why are not these roads laid down all over England, and steam engines employed to convey goods and passengers along them, to supersede horsepower?' By the mid-1820s, many were echoing that view but problems remained to be solved before steam gained ascendancy.

Weight was the key. Locomotives were still too heavy for the cast-iron track but this was largely resolved through better techniques of rolling wrought iron rails. However, there remained the need to reduce the downforce exerted by vertical cylinders. These were part-and-parcel of the beam engine-type of operation adopted by early locomotives. Finally, if the locomotive was to become competitive, the relationship between the power exerted for a given weight had to be improved. All of these topics were addressed during the late 1820s. In 1825, George Stephenson's *Locomotion No1* became the first locomotive whose wheels were linked by coupling rods, a stronger and simpler means of linking axles than the chains or gear trains used up to that point. Timothy Hackworth's *Royal George* of 1827 was the first six-wheeled engine. Its longer wheelbase allowed a larger boiler to be fitted, and improved adhesion. It was also the first locomotive where the wheels were driven directly from the cylinders, without any intermediate gearing or levers.

Above: The Stephensons' 2-2-0 Planet *was built for the Liverpool & Manchester in 1830 and was the first locomotive with outside 'sandwich' frames and outside bearings. Its cylinders were enclosed within the smokebox. This replica dates from the 1990s.*

Above: The expansion of suburban railways bred a host of small, nippy tank locomotives, among them the Great Eastern Railway's 61 class 0-4-4T. Bound for Chingford, in north-east London, engine No178 was built in 1878 and lasted until 1905.

This was taken a step further by Stephenson with *Lancashire Witch*, an 0-4-0 constructed in 1828 for the Bolton & Leigh Railway. Here, for the first time, the wheels were driven directly from the piston rod working in a crosshead. At the same time, Stephenson was examining boiler efficiency. He was not alone in concluding that, because of the greater surface area, a boiler containing a large number of heat-conducting tubes would generate more steam than a single large-diameter tube.

The multi-tubular boiler was just one of the key features that brought success to the Stephensons' *Rocket* (the design was largely the work of George's son, Robert). The blast of the exhaust was used to draw the fire through the tubes. It had a water-jacketed firebox which accelerated the process of turning water into steam. Vertical cylinders had been replaced by ones inclined at 40 degrees to the horizontal, and the driving mechanism had been simplified, with the cranks acting directly on the driving wheels. *Rocket* also resolved the power-to-weight conundrum, proving it could haul loads three times its weight.

Its triumph at the Rainhill trials of October 1829 made *Rocket* the prototype for future locomotive design. However, in contrast to the slow progress of the previous three decades, improvements and refinements now came rapidly. Differences were apparent between *Rocket* and the locomotives that Robert Stephenson delivered to the Liverpool & Manchester Railway less than a year later. One of these, *Phoenix*, had a smokebox inserted between the chimney blastpipe and the boiler. It became a universal feature of all locomotives. Stephenson's *Planet*-type 2-2-0 was noteworthy for being the first locomotive built with outside iron-and-wood 'sandwich' frames and outside bearings, characteristics that became a staple of British design practice.

Equally influential was Edward Bury's 0-4-0 *Liverpool* with its bar frames, inside cylinders and 'haycock' firebox. Inside cylinders became standard in British locomotives of the period, most importantly the classic 'single-wheeler' 2-2-2 patented by Robert Stephenson in 1833. This format was widely adopted both in Britain and abroad and became

the basis for perhaps the most famous locomotives of the 1840s and 1850s – Daniel Gooch's designs for the broad gauge Great Western Railway. In 1833, Stephenson was also responsible for introducing another British locomotive institution, the inside-cylinder 0-6-0 goods engine. Despite their less-than-easy maintenance, inside cylinders brought greater stability and were better protected from cold air, so discouraging steam from condensing.

By 1835, the characteristic form of the locomotive was established. The boiler, firebox and smokebox were mounted on frames that also supported the cylinders. The cylinders drove on to large driving wheels, while smaller wheels supplied additional support, helped distribute the engine weight, and guided the locomotive on curved track. The one thing these first locomotives did not share with their later counterparts was coal as fuel. Early boilers were unsuitable for coal-burning and instead used coke, a fuel produced as a residue from the manufacture of coal gas. However, when shortages inflated the price of coke, designers were impelled to improve the combustion processes within fireboxes to allow the use of coal.

Below boiler level, advances in metallurgy assisted the building of bigger and more powerful locomotives. Tyre wear had discouraged the building of engines with coupled

Common Steam Locomotive Wheel Arrangements

Wheels leading/driving/trailing	Type	Name (if applicable)
○●	2-2-0	–
○●○	2-2-2	Patentee
●●	0-4-0	–
●●○	0-4-2	–
○●●	2-4-0	–
○○●○	4-2-2	–
○○●	4-2-0	–
○○●●	4-4-0	–
○○●●○	4-4-2	Atlantic
●●●	0-6-0	–
●●●○	0-6-2	–
○●●●	2-6-0	Mogul
○●●●○	2-6-2	Prairie
○●●●○○	2-6-4	–
○○●●●○○	4-6-4	Hudson
○○●●●○	4-6-2	Pacific
●●●●	0-8-0	–
○●●●●	2-8-0	Consolidation
○●●●●○	2-8-2	Mikado
●●●●●	0-10-0	Decapod
○●●●●●	2-10-0	–

In the Whyte system, employed in Britain and North America, steam locomotives are described by the number of leading, driving and trailing wheels they have (in Continental Europe and elsewhere, the practice is to count the number of axles). Above are the most common British wheel arrangements, together with their nicknames, mostly of American origin. The 4-6-2 or *Pacific*, for example, has a four-wheel leading bogie, six coupled driving wheels and a two-wheel trailing truck.

Locomotive Classifications

Where appropriate, locomotives have been categorized by the classification system employed by British Railways, itself derived from LMSR practice. In this system, locomotives were classified according to their principal role (P for passenger, F for freight and MT for mixed traffic – locomotives equally suitable for passenger or freight duties). Additionally, to indicate the available power of the locomotive, these letters were preceded by a numerical index. In January 1951, this was expanded to eight ratings for passenger engines (0P to 8P) and nine for freight (0F to 9F), each beginning with the least powerful. Mixed traffic classes ranged from 2MT to 7MT. Aside from their primary use, many locomotives were given a secondary rating for other work. The LNER A4 Pacifics, for example, were rated as 6F for freight duties, although their intended role was express passenger, hence their principal rating of 8P. This applied equally to classes primarily built for goods work; another Gresley design, the J39 0-6-0 was classified as 5F but additionally rated as 4P for passenger trains. Since 'P' always preceded 'F' in the BR system, it was described as 4P5F. Locomotives featured here without a power classification either did not enter British Railways service, or were built for private industrial users.

About the specification tables

Each of the locomotive classes featured in this book is accompanied by a specification table listing the key dates and details of its design. Unfortunately, for some older locomotives, certain information is now unavailable. Among the weights and dimensions quoted, only one demands further elaboration – tractive effort.

Tractive effort is a measure of the pulling power of a locomotive, the effort it can exert in moving a train from a state of rest. Drawbar tractive effort is the force exerted at the coupling between the locomotive and the train. Here, however, we refer to cylinder tractive effort and the energy exerted at the point of the driving wheel treads.

Tractive effort is a theoretical figure expressed in pounds (lb) force and is usually calculated on the basis of 85 per cent of full boiler pressure being applied to the pistons. This reduction takes into account the loss of pressure between the boiler and the cylinders. The formula for calculating the maximum tractive effort exerted in the cylinders of a simple expansion (i.e. non-compound) locomotive is:

$$TE = \frac{N \times D^2 \times S \times 0.85P}{2 \qquad W}$$

N = number of cylinders.
D = cylinder diameter.
S = piston stroke.
W = driving wheel diameter (all in inches).
P = boiler working pressure in pounds (lb) force.

driving wheels. The substitution of steel for wrought iron in the manufacture of wheel tyres greatly reduced wear. Steel tyres lasted for up to 300,000 miles, compared to the 60,000 of wrought iron. Further incentive to build more complex machines came with improvements in lubrication and in the valve gears that controlled admission of steam to the cylinders. The Stephenson-Howe link motion, introduced in 1841, allowed expansive working in the cylinders. This increased the power developed from a given volume of steam.

Other refinements came from overseas, among them the steam injector. Up to 1860, the sole means of feeding water into a boiler was by pumps driven off an axle, or the crosshead. These, however, only operated while the locomotive was in motion. The injector invented by the

French balloonist, Henri Giffard, forced water into the boiler even while the locomotive was stationary.

On a general level, locomotives were now being designed for specific duties. Large-wheeled 4-2-2s, 4-2-0s and 2-2-2s worked express passenger trains. The 2-4-0 gained popularity as it combined speed with the adhesion offered by coupled wheels. Tank locomotives that carried their fuel on board and dispensed with tenders were built for the rapidly expanding urban and suburban lines of Britain's major cities. Powerful 0-6-0s and 0-8-0s were introduced for heavy freight work. The steam locomotive had shown itself capable of moving large loads – both goods and people – over long distances, and at previously undreamed of speeds. Transport in Britain had not undergone such a change since the building of the Roman roads, 1,400 years earlier.

Left: William Stroudley was one of the pre-eminent 19th century locomotive designers and his 80-strong E1 class 0-6-0Ts were sturdy shunting and goods engines. Originally named Burgundy, the survivor – No110 – became the 100th Stroudley locomotive built for the London Brighton & South Coast Railway, in 1877. It ended its days on colliery work in Staffordshire.

STOCKTON & DARLINGTON RAILWAY

'Locomotion' Class 0-4-0

Like most early railways – certainly those in north-east England – the role of the Stockton & Darlington was to carry coal. In key respects, however, it differed from its counterparts in County Durham, Northumberland and West Yorkshire. One was its length, over 25 miles. Another was its status. On 27 September 1825, the S&DR became the first *public* railway in the world to convey goods and passengers using steam traction. The train that could be said to have launched the railway age was hauled by the aptly named *Locomotion No1*.

The promoters of the railway wanted a means of bringing coal from Witton Park colliery near Darlington to the dockside staithes at Stockton, on the River Tees. The financial backing for the scheme came from an unusual source: an association of the Society of Friends, also known as the Quakers, and in particular from the Pease family of Darlington. When it came to placing a contract for the construction of the railway, they approached an engineer from Wylam, in Northumberland, who had made a name in colliery railways. He had also built steam locomotives, most notably for the Hetton Colliery Company. His name was George Stephenson.

Like many people, the directors of the S&DR liked the idea of a railway but were unconvinced of the merits of steam traction. It was still unproved and known to be unreliable. What advantage could it offer over tried-and-trusted horse power? Stephenson succeeded in persuading the S&DR at least to evaluate this new-fangled means of propulsion.

The locomotive he built still drew heavily on the beam-type pumping engine principle of earlier colliery engines, which included Stephenson's first design, *Blücher* of 1814. However, it did incorporate several original features. It was, for example, the first locomotive successfully to employ coupling rods to link the front and rear wheels, enabling them to turn together. Earlier engines had used chains. Its two vertical cylinders were aligned along the centre of the single-flue boiler and, through the complex arrangement of beams and rods, each drove one of the axles through the rods and crankpins on the wheels. The cranks were set at right angles, which meant that each coupling rod had to be attached to a return crank.

George Stephenson wanted to demonstrate the potential of this machine and drove the inaugural train himself. The load was considerable: six trucks filled with coal, a further six loaded wagons, a passenger 'coach', and 21 trucks crowded with people eager to sample this new way of travelling. During the journey, Stephenson got *Locomotion No1* up to a speed of 8mph.

Despite this successful debut, the S&DR management remained equivocal about steam haulage. Stephenson's company supplied three more locomotives to the railway, but it remained uncommitted. The turning point came in 1828 when Timothy Hackworth became the S&DR's first Locomotive Superintendent. Hackworth, a figure whose contribution to early locomotive development is often undervalued, set about building engines that were both reliable and powerful. It was George Stephenson,

Above: For the drive from its vertical cylinders – inserted along the centre line of the boiler – to its coupled wheels, Locomotion *relied upon an arrangement of beams, rods and cranks based upon the operating gear of stationary pumping engines. Apart from the complexity, the downforce exerted on the track was the principal drawback.*

however, who benefited most from an involvement with the Stockton & Darlington. Even before that railway's opening, he had negotiated contracts to build another, linking the rapidly-growing industrial metropolis of Manchester with the port of Liverpool.

S&DR 'Locomotion' Class 0-4-0

Built: George Stephenson*, Newcastle-upon-Tyne, 1825–26 (6 built)

Weight: 6 tons 10cwt (locomotive)
(Weight of tender unknown)

Driving wheel diameter: 3ft 11in

Boiler pressure: 50lb/psi

Cylinders: 9½in diameter x 24in stroke

Valve gear: Stephenson

Coal capacity: 10cwt

Water capacity: 240 gallons

Tractive effort: 2,050lb (at 85% boiler pressure)

(some sources credit* Locomotion *as the first engine – Works No1 – constructed by Robert Stephenson & Co. at the Forth Street workshops in Newcastle.)*

From a technical standpoint, that inaugural run marked an end as well as a beginning. As it steamed into the environs of Darlington, *Locomotion No1* was reaching the end of the line in more ways than one. It, and its breed of what were essentially mobile beam engines, had a limited future. Within four years, the Stephensons – George and his son, Robert – and other engineers were transforming locomotive design and, in the process, producing a blueprint for the ensuing 150 years.

The original *Locomotion No1* remains in Darlington, at the North Road Station Museum. A working replica, built in 1975 to mark the 150th anniversary of the formation of the Stockton & Darlington, continues to appear on preserved lines around Britain.

Below: Offering a taste of rail travel 1825-style, the replica of George Stephenson's Locomotion *has visited preserved lines, including – in 1995 – the South Devon Railway. After a day shuttling to-and-fro within the station limits,* Locomotion *stands at Buckfastleigh on the afternoon of 24 July. Aside from its Stockton & Darlington connection,* Locomotion *is significant for being the first engine to have its wheels coupled by rods. Its stovepipe chimney is connected directly to the boiler, with the exhaust entering through two horizontal pipes.*

LIVERPOOL & MANCHESTER RAILWAY

'Rocket' Class 0-2-2

By the late 1820s, George Stephenson and his son, Robert, could see that cumbersome, slow-moving colliery engines were not the way forward for steam traction. The future locomotive had to be faster, lighter and use fuel more efficiently. That meant a fresh approach to every aspect of its design, something that Robert Stephenson in particular was able to bring. The stimulus to develop a new breed of locomotive came with an announcement by the promoters of the planned Liverpool & Manchester Railway.

They were about to place contracts to build the world's first 'inter-city' railway, but first needed convincing that steam locomotives were reliable over distances (and, if so, which types of engine). Accordingly, comparative trials were arranged at Rainhill, near Liverpool, with a prize of £500 for the most successful participant. Several locomotives were entered in the trials, which were scheduled to begin on 6 October 1829 and continue for several days.

The Stephensons' entry was *Rocket*, an outside-cylinder 0-2-2 built at Robert Stephenson & Co.'s factory in Forth Street, Newcastle-upon-Tyne. Before being taken to Rainhill, *Rocket* was tested on the Kilingworth colliery railway in Northumberland. It was then dismantled, transported by road to Carlisle and taken by ship to Liverpool.

The critical test for the Rainhill entrants was one of endurance: each locomotive had to shuttle to-and-fro over the $1^3/4$-mile test track until it had covered 75 miles, the equivalent of a return trip from Manchester to Liverpool. In this exercise, *Rocket* outclassed the competition, at one point reaching a speed of 29.1mph. The Stephensons collected the £500 prize and an order for eight more engines. Crucially, *Rocket* had won over the doubters. Its triumph was the culmination of nearly 30 years' slow evolution. Now the pace of development accelerated and, in the ensuing three decades, the successors to *Rocket* – the first successful express passenger locomotive – would conquer the world.

The innovations that made *Rocket* a success became incorporated in almost all steam locomotives. Unlike the complex beam engine arrangement of early locomotives,

Above: The working replica of Rocket *approaches Horsted Keynes station on the Bluebell Railway. Robert Stephenson was mainly responsible for* Rocket's *design and several features became standard practice world-wide in subsequent locomotive design, the multi-tubular boiler and chimney blastpipe among them. In contrast to* Locomotion *of four years earlier, inclined cylinders now drove the wheels through a much simpler system incorporating short connecting rods.*

Above: The original Rocket *of 1829, which ended its days in colliery work and was left to decay for over 20 years before being saved for posterity in 1862. Normally on display in London's Science Museum, it is here the centrepiece of a 1980 exhibition in Liverpool Museum.*

Above: The replica Rocket *and its open-topped carriages contribute to the recreation of an 1830s scene for the filming of a television documentary on 11 May 1999. The location of Burrs, on the East Lancashire Railway, is not too distant from the route of the Liverpool & Manchester Railway where, until 1836,* Rocket *hauled passenger trains for real.*

L&MR 'Rocket' Class 0-2-2

Built: Robert Stephenson & Co., Newcastle-upon-Tyne, 1829–30 (7 built)

Weight: 4 tons 5cwt (locomotive)
5 tons 4cwt (tender)

Driving wheel diameter: 4ft 8½in

Boiler pressure: 50lb/psi

Cylinders: (2) 8in diameter x 16½in stroke

Valve gear: Stephenson-Wood (loose-eccentric arrangement)

Coal capacity: approx. 1 ton 0cwt

Water capacity: approx. 400 gallons

Tractive effort: 820lb (at 85% boiler pressure)

inclined cylinders either side of the water-jacketed firebox drove on to single driving wheels through short connecting rods. These were braced to the cylinders by single slidebars. This arrangement, using the single driving axle, made for exceptionally fast running. Another key feature was the multiple tube boiler, which had been developed by George Stephenson and his colleague, Henry Booth.

Instead of a single flue tube, *Rocket*'s boiler contained 25 narrow-bore copper tubes. These greatly enlarged the surface area available to heat water, so increasing steam production. A dome on top of the boiler barrel was used for drying the steam. While the multi-tube boiler contributed to *Rocket*'s unrivalled efficiency, another innovation – the chimney blastpipe – was equally significant. *Rocket* saw the first successful application of this device, which directed the exhaust steam through a narrow opening, greatly increasing its force. This, in turn, created a draught for the fire. By this means, the draught could be regulated and, importantly, with it the rate of steam generation. The snaking exhaust pipes taking steam to the chimney to create the blast were a prominent feature of *Rocket*.

In 1830, *Rocket* went to work on the newly opened Liverpool & Manchester Railway and was subsequently

joined there by six similar machines. However, the experience gained with *Rocket* rapidly saw a host of improvements introduced by Robert Stephenson into his newer locomotives. A series of modifications helped maintain *Rocket*'s usefulness but, in 1836, it was deemed surplus to L&MR requirements and sold to the Earl of Carlisle's collieries in Cumberland. Retired in 1840, it was stripped of many fittings and could easily have been broken up. However, its importance was recognized and, in 1862, *Rocket* was rescued, ultimately becoming an exhibit in the Science Museum, London. Recent inspections using fibre-optic techniques have revealed evidence of considerable accident damage.

The condition of the original *Rocket* precludes any attempt to steam it, but a working replica has been constructed. The National Railway Museum has also built a cross-sectioned replica to illustrate the inner workings of this most famous of early locomotives.

LIVERPOOL & MANCHESTER RAILWAY

No57 'Lion' 0-4-2

From pumping engine to film star, the story of *Lion* is one of the most extraordinary of any steam locomotive. At one time the 1838-built machine was the second-oldest working locomotive in the world.

Lion was one of a group of four goods engines manufactured by the firm of Todd, Kitson & Laird for the first 'inter-city' railway, the Liverpool and Manchester. All were named after big animals. It appeared at a time when a degree of standardization was coming into locomotive design. The most popular type for main-line express passenger work was the 'Patentee' 2-2-2, which Robert Stephenson – as the name suggests – had patented in 1833. It was a development of the 'Planet' 2-2-0, with the frames extended and a trailing axle added to improve stability and increase firebox area. Additionally, the 'Patentee' incorporated improvements in valve gear and boiler fabrication and, regardless of Stephenson's patent, other builders replicated the basic formula. For example, it was developed into front-coupled 0-6-0 and 0-4-2 goods engines, of which *Lion* is the most celebrated representative. Key features of *Lion*, both typical of locomotives of the period, are its round-top 'haycock' firebox and the 'sandwich' frames enclosing the wheels.

Lion remained in main-line service until 1857, by which time the Liverpool & Manchester had been absorbed into the London & North Western Railway. Renumbered No116 by the L&NWR, in 1859 the locomotive was sold to the Mersey Docks & Harbour Board for £400. After several years spent as a shunting engine, the Board installed *Lion* in Liverpool's Princes Gravity Dock, where it acted as a stationary pumping engine.

The veteran – built the year after Queen Victoria ascended to the British throne – remained in this role up to the 1920s. With the centenary of the Liverpool & Manchester approaching, in 1927, *Lion* was rescued by the Liverpool Engineering Society. It persuaded the LMSR to undertake the restoration of the locomotive at its Crewe works and, in 1930, *Lion* took its rightful place in the centenary cavalcade. After this, *Lion* went on display at Liverpool's Lime Street Station for a time.

However, in the late 1930s, it began a new career in the movies. After cameo appearances in *Victoria the Great* (1937) and 1951's *The Lady with the Lamp*, a film biography of Florence Nightingale, in 1953 *Lion* had a starring role in *The Titfield Thunderbolt*. Filmed on the recently closed Limpney Stoke to Camerton line near Bath,

Right: Profile of a remarkable survivor, Liverpool & Manchester Railway 0-4-2 No57 Lion *of 1838, which lived to play its part in the L&MR 150th anniversary celebrations in 1980. Before the event,* Lion *was domiciled at Southport and was running-in from there when pictured at Burscough on 12 May 1980.*

this told the story of a group of villagers who defied the closure of their branch line by operating it themselves with a vintage museum locomotive. The 115-year-old *Lion* certainly looked the part!

After many years stored in the paint shop at Crewe, along with other historic locomotives such as Francis Trevithick's *Cornwall* (pages 18-19), in 1965 *Lion* was transferred to the City of Liverpool Museum. After external restoration, in 1967 it went on display in a new transport gallery. Then, in 1979, the decision was taken to return it to steam for another Liverpool & Manchester anniversary, the 150th. The locomotive was taken to the Ruston Diesels plant at Newton-le-Willows (the former Vulcan Foundry) where it underwent a rapid overhaul. In the process, some six bucket-loads of rust, scale and other deposits were removed from its small boiler.

In 1980, *Lion* steamed again at the Rainhill cavalcade, accompanied by a host of its descendants from all of Britain's major railway companies. There was now only one working locomotive in the world that exceeded *Lion*'s 142 years – and that, too, was British-built. It was the Camden & Amboy Railroad's 0-4-0 *John Bull* which had been exported by Robert Stephenson & Co. to the United States in 1831.

L&MR No57 'Lion' 0-4-2

Built: Todd, Kitson & Laird, Leeds,
    1838–39 (4 built)

Weight: 18 tons 17cwt (locomotive)
    7 tons 14cwt (tender)

Driving wheel diameter: 5ft 0in

Boiler pressure: 50lb/psi

Cylinders: (2) 14¼in diameter x 18in stroke

Valve gear: 'Gab'-type (slide valves)

Coal capacity: (not available)

Water capacity: (not available)

Tractive effort: 3,325lb

*Left: With its three replica L&MR
vehicles filled with passengers,
Lion makes a return to the main
line which it served 120 years
earlier. It was operating between
Eccles, west of Manchester, and
Liverpool Road on 14 September
1980. The Leeds-built Lion was one
of a class of four goods engines
delivered to the L&MR, the world's
first 'inter-city' railway, between
1838 and 1839.*

GREAT WESTERN RAILWAY

'Iron Duke' Class 4-2-2

On 11 May 1848, the Great Western Railway's 'Iron Duke' class secured a place in the railway record books when 4-2-2 *Great Britain* attained 78.2mph at Wootton Bassett, eight miles west of Swindon. It was the fastest any steam locomotive had travelled up to that date and it was also the second occasion that the Great Western had broken its record.

The first official speed record was the 61mph of 'Fire Fly' class 2-2-2 *Ixion* in December 1845. In June 1846 that was exceeded by the 74.5mph of 2-2-2 *Great Western*, the first locomotive constructed at Swindon works. That these remarkable speeds were attainable was down to two men: Isambard Kingdom Brunel and Daniel Gooch. Brunel had engineered the broad gauge line between Paddington and Bristol for high-speed running, with gentle gradients and the minimum of curvature. The young Gooch supplied the engines that could make the most of those conditions.

The Northumberland-born Daniel Gooch was just 20 when, in 1837, Brunel recruited him as Locomotive Superintendent of the GWR. Despite his youth, Gooch had worked at iron foundries and in a drawing office, and had experience of locomotive construction: he had spent time in the employ of Robert Stephenson & Co. Before Gooch's arrival, Brunel had ordered several different locomotives for evaluation by the infant Great Western, but with mixed success. It was a matter of make-do-and-mend until Gooch's first design, the 'Fire Fly' class, entered traffic in 1840. It catapulted the GWR to the forefront of locomotive development, both in Britain and world-wide.

The most renowned of Gooch's locomotives, the 'Iron Duke' class evolved from the record-breaking *Great Western*. A few months after entering service in April 1846, the leading axle of this 2-2-2 fractured. Gooch attributed this to uneven weight distribution and successfully rebuilt *Great Western* as a 4-2-2 (or, more correctly, a 2+2-2-2). In this form, it became the model for the 'Iron Dukes', 22 of which were built at Swindon between April 1847 and March 1851. A further seven engines, delivered from Rothwell & Co. during 1854 and 1855, were notable for being named after recently fought Crimean War battles.

Top: Close-up of the driving wheel, axlebox, leaf spring and outside framing. 'Egyptian' style lettering for engine names was used throughout the lifetime of the GWR.

Above: Posing in Kensington Gardens, London, on 3 April 1985, the replica Gooch broad gauge Iron Duke *4-2-2 presents an impressive profile.*

Above: Offering broad-gauge travel to Londoners for the first time since 1892, Iron Duke sets off along its Kensington demonstration line on 3 April 1985. The replica is normally housed at the National Railway Museum.

GWR 'Iron Duke' Class 4-2-2

Built: Swindon works; Rothwell & Co., Bolton, 1847–51/1854–55 (29 built)

Weight: 35 tons 10cwt (locomotive)
17 tons 4cwt (tender)

Driving wheel diameter: 8ft 0in

Boiler pressure: 100lb/psi (subsequently increased to 115lb/psi; later engines were delivered with 120lb/psi boilers.)

Cylinders: (2) 18in diameter x 24in stroke

Valve gear: Gooch

*Coal capacity:** 1 ton 10cwt

Water capacity: 1,760 gallons (later increased to 1,880 gallons; engines were also attached to 2,700-gallon tenders.)

Tractive effort: 8,262lb
(at 85% boiler pressure)

(* the locomotives originally burnt coke)

Like *Great Western*, the 'Iron Dukes' had 8ft diameter driving wheels, but Gooch substituted round-topped fireboxes for the domed 'haycock' variety. The outside frames supported a boiler 11 feet long, 4ft 9¹/₂in in diameter and containing 303 tubes. The grate area was 21.7sq ft and the sum of the heating surfaces was 1,945sq ft. Originally, the locomotives were attached to 1,760-gallon tenders (subsequently enlarged to 1,880 gallons) but were later harnessed to 2,700-gallon tenders. These allowed the introduction of non-stop running between Paddington and Swindon. The 'Iron Dukes' became the most famous locomotives of their day and monopolized the crack Bristol and Birmingham expresses, frequently averaging over 60mph for the 53 miles between Didcot and Paddington.

Between 1871 and 1888, 24 of the class were rebuilt (or 'renewed' in GWR parlance). Their appearance changed appreciably, inviting speculation on how much of the original was retained. The 'renewals' were officially described as the 'Rover' class, from the name of the first to emerge from Swindon. The last to appear, *Tornado*, was also the last broad gauge locomotive to be built. In this form, the engines lasted until the demise of the broad gauge in 1892, when the GWR was forced to conform to the standard gauge of 4ft 8¹/₂in prevalent elsewhere in Britain.

The GWR had set aside one of the original 'Iron Dukes', *Lord of the Isles*, for preservation. However, in an act of official vandalism that has never been satisfactorily explained, it was broken up in 1906, along with the equally historic *North Star* of 1837. Almost 80 years later, however, a replica of the original *Iron Duke* itself was built for the celebrations marking the 150th anniversary of the formation of the Great Western Railway. It made its debut in April 1985, running on a section of broad gauge track laid in London's Kensington Gardens. It was an appropriate location: in adjacent Hyde Park, in 1851, the Great Exhibition had earlier acknowledged Daniel Gooch's achievements by displaying one of his celebrated broad gauge 'singles'.

LONDON & NORTH WESTERN RAILWAY

No173 (No3020) 'Cornwall' 2-2-2

Built, rebuilt, and rebuilt again, somehow *Cornwall* has contrived to survive for over 150 years, despite hauling its last revenue-earning train 80 years ago. It is a locomotive that can trace its lineage back to Trevithick – not the pioneering Richard, but his son, Francis.

No173 *Cornwall* was built at Crewe in 1847, the year after the formation of the London & North Western Railway and six years after the 2-2-2 type had been introduced on west coast passenger trains. The forerunner of this generation of single-wheelers was No26 *Aeolus*, which was constructed at the Grand Junction Railway's Edge Hill workshops in Liverpool in 1841. Although it could trace its parentage back to Robert Stephenson's 'Patentee' type of 1833, *Aeolus* was largely the work of two of the greatest Victorian engineers, William Buddicom and Joseph Locke.

Appointed Locomotive Superintendent of the Grand Junction Railway in 1840, Buddicom discovered that, due to broken crank axles, the GJR's Robert Stephenson-built inside-cylinder locomotives were spending far more time under repair than in service. *Aeolus* established a new, more reliable design whose fundamental elements – straight axles, inclined outside cylinders supported in outside framing and a deep firebox located between the rear wheels – were much imitated in Britain and beyond. Indeed, Buddicom soon quit the GJR to make his name – and a sizeable fortune – building locomotives in France. The Grand Junction Railway replaced him with Francis Trevithick.

In 1843, to quote the official statement, a new works was opened 'at the junction of Crewe' for 'the building and repairs *(sic)* of carriages and waggons as well as engines'. It was here, in 1845, that the first of Francis Trevithick's 2-2-2s with 6ft diameter driving wheels, No49 *Columbine*, was constructed. The double-framed, outside-cylindered design typified by Trevithick's *Columbine*, and the later *Cornwall*, was the culmination of the 'Old Crewe' tradition initiated by Locke and Buddicom.

Left: Close-up of the nameplate, splasher and 8ft 6in diameter driving wheel of 1847-built 2-2-2 Cornwall. The locomotive's outside cylinders drive on to the outer faces of each wheel through individual connecting rods and crankpins. The horizontal 'slots' cut into the frames gave access to the motion.

Below: At 142-years-old – at least in part! – Francis Trevithick's 2-2-2 No3020 Cornwall made a rare public appearance at a Birmingham Railway Museum open day on 14 October 1989. It carries L&NWR livery, the famous 'blackberry black'.

Above: No49 Columbine of 1845 is traditionally regarded as the first locomotive built at Crewe. It was also the first of the Grand Junction Railway's fleet of 'standard' 2-2-2s. In its L&NWR guise as No1868, the veteran stands on display at Swindon on 14 March 1990.

L&NWR No173 (No3020) 'Cornwall' 2-2-2

Built (Rebuilt): Crewe works, 1847 (1858)

Weight: 29 tons 18cwt (locomotive)
    25 tons 0cwt (tender)

Driving wheel diameter: 8ft 6in

Boiler pressure: 140lb/psi

Cylinders: (2) 17¼in diameter x 24in stroke

Valve gear: Stephenson (slide valves)

Coal capacity: 4 tons 10cwt

Water capacity: 1,800 gallons

Tractive effort: 8,700lb (at 85% boiler pressure)

The locomotives were distinguished by the combination of inner plate frames, with the cylinders mounted outside them and securely held by a double frame at the front end. To avoid a repeat of the fractured crank axle problem, drive from the cylinders was delivered to the driving wheels by means of connecting rods attached to crank pins on the wheels.

The original design of *Cornwall* showed Trevithick's debt to another British engineer who, like Buddicom, made his reputation in France. This was Thomas Crampton who devised an ingenious way of combining a low-slung boiler with large-diameter driving wheels, in such a way that the axles and cranks were not fouled by the bottom of the boiler barrel. Trevithick's version of the Crampton idea, with its low centre of gravity, certainly gave stability at the speeds generated by *Cornwall*'s 8ft 6in drivers. In other respects, however, it was an unsatisfactory arrangement and, in 1858, his successor, John Ramsbottom, replaced this boiler with one of more conventional layout.

This was to be only the first of *Cornwall*'s rebuildings. In 1897, the Ramsbottom boiler was exchanged for the one the locomotive carries today. The quoted construction date of 1847, therefore, can only truthfully be applied to the frames, motion and wheels. Even the tender was acquired from a DX class goods 0-6-0 in 1920.

Though placed on the L&NWR's 'Duplicate List' (essentially, its reserve stock) in 1885, where it was renumbered No3020, *Cornwall* remained in everyday service until 1905. What enabled it to outlive the rest of its type was its selection in 1907 as the engine exclusively maintained to transport the L&NWR's Chief Mechanical Engineer around his domain. On 20 July 1920, the occupant of that saloon was Charles Bowen-Cooke, CME since 1909. Having brought Bowen-Cooke to Euston, *Cornwall* returned north. It piloted 'Claughton' class 4-6-0 No1914 *Patriot* on the 'Midday Corridor' on what would prove its last revenue-earning journey.

Officially retired in 1922, *Cornwall* was kept at Crewe works, but ventured to the Stockton & Darlington centenary celebrations of 1925, and those marking the 100th anniversary of the Liverpool & Manchester Railway in 1930. Like its L&NWR counterpart, *Columbine*, No3020 *Cornwall* is now part of the National Collection.

MIDLAND RAILWAY

'156' Class 2-4-0

The Midland Railway's preference for 'building small' led to the construction of several classes of 2-4-0 passenger engines. Small engines cost less to build and maintain, and inflicted less wear-and-tear on the track. If train loadings outstripped the capability of one locomotive, then two would be used (and, in the case of the heaviest freight workings, three). According to the Midland's bookkeepers, the savings would outweigh additional operational costs. The policy was already in place when, in 1844, Matthew Kirtley became the Midland's first Locomotive Superintendent. Kirtley, then aged only 31, had been promoted from one of the Midland's constituent companies, the Birmingham & Derby Junction Railway.

The first of Kirtley's 2-4-0s appeared in 1856, and was followed by five variations on this initial design. Deficiencies in Derby works' idea of sound frame construction limited their usefulness, and their working lives. Both, however, were improved with the introduction of deeper, slotted-plate double frames, and Kirtley's next 2-4-0s were to prove one of the Midland's best investments.

Some gave over 80 years' service, and Kirtley's belief that the locomotives could handle the Midland's heaviest trains was shown to be justified. They daily hauled expresses leaving Derby for Manchester and London.

Between 1866 and 1873, Derby works constructed 27 '156' class 2-4-0s, the final five appearing under Kirtley's successor, Samuel Waite Johnson. The reconstruction of earlier engines then enlarged the class by a further two. For the period, the substantial frames, small boiler and simple cab design left the '156' looking a little old fashioned. In his use of coupled wheels for high-speed running, though, Kirtley was ahead of the field. Elsewhere, the behaviour and reliability of coupling rods under stress was still questioned, hence the continued preference for single-wheeler designs (4-2-2s, 4-2-0s, 2-2-2s and 2-2-0s).

Inevitably, the 2-4-0s were downgraded as newer engines became available. Some took to the Midland's branch lines; others found refuge on cross-country routes. Although withdrawals began in 1894, rebuilding with larger cylinders and new-pattern boilers prolonged the

lives of many of the '156' class and 21 survived to become part of the locomotive fleet of the London Midland & Scottish Railway in 1923. By now, though, they were reduced to the humblest of roles. No20008, for example, replaced a L&NWR 2-4-0 in the guise of *Engineer Watford*, based at the eponymous permanent way depot to undertake works train duties.

The historic significance of the '156' class was recognized when, after withdrawal in 1930, No156 itself – which had become No1 in the Midland Railway's stock list – was retained for preservation. Somehow this decision was overturned and the 66-year-old was broken up in 1932. Fifteen years later, however, one of its classmates was spared.

Midland Railway No158A, renumbered MR No2 in 1907, was outshopped from Derby in September 1866. In June 1892, it was working out of Ilkley shed in Yorkshire and, by April 1914, had migrated south to Gloucester. As LMSR No20002, the Kirtley veteran was still on the books of Bourneville shed in Birmingham in September 1935 and was only retired in 1947, after 81 years' service. The decision was taken to preserve this last representative of the Midland 2-4-0 classes, even though it was in far from original condition. It had been rebuilt by Johnson in 1881 with a 'C'-type boiler and subsequently exchanged that for a 'B'-type boiler in 1897. Johnson's successor, Richard Mountford Deeley, had rebuilt the 'front end' (the cylinders and exhaust system) and, before 1900, the locomotive had been parted from its original tender. This was by no means unusual: seemingly all Midland tenders, regardless of their capacities, were viewed as interchangeable between a variety of classes.

This hybrid condition, however, does not detract from No158A's status in representing the mid-Victorian era passenger locomotive, or the work of that outstanding locomotive engineer, Matthew Kirtley. Currently, the old-timer could be in no better hands: it is entrusted to the safe-keeping of the Midland Railway Trust, and can be viewed at its base in Butterley, Derbyshire.

Right: Built in 1866, No158A is the sole surviving outside-framed Midland Railway 2-4-0, although by no means in as-built condition. It has twice been reboilered and the front end rebuilt, and last saw its original tender a century ago! Resplendent in crimson lake livery, No158A poses at Butterley, Derbyshire, on 26 May 1978.

Left: 43 years earlier, No158A – as LMSR No20002 – stands outside the roundhouse at Bourneville, Birmingham, on 2 March 1935. It lasted in LMSR stock for a further 12 years, ending its days in the Nottingham area.

Below: The exhaust emitted by No158A is strictly for effect: sadly, the 134-year-old has not been in steamable condition for decades. It was photographed in the Midland Railway Centre's museum at Swanwick, Derbyshire, on 1 September 1993.

MR '156' Class 2-4-0

Built: Derby works, 1866–74 (29 built)

Weight: 41 tons 5cwt (locomotive)
33 tons 15cwt*/35 tons 6cwt** (tender)

Driving wheel diameter: 6ft 2½in

Boiler pressure: 140lb/psi

Cylinders: 16½in diameter x 24in stroke
(later enlarged to 18in diameter)

Valve gear: Stephenson (slide valves)

Coal capacity: 3 tons 10cwt

Water capacity: 2,750* or 2,950** gallons

Tractive effort: 12,340lb (at 85% boiler pressure)

(*/** these were the principal tender types harnessed to the Kirtley '156' class 2-4-0s)

GREAT NORTHERN RAILWAY

G Class '8-foot Single' 4-2-2

It remains one of the most impressive exhibits at the National Railway Museum, a breathtakingly graceful machine dominated by its towering driving wheels. As an example of engineering artistry, among surviving locomotives Patrick Stirling's '8-foot Single' is matched only by its fellow NRM occupant, Wainwright's D class 4-4-0 (pages 66-67).

Stirling joined the Great Northern Railway in 1866, having been Locomotive Superintendent of the Glasgow & South Western Railway since 1853. One of his first actions upon arrival at the GNR's Doncaster works was to instigate a policy of standardization. Another was to borrow a single-wheeler, one with 7ft diameter drivers, from the Great Eastern Railway. Evidently impressed by this machine, in 1868 Stirling produced two small classes of 2-2-2s with 7ft 1in driving wheels. Two years later came the design that is generally regarded as his masterpiece, the G class 4-2-2 with its 8ft 1in drivers. Built to be racers, the 'Stirling Singles' became first choice for the GNR's prestige expresses on the London to York run, including the 10.00am from King's Cross – the then-unofficially named 'Flying Scotsman'.

Stirling elected to use outside cylinders, but with inside valve chests. He had little choice in the matter: inside cylinders would have dictated a boiler centre line height of 8ft to clear the cranks – hardly a recipe for stability at speed. Additionally, the inside cylinders would have exerted such lateral force on the wheel flanges that the resultant leverage of the cranks could have led to fractures. On the plus side, outside cylinders presented the potential for greater horsepower output. Although unorthodox for the period, the domeless boiler was typical Stirling, but the sum of the heating surfaces was surprisingly low for the comparatively large cylinders.

Another feature of the '8-foot Single' was its use of a four-wheel leading bogie in preference to the normal two-wheeler. Stirling argued that the combination of outside cylinders and a single-axle bogie could produce 'hunting', a side-to-side motion of the locomotive at speed. Pivoting horizontally about a pin situated a few inches behind its centre, the chief asset of the four-wheel bogie was its ability to 'nudge' the front end of an engine into a curve more gently than was possible from the front wheels of a

Stirling 'Single' No1 was overhauled to working order for the third time in preservation in 1981. It had been retired by the GNR in 1907, and was restored as closely as possible to its original condition, but retaining the new, longer frames fitted in 1880 and its larger boiler. It returned to steam in 1925, and again in 1938. On 6 December 1981, now aged 111, No1 makes a spirited start from Loughborough, on the Great Central Railway.

2-2-2. Additionally, Stirling located the cylinders between the bogie wheelsets, aligning them horizontally with the driving wheel centres. This avoided excessive weight on the front axle.

Construction of the class occupied an extraordinarily long period, with only two or three locomotives appearing each year. The final total of G class 4-2-2s was 37, to which were added ten of the G2 class of 1884 and six of the G3 class of 1894. The last appeared in 1895, the year in which Patrick Stirling died in office, aged 76.

Given this 25-year production span, it was predictable that there would be modifications to the design. Running counter to Stirling's standardization scheme, it is doubtful if any two 'Singles' were identical. Some received larger fireboxes and grates. Engines Nos1003-1007 had their cylinder diameter increased by half-an-inch to 19½in and working pressure raised from 140lb to 160lb/psi.

Despite this tinkering, the 'Singles' remained remarkable engines, as their contribution to the 1895 'Races to the North' testified. Their capabilities were regularly evident in everyday service, too.

A 275-ton load and an average speed of 50mph were within their range and, on lighter trains, speeds up to 85mph were recorded (those locomotives with the higher boiler pressure were the fastest). During the early 1900s, a reboilered single was entrusted with 5.30pm 'express goods' from London to Glasgow which it took as far as Peterborough. Amounting to 24 vehicles weighing around 340 tons, this was a fair load for a single-wheeler and suggests they had muscle, and good adhesive properties, as well as speed. Eventually, though, they were outstripped by heavier loadings and downgraded to secondary duties. By 1916, all had been scrapped, except for the doyen of the class, No1, which the Great Northern had the foresight to save for posterity.

GNR G Class '8-foot Single' 4-2-2

Built: Doncaster works, 1870–95 (G, G2, G3 classes) (53 built)

Weight: 38 tons 10cwt (locomotive)
30 tons 0cwt (tender)

Driving wheel diameter: 8ft 1in

Boiler pressure: 140lb/psi

Cylinders: (2) 18in diameter x 28in stroke

Valve gear: Stephenson (slide valves)

Coal capacity: 3 tons 10cwt

Water capacity: 2,900 gallons

Tractive effort: 11,130lb (at 85% boiler pressure)

(Specification relates to engine No1; detail alterations made with later examples)

Above: Illustrating Patrick Stirling's 2-2-2 designs is G3 class 2-2-2 No879, one of a batch of 11 engines built between 1892 and 1894. The G3s had 7ft 7in diameter driving wheels and were harnessed to huge tenders that, in working order, weighed more than the locomotives. Dated 1894, the location of this photograph is believed to be Wakefield.

Right: Unquestionably, one of the most graceful and impressive of Victorian designs, Stirling 'Single' No1 with its rich apple green livery and imposing 8ft 1in diameter driving wheel. Not all of the 'Singles' boasted the decorative slotted splasher; some were solid castings.

LONDON BRIGHTON & SOUTH COAST RAILWAY

A1/A1X Class OP 0-6-0T

Among British steam locomotives, it is unlikely any can compete with William Stroudley's A1/A1X tanks for length of service or variety of roles. Introduced in 1872, they began life on London suburban services but many later saw service well beyond south-east England. They were used as far apart as Shropshire, Scotland and South America, and – at an age of 125-plus – one, No55 *Stepney*, is still earning its keep on ex-LB&SCR metals.

Upon joining the London Brighton & South Coast Railway in 1870, one of William Stroudley's first tasks was to produce a new design of suburban tank locomotive. It had to combine the normally contradictory attributes of low weight and high power. The low axleloading was essential to allow it to run safely over the lightweight rails and shallow ballasting of many lines in the London area. The power was needed to handle heavy commuter trains on steep gradients, particularly on the East London Railway. It burrowed beneath the Thames through a tunnel built by Marc Brunel, father of Isambard, and was used by LB&SCR trains serving the City.

The year before joining the LB&SCR, Stroudley had produced a small six-coupled tank for his previous employers, the Highland Railway and this supplied the model for his LB&SCR design. After three attempts at getting the boiler dimensions right, the first six entered traffic between September and December 1872. They were allowed time to prove themselves before a second, much larger batch was ordered. Brighton works delivered a further 44 between 1874 and 1880.

For their size, they were astonishing engines. They happily handled 12-coach trains on demanding stop-start workings, where rapid acceleration rather than sustained speed was the key. On 100-ton trains, the Stroudley tanks were allowed 35 minutes for the 9.75-miles journey, but this included ten station stops. Little wonder that such snappy performances should earn them the nickname of 'Terriers' (although some footplatemen also knew them as 'Rooters'). In 1878, 'Terrier' No40 *Brighton* was sent to the Paris Exhibition, where it became the first (but not the last) Stroudley design to gain a gold medal.

Unfortunately, the success of Stroudley's design was its undoing. Their efforts made LB&SCR's south London services so popular, longer trains had to be introduced that were beyond the capacity of the 'Terriers'. Other work was found for them – shunting, piloting, light goods and branch line duties – but, in 1898, the LB&SCR decided 15 were surplus to requirements. Four were sold and the remainder scrapped. The rest would have suffered similar fates (some were already in storage) had not the LB&SCR decided to inaugurate 'motor train' workings. The 'Terriers'

Above: The single-line token is collected as one of the three Stroudley 'Terriers' based on the Kent & East Sussex Railway, 1876-built No32650, starts away from Rolvenden for Northiam.

LB&SCR A1/A1X Class OP 0-6-0T

Built: Brighton works, 1872/1874–80 (50 built)

Weight: 24 tons 7cwt (A1)/28 tons 10cwt (A1X)

Driving wheel diameter: 4ft 0in

Boiler pressure: 140lb/psi (A1)/150lb/psi (A1X)

Cylinders: (2) 13in diameter* x 20in stroke

Valve gear: Stephenson (slide valves)

Coal capacity: 1 ton 0cwt

Water capacity: 500 gallons

Tractive effort: 10,410lb** (at 85% boiler pressure)

(* cylinder diameters of A1X class varied between 12, 13 and 14in)

(** certain locomotives had reduced tractive efforts of 8,890lb or 7,650lb) were ideal for this undemanding role and 20 were fitted for push-pull working.

Between 1911 and 1913, their continued usefulness saw 12 'Terriers' receive new boilers, becoming the A1X class. Four more were reboilered after World War I. Nevertheless, between 1898 and 1920, the LB&SCR disposed of 21 engines to organizations as diverse as the Admiralty, the Newhaven Harbour Co., minor railway companies (including two on the Isle of Wight) and collieries. Five were bought by the civil engineering contractors, Pauling & Co., and were used in the construction of the Great Central Railway. Three of these were broken up in 1909, but two were sold on and were last heard of working on a tramway in South America!

The 'Terriers' remained at work on the Isle of Wight into the British Railways era, as well as becoming the mainstays of the Hayling Island branch in Hampshire and Newhaven harbour tramway in Sussex. In all BR inherited 15 'Terriers', two of which were in departmental service at Brighton works and at Lancing carriage works. The last was retired in 1963, but ten of the original 50 have been preserved. In May 1960, No55 *Stepney* became the Bluebell Railway's first locomotive, being joined by No72 *Fenchurch* four years later. Three more 'Terriers' (BR Nos32650, 32670 and 32678) are based on the Kent & East Sussex Railway and two (BR Nos32640 and 32646) on the Isle of Wight Steam Railway. LB&SCR No62 *Martello* is at the Bressingham Steam Museum in Norfolk, and No82 *Boxhill* is part of the National Collection at York. To see No54 *Waddon*, however, it is necessary to travel to the Canadian Historical Museum in Montreal.

Left: Pictured at Havenstreet, on the Isle of Wight Steam Railway, on 20 July 1991, NoW8 Freshwater entered service in 1877 as No46 Newington. It first arrived on the Isle of Wight in 1914, returning to the mainland in 1949. Withdrawn in 1963, the engine was displayed in a Hampshire pub car park for many years!

Below: Wearing its LB&SCR livery – officially described as 'improved engine green' – No55 Stepney undergoes cleaning. Brighton-built in 1875, upon retirement in 1960, it became the first locomotive acquired by the embryo Bluebell Railway.

BLACK HAWTHORN & COMPANY

'12-inch Standard' 0-4-0ST

Black Hawthorn & Company was formed in 1865, the main partners being William Black and Thomas Hawthorn. Based in Gateshead, it was a general engineering business producing steam engines of all types. Alongside railway locomotives, it made marine, colliery and other types of stationary engine, and supplied customers on every continent. Its largest products were 4-6-0 tender engines exported to South America.

On a smaller scale, designs such as its 'Standard' 0-4-0 saddletank, with 12in diameter cylinders, were usually built in batches and held 'in stock'. Locomotives could wait around for a year or more before being sold. Many engines were subsequently resold by the first buyer, but few of these Black Hawthorn saddletanks saw service outside industry. The North Eastern Railway bought four, and the East & West Junction Railway in Yorkshire acquired

a second-hand example. Another second-hand locomotive – still unidentified – was taken into Great Western stock in 1923 and used up to 1946.

William Black retired in 1896 and the business was sold to Chapman & Furneaux, who continued with locomotive building. Six years later, however, Chapman & Furneaux closed down and the goodwill of the firm was sold to Hawthorn Leslie of Newcastle-upon-Tyne. Among the major customers for Black Hawthorn's saddletanks was a Middlesbrough steel company, Bolckow, Vaughan & Co., which took no less than 20 engines. Nine more were sold to the Consett Iron Company in County Durham, and four were deployed by Head Wrightson & Co. in its Teesdale Iron Works at Thornaby-on-Tees. Another Teeside company, North Eastern Steel of Middlesbrough, also bought four. The Newcastle-based civil engineers, Walter Scott, owned three, as did the Tyne Coal Co., which used them at its colliery in Hebburn.

Outside north-east England, Black Hawthorn sold six engines to Birmingham Corporation's gas department. The largest overseas order came from the Libau Harbour Authority in the Baltic state of Latvia. The Mount Kemble Coal Co. of New South Wales, Australia, employed two, as did Orconera Iron Ore of Luchana, near Vizcay, in Spain. Uruguay's Great Eastern Railway owned one.

Black Hawthorn No266 *Wellington*, now preserved on the Tanfield Railway, close to its Gateshead birthplace, enjoyed the typically varied working life of one of these saddletanks. Beginning in 1873, it earned its keep for over 100 years. The name *Wellington* was applied by the locomotive's first owners, Walter Scott & Co. During the 1870s, the company had contracts to construct harbours at Hartlepool, and at Burntisland, in Scotland. In addition, it undertook railway engineering work for the North Eastern and London & North Western Railways. *Wellington* would certainly have seen employment on some of these contracts.

By the 1890s, the locomotive was in the service of the Holwell Iron Co. at its quarry in Leicestershire, where it was renamed *Holwell No3*. By 1895, it had been transferred to South Witham quarry in Lincolnshire but, around 1912, returned to Leicestershire, this time to Buckminster quarry. During the 1920s, *Wellington* went on loan to the Frodingham Iron & Steel Co. but, by the outbreak of war in 1939, it had been reclaimed by Holwell Iron for use at its Leicestershire quarries.

The Holwell Iron Co. passed into the ownership of the Stanton Iron Co., one of whose subsidiaries ran Wirksworth quarry in Derbyshire. It was here, in 1978, that *Wellington* completed a 105-year working life, although its later years were mainly spent as spare engine to a 1912-built Peckett saddletank. By this time, Wirksworth quarry – and

Above: Tackling the gradients of the historic Tanfield Railway, Wellington *climbs away from Causey Arch Halt on its way to Andrews House and Sunniside on 23 October 1993.*

Wellington – belonged to Tarmac Roadstone who agreed to sell the locomotive for preservation. By then, it was the sole survivor of a once 151-strong class.

Many detail alterations were introduced into the '12-inch Standard' over the years. For example, it is believed the initial batch did not have cabs. The first style of cab – narrow in width and with rounded front-and-back corners – was being fitted by the time *Wellington* was built in 1873. Wheel dimensions underwent a minor change in 1886 when the diameter was increased from 3ft 2in to 3ft 3in. This was not for any technical reason, merely a consequence of altering the design of the wheel casting. It is also thought that the later engines were some two-and-a-half tons heavier. The accompanying table gives the weights and dimensions for a typical Black Hawthorn saddletank.

Above: After a diverse career in industrial use, when pictured in the autumn of 1993, Wellington was – at age 120 – Britain's oldest working locomotive.

Above: Wellington's footplate, with the water gauge glass prominent. These engines had the minimum of controls – just as well, as the cab also housed the coal supply!

BH&C '12-inch Standard' 0-4-0ST

Built: Black Hawthorn & Company,
Gateshead-on-Tyne, 1866–1901 (151 built)

Weight: 13 tons 6cwt

Driving wheel diameter: 3ft 2in (later 3ft 3in)

Boiler pressure: 140lb/psi

Cylinders: (2) 12in diameter x 19in stroke

Valve gear: Stephenson

Coal capacity: 20 cubic feet

Water capacity: 470 gallons

Tractive effort: 7,366lb (at 85% boiler pressure)

HAYDOCK FOUNDRY COLLIERIES RAILWAY

NoC 'Bellerophon' 0-6-0WT

Colliery workhorse it may have been, but the venerable *Bellerophon* represents a watershed in locomotive design. It was the work of a remarkable, yet largely unknown Victorian engineer, and serves as a reminder of an equally noteworthy industrial enterprise that once dominated south-west Lancashire.

Today, Haydock is best known for its racecourse. However, a century ago it lay at the heart of the Lancashire coalfield and its mines produced around two million tons annually. Moving that quantity of coal required a railway network of considerable complexity and, at their height, the colliery lines totalled 60 miles.

Richard Evans had become a partner in the Haydock Collieries Co. in 1833 and, upon assuming sole control in 1847, renamed it Richard Evans & Sons. Two of his four sons made their mark in the family business. One of the pair, Josiah, studied engineering, mathematics and classics in London, but returned to the Lancashire firm of Jones & Potts to take his apprenticeship. The company was a sub-contractor to Robert Stephenson & Co. of Newcastle-upon-

Tyne and supplied parts for the 'Firefly' class engines that Stephenson was building for the Great Western Railway. Evidently, Josiah Evans was impressed with this Daniel Gooch design, and by its Gooch-Stephenson valve gear.

Joining his father's company, Evans was placed in charge of the foundry that supplied the collieries with its rails, tubs, wagons and even the carriages to carry the miners to and from the pithead. Just about the only items the colliery railway imported were its locomotives. However, by the late 1860s, its fleet of 25 new and second-hand engines was proving inadequate for the task. Josiah Evans was convinced his foundry could build better machines. Taking a four-coupled tank design as his starting point, and drawing on his experience with the Gooch engines, Evans produced the first of his six-coupled well tanks in 1868. In one significant area, however, Evans broke new ground. His was the first successful application of the piston valve. He had overcome the lubrication problems that had blighted previous attempts, and many now credit Josiah Evans with the invention of the piston valve.

Evans was also ahead of contemporary British practice in fitting his engines with outside cylinders and motion. The valve gear was an adaptation of the Gooch-Stephenson arrangement, with the cylinder piston valves activated by rocking levers working off a modified version of the Gooch reversing link motion. This was driven by Stephenson-type eccentrics worked from return cranks on the rear axle.

Bellerophon was the third of the six locomotives built by the Haydock Foundry. Outshopped in 1874, it differed from its predecessors in several respects. The steam pressure was increased from 120lb to 140lb/psi, and there were changes to the type of springing used, and to the injectors. Most significantly, the valve gear was revised, with Gooch-type box links replacing the rocking shafts. They were attached vertically, with the long, horizontal valve stems hinged at the front.

The six Josiah Evans engines remained the principal motive power at Haydock for over two decades. They

were strong enough to dispense with double- and triple-heading, allowing a reduction in the locomotive fleet from 25 to 15. Loads of 1,000 tons were within their capability, but by far their most exotic workings were the annual works outings to Blackpool. Improbable as it seems, Josiah Evans's colliery tank engines would double-head with locomotives of the Lancashire & Yorkshire Railway.

Following the nationalization of the coal industry in 1947, the surviving Evans engines were dispersed to other Lancashire collieries. *Bellerophon* first went to Bold Colliery and then to Lea Green. One-by-one its classmates were cut up and, in 1964, the torch was poised over 'Owd Bell', as enginemen fondly referred to the veteran. The last-minute intervention of the Industrial Locomotive Society prevented the destruction of this historic machine and, in 1966, it found a new home across the Pennines, on the Keighley & Worth Valley Railway. After 15 years in storage, the K&WVR-based Vintage Carriages Trust undertook the restoration of *Bellerophon* and, at the age of 111, it steamed again on 1 May 1985. Fifteen years on, 'Owd Bell' remains at work, a tribute both to the skill of Josiah Evans and the dedication of its restorers.

HFCR NoC 'Bellerophon' 0-6-0WT

Built: Haydock Foundry, Lancashire, 1874 (6 built)

Weight: 35 tons 0cwt

Driving wheel diameter: 4ft 0in

Boiler pressure: 140lb/psi (later increased to 160lb/psi)

Cylinders: (2) 15in diameter x 22in stroke

Valve gear: Gooch-Stephenson (piston valves)

Coal capacity: 2 tons 10cwt

Water capacity: 600 gallons

Tractive effort: 11,000lb (at 85% boiler pressure)

Above: Josiah Evans's employment of the outside Gooch-Stephenson valve gear arrangement was noteworthy for driving on to the rear axle of his six-coupled Haydock Foundry well tanks.

Opposite: When 1874-built Bellerophon *partnered the Bluebell Railway's red-liveried Fletcher Jennings 0-4-0T No3* Baxter *on 5 August 1990, their combined ages added up to 229 years.*

Right: The Vintage Carriages Trust's Bellerophon *pilots LMSR Fowler 3F 0-6-0T No47279 out of Haworth with a Keighley & Worth Valley service for Oxenhope on 25 February 1996.*

LONDON & NORTH WESTERN RAILWAY

'Precedent' Class 2-4-0

'Wonderful little engines' was how the railway journalist, Charles Rous-Marten, described Francis Webb's 'Precedent' 2-4-0s. He certainly experienced some sparkling runs behind them. However, it was during the 'Races to the North' in the summer of 1895 that the achievements of the 'Precedents', and in particular the now-preserved No790 *Hardwicke*, became legendary.

Francis Webb had been Chief Assistant to the L&NWR's John Ramsbottom when the latter introduced his 'Newton' class 2-4-0s in 1866. That year, Webb quit the L&NWR, a move variously attributed to his lack of prospects, or a personality clash with his chief. Five years on, Ramsbottom announced his retirement and Webb returned to the fold. If there was a rift between the two men, it was not evident in Webb's first act as Chief Mechanical Engineer, which was to continue the construction of four Ramsbottom designs, including the 'Newton' class 2-4-0s. By this time, the 2-4-0 was replacing the single-driver as the pre-eminent express passenger type. It possessed a similar potential for high-speed running, but with the greater adhesion offered by four coupled wheels.

The 'Precedents' owed much to the 'Newtons', although significantly Webb opted for a larger boiler. With its 6ft 7½in diameter driving wheels, the 'Precedent' was intended for fast running on the gentler southern grades of the West Coast route. For the stiff climbs north of Crewe,

Webb put his faith in the smaller-wheeled 'Precursor' 2-4-0. Paradoxically, while the 'Precursors' fell short – both of steam, and of expectation – the 'Precedents' astonished many by taking the ascent of Shap Fell in their stride, admittedly with comparatively light train loadings.

In true L&NWR fashion, Webb opted for simplicity and cheapness in the 'Precedents', but was sufficiently astute to see they had free-flowing, amply proportioned steam passages. In that way, these small engines were able to cope with being worked hard. Testifying to the inherent reliability of the design, No955 *Charles Dickens* was credited with the phenomenal figure of one million miles worked in just nine years and 219 days.

Between 1874 and 1882, 70 'Precedents' were outshopped from Crewe. Though small engines by the standards of other main-line railways, they were the

Above: Side view of the preserved Webb 'Precedent' 2-4-0 No790 Hardwicke showing the L&NWR lined black livery in all its glory, along with the distinctive style of name- and number-plates used by the company. The semi-circular cut-outs allow lubrication of the motion.

Left: During the 1970s, Hardwicke emerged from the National Railway Museum to make a welcome return to the main line. On 23 May 1976, the 1892-built locomotive makes light work of a Cumbrian coast special between Carnforth and Grange-over-Sands.

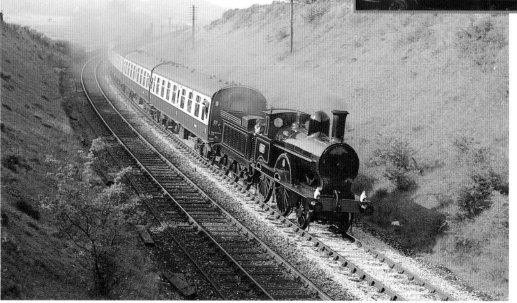

Below: 'Improved Precedent' No5092 (and crew) pose for the camera at the engine's birthplace of Crewe on 16 June 1929. Outshopped as 'Newton' class 2-4-0 No1684 Speke *in May 1868, No5092 was rebuilt in June 1891 and condemned in July 1931. The 'Improved (or 'Renewed') Precedent' class was rendered extinct – apart from the preserved* Hardwicke *– in October 1934.*

L&NWR's largest and were pressed into service on important workings out of London's Euston. These included all but two of the Anglo-Scottish trains, which they took as far as Rugby. By 1881, 'Precedents' were in sole charge of 16 of the prestige services to Birmingham, Manchester and Liverpool.

In the late 1880s, Webb's 3-cylinder compounds were introduced to replace the 'Precedents' on front-rank services. Such was their unreliability, however, that the 2-4-0s were reinstated and, between 1893 and 1901, 62 of the first batch were rebuilt as 'Renewed (or 'Improved') Precedents'. They received 150lb/psi boilers and larger tyres, which increased the nominal diameter of the driving wheels to 6ft 9in.

The problems with Webb's compounds presented the 'Precedents' with their opportunity for immortality. In 1895, the East Coast companies threw down the gauntlet by accelerating their Anglo-Scottish night services. The L&NWR responded by retiming its Aberdeen sleeper, which it operated in conjunction with the Caledonian Railway. 'Precedents' worked the train from Euston to Crewe and from Crewe to Carlisle, and No790 *Hardwicke* was one of the engines given the taxing northern leg. In the ensuing weeks, as the 'racing' intensified, the average speed over the 141 miles between Crewe and Carlisle continued to rise. The climax came on 22 August when *Hardwicke* averaged 67.2mph with a 70-tons train, and went over Shap at an astonishing 65.3mph. In six weeks, the fastest journey time between London and Carlisle was

reduced by 1 hour 15 minutes. The loads may have been light, but then so were the locomotives.

In their later years, the 'Precedents' pottered around the L&NWR system on secondary work. Six were based at Rugby for Stamford and Peterborough services. The last was withdrawn, as LMSR No25001, in October 1934, but the record-breaking *Hardwicke* was rightly spared and even enjoyed a return to steam during the 1970s. It is preserved at the National Railway Museum in York.

L&NWR 'Precedent' Class 2-4-0

Built: Crewe works, 1874–82 (70 built)

Weight: 32 tons 15cwt (locomotive)
25 tons 0cwt (tender)

Driving wheel diameter: 6ft 7½in* (later 6ft 9in)

Boiler pressure: 140lb/psi (later 150lb/psi)

Cylinders: (2) 17in diameter x 24in stroke

Valve gear: Allan (straight link) (slide valves)

Coal capacity: 4 tons 10cwt

Water capacity: 1,800 gallons

Tractive effort: 10,920lb (at 85% boiler pressure)

(* *early L&NWR records usually listed wheel diameters minus tyres, hence some references show the original 'Precedent' coupled wheels as 6ft 6in)*

NORTH EASTERN RAILWAY

1001 Class 'Long Boiler' 0-6-0

The North Eastern Railway's 1001 class embraced a large number of six-coupled goods engines that could trace their origin back to the Stockton & Darlington Railway. Although they came from several different engine builders, shared several sizes of cylinder and three sizes of driving wheel, these locomotives had one thing in common: the 'short wheelbase-long boiler' principle. A form of this was patented by Robert Stephenson in 1841, although there were earlier engines that had 'long boiler' characteristics.

In 1846, the Locomotive Superintendent of the Stockton & Darlington, William Bouch, built three 'long boiler' 0-6-0s. These were followed in 1852 by another Bouch 0-6-0 with 17in diameter cylinders and 4ft 2½in coupled wheels. The S&DR initially ordered only two engines, both from the Tees Engine Works of Gilkes Wilson & Co. (which was effectively part of the S&D empire). By 1854, it had added a further nine, fitted with 18in diameter cylinders and, like their predecessors, carrying names.

With the class standardized on 17in diameter cylinders, 5ft 0½in coupled wheels and a working pressure of 130lb/psi, volume production began in 1860. Again

Gilkes, Wilson was involved in the construction, but had to share the order with other north-east companies, and with the Stockton & Darlington's workshops at Darlington and Shildon, in County Durham. Construction of this batch continued up to 1868, five years after the S&DR had merged with the North Eastern Railway.

Their most distinctive feature, of course, was the boiler, which was an impressive 13 feet or more long and four feet wide. Although the use of such a large steam-raiser with a relatively small firebox became the antithesis of locomotive design in the 20th century, it was wholly appropriate for conditions a century earlier. The case for the 'long boiler' was that it obtained the maximum transfer of heat from the hot gases as they were drawn through the tubes. There was also an operational benefit.

On a railway such as the Stockton & Darlington, very few of its goods and mineral trains enjoyed uninterrupted journeys. Long periods would be spent in holding loops waiting for a path between other services. In these situations, the long boiler acted as a reservoir for the substantial volume of steam required to restart heavy

NER 1001 Class 'Long Boiler' 0-6-0

Built: Darlington and Shildon works; Avonside Engine
  Co., Bristol; Dübs & Co., Glasgow; Gilkes, Wilson,
  Middlesbrough; Hawthorn & Co., Newcastle-upon-
  Tyne; Hopkins, Gilkes, & Co., Middlesbrough;
  Kitching & Co., Darlington; Robert Stephenson &
  Co., Newcastle-upon-Tyne, 1852–75 (192 built)

Weight: 35 tons 4cwt (locomotive)
  22 tons 2cwt (tender)

Driving wheel diameter: 5ft 0½in*

Boiler pressure: 130lb/psi

Cylinders: (2) 17in diameter x 24in stroke**

Valve gear: Stephenson (slide valves)

Coal capacity: 5 tons 0cwt

Water capacity: 1,600 gallons

Tractive effort: 13,720lb (at 85% boiler pressure)

(some locomotives had driving wheels of 4ft 0in
  or 4ft 2½in diameter)*

*(** certain locomotives had 18in diameter
  cylinders; others had a cylinder stroke of 26,
  28 or 30in)*

Right: Distinctive features of the front end of preserved 1001 class 0-6-0 No1275 include the scalloped-edged bufferbeam, large sandboxes, robust smokebox door hinge, stovepipe chimney and unusual style of lamp bracket.

Above: 'Long Boiler' No1275 at Swindon works during the 'National Railway Museum on Tour' exhibition in April 1990. No1275 was one of 10 engines built under NER auspices to William Bouch's original Stockton & Darlington design by Dübs of Glasgow in 1874. No1275 became the last of class in service, being retired from Malton shed, in Yorkshire, in 1923.

Right: Steam dome, splasher, driving wheel and rods of No1275. The engine carries the NER Gateshead works passenger livery with its running number applied to either side of the dome. Note the distinctive Dübs & Co. diamond-shaped worksplate on the running board.

trains. While idle, the small firegrate would have kept the amount of fuel consumed to a minimum. The same benefits accrued while shunting.

A further 70 'long boiler' 0-6-0s were delivered between 1870 and 1875, and from contractors outside north-east England. The 1874 batch, which included the now-preserved No1275, came from Dübs of Glasgow and the Avonside Engine Co. of Bristol was responsible for the last ten, completed in 1875. The usefulness of the 'long boilers' saw them undergo general rebuilding under the Worsdell brothers' (Thomas and Wilson) regimes (1885–1910), and this included the provision of new 14ft long boilers and replacement chimneys.

By the mid-1890s, they had become concentrated in the Darlington area, with a handful operating out of Rosedale, a remote depot in the heart of the North York Moors. Here, they worked the branch from Battersby, which could reached solely by the rope-worked Ingleby incline. Elsewhere on the Moors, locomotives based at Whitby and Malton, including No1275, worked the route through Newtondale, today's North Yorkshire Moors

Railway. Other members of the class to 'scale the heights' were those stationed at Shildon. They undertook trips as far west as Cockermouth, hauling coke to the blast furnaces of west Cumberland.

In 1894, regardless of variations in cylinder and wheel dimensions, the NER elected to include all the 'long boiler' 0-6-0s of Stockton & Darlington origin within its 1001 classification. The total came to 192 engines, the oldest of which, *Aberdeen,* was a Gilkes, Wilson product of 1852. It lasted in traffic until 1903. Large numbers were withdrawn between 1905 and 1908, but some of the 1001s soldiered on into the 1920s. The last to be retired was No1275, one month after the Grouping in February 1923.

NORTH EASTERN RAILWAY

'901' Class 2-4-0

Edward Fletcher's tenure as Locomotive Superintendent of the North Eastern Railway lasted almost 30 years, from the formation of the company in 1854 until his retirement in 1883. Fletcher was Northumberland born-and-bred, and grew up in that crucible of early locomotive engineering north of the River Tees. He was apprenticed to no less a figure than George Stephenson. However, Fletcher's early career was relatively unspectacular. He was 37 before attaining his first senior position, being appointed Locomotive Superintendent of a minor north-eastern concern, the Newcastle & Darlington Junction Railway, in 1845. Nevertheless, it proved the stepping-stone to greater things.

Fletcher's inheritance from the three constituent companies that formed the NER amounted to 387 engines. Of those, 244 came from the York, Newcastle & Berwick Railway and included a large number of 2-4-0 passenger engines. It was a type that Fletcher was happy to perpetuate in his designs, the most celebrated – and longest-lived – of which was the 901 class. It was, without doubt, the best of the North Eastern 2-4-0s.

NER '901' Class 2-4-0

Built: Gateshead works; Beyer Peacock & Co., Manchester; Neilson & Co., Glasgow, 1872–82 (55 built)

Weight: 39 tons 14cwt (locomotive)
29 tons 17cwt (tender)

Driving wheel diameter: 7ft 0in

Boiler pressure: 160lb/psi

Cylinders: (2) 17in/17½in/18in diameter* x 24in stroke

Valve gear: Stephenson

Coal capacity: 5 tons 0cwt

Water capacity: 2,500 gallons

Tractive effort: 12,590lb (at 85% boiler pressure)

(cylinder diameters varied. The NER's 1894 register of engines lists 22 of the 901 class with 17in x 24in, 17 with 17½in x 24in, and 16 with 18in x 24in cylinders)*

Below: Withdrawals of the 901 class 2-4-0s began in 1913 and No928, here, lasted only until May 1914, when it was retired from Hull depot. Note the Westinghouse air brake pump next to the cab.

The NER's Gateshead workshops on Tyneside produced two prototypes for the class in 1872. After trials, orders for ten apiece were placed with two outside builders, Beyer Peacock and Neilson & Co. The former delivered its quota between May and July of 1873, and the latter during November and December of that year. At a more leisurely pace, 33 further examples were delivered from Gateshead over an eight-year period from 1874 until 1882.

There were detail differences between the batches – most noticeably the square-edged cabs of the Beyer Peacock engines – but all were distinguished by being massively built and soundly designed. The slide valve dimensions gave generous steam port openings, making the 901s very free-running. The bearings on all axles were generously proportioned and, although the footplate controls were simple, they did include two ingenious devices. One was a development of the combined lever and screw reverser that Robert Stephenson & Co. had introduced in 1867. Using the wheel and screw, the lever moved slowly to any chosen cut-off position. However, it was also possible to manipulate the lever directly, allowing a rapid switch from forward to reverse. The other innovation was Fletcher's own. He arranged the exhaust cocks so that, if desired, the driver could soften the blast at the chimney by diverting some of the exhaust beneath the cylinders. The aim was to reduce coal consumption.

From their introduction, the 901 class 2-4-0s put in excellent service on the Newcastle-Edinburgh and Newcastle-York-Leeds runs, hauling 160-170-ton loads. During 1884, engines based at Gateshead depot were averaging 4,400 miles per month. Apart from minor instances of updating, only two of the class underwent extensive rebuilding. One of the Gateshead engines, No167, received a larger boiler and had its wheelbase lengthened accordingly. More substantial modifications were made to the last of the Neilson-built engines, No933, which in 1907 was not only reboiled, but converted to a 4-4-0. It seems the experiment was unsuccessful, as the locomotive was scrapped in 1914.

It became one of 29 of the class withdrawn between 1913 and 1914 and, but for the onset of World War I, the rest would have followed. Instead, the curtailing of new construction led to a shortage of motive power and new work was found for the 2-4-0s. Some were drafted on to the coastal line between Scarborough and Bridlington, but the majority were stationed at Darlington. From here, they worked passenger services over the Stainmore route to Kirkby Stephen, Penrith and Tebay. Darlington also kept 2-4-0s on standby as main-line pilots.

By 1923 only ten of the 901s remained, shared between Barnard Castle, Darlington, Kirkby Stephen and York. Among the final five withdrawn in 1925 was No910 which, after being outshopped from Gateshead in April 1875, had participated in the celebrations marking the 50th anniversary of the opening of the Stockton & Darlington Railway. Since then, repeat appearances have graced the 100th anniversary in 1925 and the 150th in 1975. It remains to be seen whether No910, now part of the National Collection, will adorn the cavalcade marking the S&DR's 175th birthday.

Above: Thanks to the foresight of the LNER, No910, pictured in the old Queen Street Museum in York on 30 April 1949, survives to represent Edward Fletcher's masterpiece, the 901 2-4-0. Built at Gateshead in 1875, No910 enjoyed a working life of 50 years.

Above: The 901 class was massively constructed, with sturdy frames and generous bearings. The NER was similarly generous in the exterior finish, with lavish use of brasswork and a glorious livery. The basic pea-green was set off with broad, dark bands on the boiler barrel and myrtle-green surrounds to the tender and cabsides.

MIDLAND RAILWAY

1377 Class 1F 0-6-0T

Enthusiasts knew them as 'half-cabs', but to the Midland Railway they were the 1377 class, one of four classes of six-coupled tank engines introduced by Samuel Waite Johnson. The precedent had been set by Johnson's predecessor, Matthew Kirtley, with a series of 0-6-0Ts intended to work trip freights to goods depots in east London. These appeared during 1871 and, in the ensuing 31 years, the number of six-coupled tanks on the Midland's books climbed to 350.

The first Johnson-designed engines appeared a year after he had replaced Kirtley. Forty were delivered between 1874 and 1876. With their 'A type' boilers, 17in x 24in cylinders and 140lb/psi working pressure, these locomotives set the pattern for future construction. The design evolved into the 1377 class, the first of which, No1377 itself, was outshopped from Derby in May 1878. Noteworthy changes from the 1874 design were an enlargement of the coal bunker and a reduction in water capacity. Additionally, the frames were extended, although the wheelbase length was unaltered. The majority were fitted with open-backed cabs, 'half-cabs', as they became known. However, about 40 of the class received full cabs, including five built in 1883 for the Worth Valley branch in West Yorkshire.

Construction of the 1377 class continued until 1892, with Derby contributing 165 and a final 20 being ordered from Vulcan Foundry. They were distributed throughout the Midland's extensive system, which reached into East Anglia, and beyond Bristol and Gloucester into South Wales. Here, examples were employed on secondary passenger services in the Swansea area. In the main, though, their duties embraced pilot work around motive power depots, goods yards and stations, together with local freights. Engines used on passenger services had their regular steam brakes supplemented with vacuum brakes and, altogether, about 25 examples were vacuum-fitted.

1377 class tanks based at Kentish Town in London were regularly employed on empty stock workings

Right: Fulfilling the terms of a contract signed in 1866, Johnson 1377 class 0-6-0T No41835 undertakes shunting at Staveley Ironworks in April 1964. Built by Vulcan Foundry in October 1892 as Midland Railway No2003, this became the last of its class to be fitted with a G5-type boiler (in September 1961).

into and out of St Pancras and, in 1900, nine were equipped with carriage warming apparatus. Subsequently this was added to a number of the other vacuum-braked examples. The entire class of 185 entered LMSR stock in 1923. Generally, they remained in ex-Midland territory, but a few ventured further afield – Birkenhead, Shrewsbury and Walsall, for example.

Withdrawals began in 1928, with 76 retired by 1933. As the pace of scrapping accelerated, vacuum brake and carriage warming equipment was salvaged from condemned engines and re-fitted to the surviving members of the class. In a surprising move, however, five locomotives were lent to the War Department during World War II and sent to the Melbourne Military Railway in Leicestershire. There, they were fitted with Westinghouse air braking to allow Army footplate crews to become familiar with its operation. The loan period extended from early 1940 until December 1944. The most unusual 'modification' of a 1377 tank, though, had occurred in 1932. No1831 was selected for conversion to a 400 horsepower diesel-hydraulic shunter. The experiment was not particularly successful but it did mark the beginning of the LMSR's interest in diesel traction.

Following nationalization, the total of 1377 tanks was steadily reduced and, by the winter of 1960–61, only 11 remained in British Railways stock. However, entirely due to a contract signed by the Midland Railway in 1866, a handful of those were guaranteed a further five years' work. The Midland had undertaken to supply shunting locomotives to the Staveley Ironworks in Derbyshire for no

Above: Clearly demonstrating why the 1377 tanks became known as 'Half-Cabs', the surviving example, No41708, is pictured masquerading as one-time Gloucester-based classmate No1720 during a Dean Forest Railway gala on 13 August 1994.

Left: Wearing its correct identity, No41708 approaches Mytholmes tunnel at the head of a Worth Valley service in September 1997. Outshopped from Derby works in June 1880 as No1418, the 'Half-Cab' had a working life of 86 years.

MR 1377 Class 1F 0-6-0T

Built: Derby works; Vulcan Foundry, Newton-le-Willows, Lancashire, 1878–91 (185 built)

Weight: 39 tons 11cwt

Driving wheel diameter: 4ft 6½in (later 4ft 7in)

Boiler pressure: 140lb/psi or 150lb/psi, depending on boiler type

Cylinders: (2) 17in diameter x 24in stroke

Valve gear: Stephenson (slide valves)

Coal capacity: 2 tons 2cwt

Water capacity: 740 gallons

Tractive effort: 15,005lb or 16,080lb, depending on boiler type (at 85% boiler pressure)

less than 100 years. The LMSR and British Railways inherited that obligation, and the Johnson 1377 class remained the most suitable locomotives to meet it.

Steam working ceased at Staveley in 1965 and the five surviving 'half-cabs' were stored. They ended up clustered around sidings near Rotherham Masboro Station and were officially condemned in December 1966. Thankfully, with assistance from the Association of Railway Preservation Societies, the Midland Railway Locomotive Fund was able to secure the future of one of the Staveley Ironworks engines, No41708 of 1880. Appropriately, it made its preservation debut on one of the stamping grounds of the 1377 class, the Keighley & Worth Valley Railway. No41708 is currently based on the Swanage Railway in Dorset.

LONDON & NORTH WESTERN RAILWAY

'Coal Tank' 2F 0-6-2T

Nearly a century after his reign at Crewe ended, Francis Webb – locomotive overlord of the London & North Western Railway for 32 years – still gets a bad press. It is true that the L&NWR paid dearly for his intransigence, and his rejection of criticism (not that there was much of that, such was the awe in which Webb was held). However, no one would dispute the success of the fast, free-steaming 'Precedent' 2-4-0s; or that the 'Teutonics' and 'Coal Engines' were reliable, hard-working locomotives. It is simply that these achievements continue to be overshadowed by Webb's more idiosyncratic conceptions.

The 'Coal Tank' of 1881 was another Webb classic. These were strong engines whose 17in diameter cylinders supplied the muscle to get a long rake of heavily loaded wagons on the move. They proved popular engines all over the L&NWR network, despite incorporating a few Webb 'quirks'. The cab was narrow, due to the extension of the water tanks, and there was little standing room (this was before crews enjoyed the luxury of seats). Webb's patent lifting injector was fitted, operated by lever-operated steam valves – not an especially efficient use of steam when compared to the universally adopted Giffard injector. Moreover, stopping a 'Coal Tank' must have been

quite an experience. The brake application valve was a simple flap in the 2in diameter train pipe. It reduced to a quarter-inch bore in the vacuum cylinder and, consequently, hampered the rate of brake application.

Essentially, these Webb-designed locomotives were a side-tank version of his 0-6-0 'Coal Engines' of 1873. This was the origin of the classification 'Coal Tank', rather than any intended role, since they were widely used on passenger as well as goods work. Following the 1923 Grouping, the LMSR fitted many of the class with vacuum controls to operate motor-trains.

Only seven of the 300-strong class were retired before 1923, and the LMSR renumbered the rest in the series 7550-7841. However, only 64 made it to nationalization in 1948, and even some of those were not allocated British Railways numbers. Their life expectancy was too short to warrant the effort, but 56 were reprieved and renumbered Nos58880-58935.

By this time, many of the 'Coal Tanks' had gravitated towards the one-time L&NWR outpost of South Wales. Nine were on the books of Abergavenny depot, while Tredegar was home to seven and Swansea five. Others were based in North Wales, south Lancashire and around Birmingham. Despite the influx of new Stanier engines, a trio of 'Coal Tanks' was still working out of Bletchley shed in Buckinghamshire. Eleven were allocated to Edge Hill, Liverpool, and mainly used on Lime Street to Bootle services. They also appeared on boat train workings to Liverpool Riverside, although their wheelbase was not especially suited to the sharply curved quayside tracks.

L&NWR 'Coal Tank' 2F 0-6-2T

Built: Crewe works, Cheshire, 1881–97 (300 built)

Weight: 43 tons 15cwt

Driving wheel diameter: 4ft 5½in

Boiler pressure: 150lb/psi

Cylinders: (2) 17in diameter x 24in stroke

Valve gear: Stephenson (slide valves)

Coal capacity: 3 tons

Water capacity: 1,120 gallons

Tractive effort: 16,350lb (at 85% boiler pressure)

Right: Sole survivor of a once 300-strong class, Webb 'Coal Tank' No1054 stands on the turntable at Keighley on 27 October 1990. Outshopped in 1888, it became LMSR No7799 and BR No58926 before withdrawal in January 1958.

Above: Appropriately with a rake of LMSR-built vehicles in tow, No1054 awaits departure from Hampton Loade with a train for Bridgnorth during a visit to the Severn Valley Railway on 20 September 1986. The 'Coal Tanks' were essentially side-tank versions of Webb's six-coupled 'Coal Engines' – despite the name, coal traffic was never their intended role – but the true inspiration for the design came from Barton Wright's 0-6-2 tanks on the Lancashire & Yorkshire Railway.

Right: In sparkling condition, No1054 runs round its train at Bridgnorth on the morning of 21 September 1986. The class was widely used on passenger work and, after entering LMSR stock in 1923, many were equipped for motor-train working. Their chief haunts became North and South Wales, south Lancashire and the Birmingham area.

The last of the 'Coal Tanks', BR No58926 (L&NWR No1054) was retired in January 1958, after 78 years' service. With no official commitment to saving the engine, it took the efforts of the late J.M. Dunn, then shedmaster at Bangor, in North Wales, to ensure its survival. In a year, he raised the money to buy the locomotive – by then a forlorn sight at Crewe – from British Railways. The 'Coal Tank' was then given a cosmetic restoration at its birthplace.

Finding a home proved difficult, but in 1963 the National Trust accepted the 'Coal Tank' for display at its Penrhyn Castle Museum in Wales. In 1973, No1054 went on loan to the now-defunct Dinting Railway Centre and it was here that it was overhauled to working order in time to appear at the Liverpool and Manchester Railway 150th anniversary celebrations in 1980.

Subsequently, the veteran enjoyed a few outings on the main line. It was hired by a Manchester brewery to haul trains commemorating the company's anniversary, and then worked a return railtour between Dinting and the Severn Valley Railway. These were the first occasions a 'Coal Tank' had hauled passenger trains since the 1950s. In recent years, No1054 has been a notable member of the locomotive fleet on the Keighley & Worth Valley Railway in West Yorkshire.

NORTH EASTERN RAILWAY/NORTH LONDON RAILWAY

Dock Tanks

The North Eastern Railway had an interest in nine major ports along the east coast, some of which could only accommodate short wheelbase locomotives. It was for this role that Thomas Worsdell designed the diminutive H class 0-4-0 tank, the first six of which appeared in 1888. A further ten were delivered in 1890, and three more in 1897, all built at the NER's Gateshead works. Surprisingly, 25 years on, the NER ordered a further five and this final batch, re-classified Y7 by the recently formed LNER, emerged from Darlington in 1923.

Their role as dock shunters saw the class chiefly allocated to the Hull depots of Alexandra Dock and Dairycoates. Further north, examples were based at South Shields and, during the 1930s and 1940s, 13 worked out of Tyne Dock. Away from dock work, two were employed as yard shunters at Darlington.

During 1929 and 1930, the LNER sold three of the oldest Y7s. The following year, a further six engines were bought by R. Frazer & Sons of Hebburn-on-Tyne who then auctioned them to colliery companies in Northumberland and County Durham. Later, the LNER disposed of three of the 1923-built engines. No984 joined the Army in 1939 and was first stationed at Woolwich Arsenal. Subsequently, it worked at other Royal Ordnance factories before being broken up in 1947. The second, No986, worked on a harbour project at Morecambe before being scrapped in 1955. The last of this trio, No985, enjoyed a happier fate.

After 16 years in the Hull area, it was reallocated to Tyne Dock in 1939. It then left ex-NER territory altogether and became a shunter at the ex-Great Eastern Railway works at Stratford in east London. Renumbered BR No68088 and, subsequently, Departmental No34, it was withdrawn in 1952 and sold to the National Coal Board. After a time at Bentinck Colliery, Nottinghamshire, No68088 was sold to the Y7 Preservation Fund and has maintained this East Midlands connection ever since. First steamed in preservation in 1983, it currently lives at the Great Central Railway's 'Northern Extension' base at Ruddington.

The other surviving Worsdell H class tank, No1310, belongs to an earlier batch. Built at Gateshead in 1891, it was withdrawn from Tyne Dock in 1931 and sold to Pelaw Main Collieries. As National Coal Board (Durham Area) No64, the veteran remained on colliery shunting until 1964. Bought by the Steam Power Trust '65 group, No1310 can now be seen on the Middleton Railway in Leeds.

In the south, the prime function of The North London Railway was to act as a link between the London & Birmingham Railway and the docks at Poplar, in east London. The NLR possessed a mixed bag of locomotives, the most celebrated of which were the 4-4-0 tanks designed by William Adams. The longest-lived, however, was a class of 0-6-0 dock tanks, the work of Adams's successor, John C. Park.

Park took over as Locomotive Superintendent of the NLR in 1873 and, six years later, introduced the 75 class 0-6-0T. To negotiate the tightly curved track in the docks area, they had to have short, rigid wheelbases and this made them notoriously rough-riding. However, they were remarkably powerful machines: on test one started a 699-ton goods train on a 1 in 100 gradient. Based at Devons Road in Bow, the 75 class tanks continued to work at Poplar until the mid-1950s. When Devons Road became Britain's first all-diesel depot, it should have spelled the end for these, the last active locomotives built at the NLR's Bow works.

However, as far back as 1931, the LMSR had despatched two of the class to the Cromford & High Peak line in Derbyshire, where their short wheelbase was ideally suited to the terrain. With a tractive effort of 18,140lb, the North London tanks were also powerful enough for the gradients of the C&HP, and British Railways followed the LMSR in relocating engines from London. They continued to work on the Cromford & High Peak until 1960 when one of four survivors, No58850, was saved for preservation. Built in 1881, as North London Railway No116, and now on the Bluebell Railway, it is the only remaining Bow-built locomotive.

Below: North London Railway 75 class 0-6-0T No58850 climbs away from Sheffield Park with a five-coach train for Horsted Keynes on 12 May 1991. Their short, rigid wheelbases made these locomotives notoriously rough-riding. The Bluebell Railway has been home to this last surviving NLR engine for some 30 years.

Above: When its days as a colliery shunter ended at the Watergate pit on Tyneside in 1964, Y7 class 0-4-0T No1310 had outlived the last of its British Railways-owned classmates by no less than 12 years. After preservation in 1965, it briefly saw service on the Middleton Railway in Leeds but its next overhaul was a protracted one, beset by unforeseen mechanical problems. No1310 was not recommissioned until 31 May 1993, the date it was pictured at the Middleton's Moor Road terminus.

Left: Notwithstanding its Victorian demeanour, Worsdell Y7 class 0-4-0T No68088, pictured at Loughborough, on the Great Central Railway, was constructed as late as 1923 at the North Eastern Railway's Darlington workshops. Retired from its role of Stratford works shunter in 1952, the engine was sold to the National Coal Board.

Dock Tanks

	North Eastern Railway H class (LNER Y7) 0-4-0T	North London Railway 75 class (LMS/BR 2F) 0-6-0T
Built:	Gateshead works, 1888–97; Darlington works, 1923 (24 built)	Bow works, 1879–1905 (30 built)
Weight:	22 tons 14cwt	45 tons 10cwt
Driving wheel diameter:	3ft 6¼in	4ft 4in
Boiler pressure:	160lb/psi	160lb/psi
Cylinders:	(2) 14in* diameter x 20in stroke	(2) 17in diameter x 24in stroke
Valve gear:	Joy (radial gear)	Stephenson (slide valves)
Coal capacity:	6½cwt	25cwt
Water capacity:	500 gallons	956 gallons
Tractive effort:	11,041lb (at 85% boiler pressure)	18,140lb (at 85% boiler pressure)

(* some locomotives had a cylinder diameter of 13in)

LONDON BRIGHTON & SOUTH COAST RAILWAY

B1 Class 'Gladstone' 0-4-2

The railway commentator, J.N. Makselyne, described the Stroudley B1 class 0-4-2 as 'a special type of locomotive to meet somewhat special requirements'. The observation was made in 1928, when the survivors had less than five years' service remaining and that, inevitably, on secondary duties. Yet, for over two decades, the 'Gladstones', as the engines were known, had worked the majority of express services on the London Brighton & South Coast Railway.

The LB&SCR had tempted the brilliant William Stroudley away from the Highland Railway in 1871. Its directors were rewarded with locomotive designs that met the LB&SCR's needs efficiently and economically. The London to Brighton services were entrusted to the D3 class and the Class B 'Richmonds' but, by 1880, accelerated services and heavier loadings called for more power. Stroudley's solution, the B1 0-4-2, was a development of those two classes, incorporating a larger boiler and cylinders.

Stroudley based his case for employing an 0-4-2 wheel arrangement, rather than the single-driver 2-2-2 and 4-2-2 favoured elsewhere, on a combination of theory and practicality. On the practical side, any new design had to be able to operate over the existing permanent way, and fit on existing turntables. Theorists argued that, without

leading guiding wheels, the 6ft 6in diameter driving wheels of the B1 would derail as they rode up-and-over the rails at high speeds. Stroudley countered by pointing out that the heaviest weight of a locomotive was towards the front end and that, on the well-laid tracks of the Brighton line, the discrepancy in rail level over the length of a locomotive would not require the addition of a front bogie. Nevertheless, he put much thought into the balancing and profiling of the leading coupled wheels and the trailing truck. The tyres of the driving wheels were of a harder steel than normal, and special attention was paid to the springing. Leaf springs were used on the leading axle,

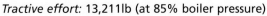

LB&SCR B1 Class 'Gladstone' 0-4-2

Built: Brighton works, Sussex, 1882–91 (36 built)

Weight: 38 tons 14cwt (locomotive)
    27 tons 7cwt (tender) (before modification)

Driving wheel diameter: 6ft 6in

Boiler pressure: 140lb/psi (later increased to 150lb/psi)

Cylinders: (2) 18¼in diameter x 26in stroke

Valve gear: Stephenson (slide valves)

Coal capacity: 2 tons (later increased to 4 tons)

Water capacity: 2,250 gallons

Tractive effort: 13,211lb (at 85% boiler pressure)

Above: Stroudley B1 class 0-4-2 No192 was outshopped from Brighton works in November 1888 and originally named Jacomb-Hood. Photographed at Battersea, London, on 17 May 1924, it had lost the name but retained the oval brass numberplate on the cabside. It had also been repainted in the umber livery devised by one of Stroudley's successors, Earle Marsh.

Right: After the Stephenson Locomotive Society paid to have No214 Gladstone restored to its original condition, the locomotive was brought to Battersea for inspection and photography by SLS members. On 21 May 1927, the 1882-built engine is being shunted into position by classmate No197 which became the penultimate B1 to be withdrawn, in June 1932.

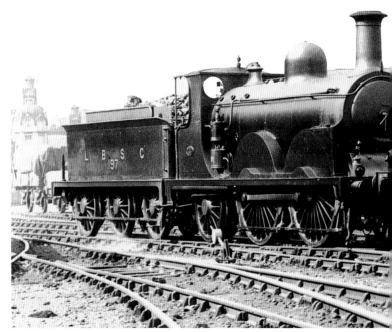

but more flexible coil springs were fitted to the centre axle. No accident involving the 'Gladstones' was attributable to their unconventional wheel arrangement.

The overall robustness and simplicity of the B1s added to their success, although Stroudley indulged in two innovations that he thought would prove beneficial. A device was fitted that condensed exhaust steam to feedwater, so allowing some of the waste heat to be recovered. He also took advantage of the air supply provided for the Westinghouse brake to bring air-powered assistance to the screw reversing gear.

The boiler of the B1 was a superb steam generator. This owed much to the large firebox, itself made feasible by the

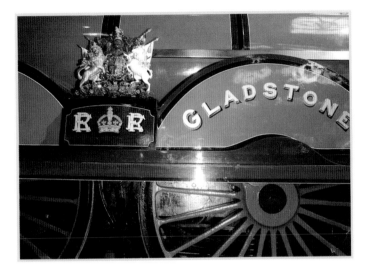

placing of the coupled wheels at the front of the locomotive. Perhaps the only impractical aspect of the design concerned the tender, where the absence of coal rails led to fuel being lost 'overboard'. Lawson Billinton, one of Stroudley's successors, added fenders to overcome this and simultaneously incorporated a well tank under the tender to increase water capacity. For its time, the Stroudley cab was both comfortable and sophisticated. Its water gauges were lit at night; the LB&SCR's electric passenger alarm was fitted; and the drivers enjoyed the benefit of Stroudley's patent speedometer.

The prototype for the B1, No214 *Gladstone*, ran for a year before the class went into production. Subsequently, in 1889, one of the series, No189 *Edward Blount*, won a gold medal at the Paris Exhibition. Afterwards it undertook trials on the Paris-Lyon-Mediterranée railway, impressing its French hosts with a speed of 69.5mph on level track with a heavy train.

Displaced from the Brighton expresses by new Earle Marsh Atlantics, withdrawals of the 'Gladstones' began in April 1910 with No215 *Salisbury* (it had a mileage of 909,132). By 1931, only two remained, and the last – No172 – was retired in 1933. However, in 1927 the Stephenson Locomotive Society had succeeded in rescuing the prototype, almost certainly the first instance of a main-line express engine being bought privately. The Southern Railway's price of £140 included reboilering and other remedial work necessary to return the locomotive to its original condition, which is how *Gladstone* is currently displayed at the National Railway Museum in York.

Above: Close-up of the nameplate splasher and coat of arms of King Edward VII mounted on the running plate of No214 Gladstone. *As now displayed in the National Railway Museum, the locomotive carries the yellow ochre livery that Stroudley interpreted as 'improved engine green'.* Gladstone *is the only surviving LB&SCR-built passenger tender engine.*

LONDON & SOUTH WESTERN RAILWAY

415 (0415) Class 1P 4-4-2T

William Adams, who joined the London & South Western in 1878, was the first British engineer of note to advocate the use of guiding bogies in a locomotive chassis. Adams's first design for the L&SWR was a 4-4-0 suburban tank that was subsequently extended to a 4-4-2 to accommodate an enlarged coal bunker. It was from this 46 class that the 415 class of 1882 was derived, specifically for London suburban services. Soon after their introduction, the 415s gained the nickname 'Radial Tanks' from another Adams trademark, the trailing radial axle.

Four companies were awarded contracts to build the 415 class. A total of 59 was shared between Robert Stephenson & Co. (28), Dübs & Co. (20) and Neilson & Co. (11). Only 12 were ordered from Beyer Peacock, which was surprising as they had been the L&SWR's principal locomotive supplier. The preserved No488, which entered traffic in March 1885, was a Neilson product.

However, the time spent by the 415 class serving the capital's Victorian commuters was comparatively brief. Within ten years they had been downgraded to rural branch duties and other secondary traffic. For No488, this meant moves to Exeter, Bournemouth and, in 1905, Eastleigh. The locomotive affairs of the L&SWR were now in the hands of Dugald Drummond, who appears to have been content to let the 415 tanks see out their time. His only significant modification (apart from re-boilering some engines) was to exchange Adams's stovepipe chimney for a lipped variety of his design.

By 1914, along with many of the 'Radial Tanks', No488 had been declared surplus to requirements. It was renumbered No0488, placed on the 'Duplicate List', and stored. However, that summer, Kaiser Wilhelm invaded Belgium, Britain went to war, and the need was for more motive power, not less. Sold to the Ministry of Munitions in 1917 for £2,107, No0488 was drafted into service at the Ridham salvage depot near Sittingbourne in Kent. Its 'military service' lasted three years, at which point the locomotive could well have gone to the breaker's had it not been for the intervention of that pioneer of light railways, Colonel Holman F. Stephens.

Stephens was engaged in building the East Kent Railway, principally to serve what appeared to be some promising coal deposits. For a knockdown price of £900, the EKR bought No0488 from the government and, renumbering it No5, restored it to L&SWR livery. The majority of its classmates were not so fortunate, and the bulk of the 415 class was scrapped between 1921 and 1928. Withdrawals had begun in 1916. Some years earlier, in 1903, the L&SWR had found the 'Radial Tank' to be the ideal motive power for the difficult five-and-a-quarter mile branch between Axminster, in Devon, and the Dorset

coastal resort of Lyme Regis. With its arduous gradients and twisting curves, this line had taken its toll in flange wear and frame stress of other classes, including the Stroudley 'Terriers' and 02 class 0-4-4 tanks. The 415 class 4-4-2T, on the other hand, with is shorter wheelbase and fore-and-aft guiding wheels, was tailor-made for the task.

Two of the class monopolized the Lyme Regis run for over 30 years, working alternate weeks. This arrangement worked well as long as both engines were serviceable, otherwise unsuitable substitutes had to be commandeered. It was to avoid this situation that, in 1946, the Southern Railway made an offer for the now-redundant No0488. It bought the engine for just £120 but, as it had been unused for seven years, was forced to spend £1,500 refurbishing the veteran.

Above: Wearing a 72A (Exmouth Junction) shedplate, Adams 0415 4-4-2T No30584 awaits departure from Axminster on 31 July 1960. It was one of three of the class (Nos30582 and 30583 were the others) kept on the books of British Railways' Southern Region to work the tortuous and steeply-graded branch line to the picturesque Dorset resort of Lyme Regis.

No0488 joined its two companions and put in 15 years' service on the Lyme Regis branch. At the age of 75, the trio was still averaging 18,000 miles a year; the final mileage for No0488 (BR No30583) was 1,604,703. Displaced in 1961 by LMSR Ivatt 2-6-2Ts, two of the three 'Radial Tanks' were broken up, but No488 again cheated the cutter's torch. It was bought by the fledgling Bluebell Railway for £850 and ran there under its own steam from Brighton on 12 July 1961.

Above: Built by Neilson's of Glasgow in 1885, Adams 0415 4-4-2T No488 enjoyed an extraordinarily diverse career before taking up residence on the Bluebell Railway in July 1961. Seen piloting Stroudley LB&SCR A1X class 'Terrier' No72 Fenchurch on Freshfield bank with a train for Horsted Keynes, the 'Radial Tank' saw service during the early 1990s but currently awaits overhaul.

Below: Profile of the surviving 'Radial Tank' No488, in its BR guise as No30583, at Axminster on 21 August 1954. Comparison with the photograph above indicates that, in preservation, the locomotive has exchanged its lipped chimney for the L&SWR-style stovepipe variety. Water capacity appears minimal, but the comparatively small sidetanks were augmented by a well tank beneath the bunker.

L&SWR 415 (0415) Class 1P 4-4-2T

Built: Beyer Peacock & Co., Manchester; Dübs & Co., Neilson & Co., both Glasgow; Robert Stephenson & Co., Newcastle-upon-Tyne, 1882–85 (71 built)

Weight: 55 tons 2cwt

Driving wheel diameter: 5ft 7in

Boiler pressure: 160lb/psi

Cylinders: (2) 17½in diameter x 24in stroke

Valve gear: Stephenson (slide valves)

Coal capacity: 1 ton 0cwt

Water capacity: 1,200 gallons

Tractive effort: 14,919lb (at 85% boiler pressure)

WIGAN COAL & IRON COMPANY

'Lindsay' 0-6-0ST

In the late 19th century, the Wigan Coal & Iron Company was one of the largest joint stock enterprises in Britain, with a capital of around £2 million. The company owned and operated more than 30 locomotives, most of them built to its designs at its Kirkless workshops. However, all revealed a strong London & North Western influence. This was no surprise since the WC&I's workshop staff received its training at Crewe, where they came under the direction of the omnipotent and formidable Francis William Webb.

Six-coupled saddletank *Lindsay* is the sole survivor from the engines constructed in and around Wigan. As well as at Kirkless, locomotive-building was undertaken at Haigh Foundry, the Pagefield Ironworks of Walker Brothers and at Wilkinson's foundry at Holme House, the last best-remembered for its street tramway engines.

The standard-gauge *Lindsay* became the third locomotive to carry that name. The first dated from the 1840s, a product of Haigh Foundry, and was named after the eldest son of the Foundry's owner, the Earl of Crawford and Balcarres. It was employed on the network of lines serving the Earl's collieries at Haigh, Blackrod and Aspull. In 1868, this locomotive was replaced by a tender engine, also called *Lindsay*, that used the boiler and other components from its predecessor. Unfortunately, this second locomotive was something of a 'rogue' and suffered frequent derailments. One derailment, in 1869, resulted in the death of the driver. Four years earlier, the Earl had amalgamated his colliery and engineering companies with those of John Lancaster. The latter owned coal mines at Kirkless, Standish, Hindley and West Leigh. The new, enlarged company became the Wigan Coal & Iron Company.

The third *Lindsay* – the one depicted here – spent most of its working life near its birthplace, employed on colliery workings around Wigan and the Kirkless Iron & Steel Works. During the 1960s, and now well over 70 years old, it was to be found pottering around Chisnall Hall Colliery at Coppull, the last operational pit in the Wigan area. It was not until 1967, following Chisnall Hall's closure, that *Lindsay* left Lancashire for the first time. It became stand-by engine at Hafod Colliery in north Wales.

Eventually *Lindsay* was bought by a Preston metal merchant and stored in a scrapyard but, in 1978, the Locomotive 'Lindsay' Partnership succeeded in its aim of preserving the last surviving Wigan-built steam locomotive. During 1979 and 1980, *Lindsay* underwent a complete rebuild, undertaken by engineers and fitters from the National Coal Board. This team became responsible for subsequent repairs and maintenance, including – up to 1993 – two major overhauls. While, rebuilding was underway, the opportunity was taken to restore the locomotive to its original condition. Later accretions, such as the enclosed cab, were removed.

WC&I 'Lindsay' 0-6-0ST

Built: Kirkless works, Wigan, Lancashire, 1887 (1 built)

Weight: 39 tons 0cwt

Driving wheel diameter: 4ft 4in

Boiler pressure: 140lb/psi

Cylinders: (2) 16in diameter x 26in stroke

Valve gear: Stephenson

Coal capacity: (not available)

Water capacity: (not available)

Tractive effort: (not available)

Right: The epitome of the Victorian industrial locomotive, six-coupled saddletank Lindsay remained at work in the Wigan area until 1967. However, many major components – including the boiler, firebox and smokebox – have had to be renewed during the locomotive's 22 years in preservation.

Above: With the twin white star emblem of the Wigan Coal & Iron Company on its bufferbeam, Lindsay is not all that far from its roots as it stands outside the running shed at Steamtown Carnforth, in north Lancashire. Note the large steam dome, indicative of a saturated (i.e. non-superheated) locomotive. The L&NWR influence in its design is evident.

Right: Close-up of the saddletank, nameplate, wheel splashers, springs, coupling rod and 4ft 4in diameter driving wheels of Lindsay. The reversing rod is located above the running plate, while the brake rigging can be glimpsed below the coupling rod. Typical of the period, Lindsay has inside cylinders.

Much of the locomotive had to be renewed, including the boiler, firebox, coal bunker, smokebox, chimney, spectacle plate and copper dome. Finally, *Lindsay* was repainted in the colours of the Wigan Coal & Iron Company, a livery officially described as 'dark chocolate'. The WC&I's twin white star motif was applied to the buffer beam, and the original brass worksplates and nameplates refitted.

In 1981, *Lindsay* joined the collection at Steamtown Carnforth and it was there, on 31 May 1987, that it celebrated its 100th birthday. Taken out of service in October 1988, the veteran underwent a further overhaul – including a boiler retube – in the workshops of Carnforth Railway Restoration, returning to steam in June 1990.

Evolution and Elegance
1885–1920

L&YR 27 class • Six-coupled Goods

MR 115 class 'Spinner' • GNR J13 (J52) class

L&SWR 02, M7 classes • Metropolitan Railway E class

L&SWR T9 'Greyhound' • SE&CR D class 'Coppertop'

GNR C1, C2 'Atlantics' • MR 4P Compound

GWR 3700 'City' class • GWR 2800/2884 classes

GWR 4500/4575 Prairie tanks • Two Tank Types

GWR 4200/5205 classes • GWR 4300 class

GCR 8K (04) class • MR 4F class • S&DJR 7F class

GER L77 (N7) class • GCR 11E/11F (D11) 'Director'

NER Q7 class

1885–1920

Evolution and Elegance

Forty years after the opening of the Liverpool & Manchester Railway, there were 13,500 route miles of railway in Britain. All major towns and cities could be reached by train and branch lines snaked into the remotest parts of the country. This growth was largely uncontrolled, leading to a proliferation of companies and a duplication of lines that was later to have serious commercial repercussions. Few gave that much thought, however, in the 1870s and 1880s. There were more pressing questions, such as how to cope with the demand for train travel. What had begun as principally a means of conveying goods had developed into the most popular means of public transport.

The Great Western and Great Northern Railways, among others, demonstrated how fast their passenger services could run, but primitive braking systems limited the trains' capacity. Consequently, there was no pressing need to build bigger, more powerful (and, inevitably, more expensive) locomotives. By the late 1880s, that argument no longer held. Continuous braking, whether using the compressed-air Westinghouse system or vacuum brakes, could now be applied to every wheel. This allowed heavy trains to run safely at high speeds. Moreover, the lightweight, wooden-bodied coaches used up to that point were being replaced by heavier, better-appointed steel-bodied vehicles. More powerful locomotives were essential.

In other countries, especially the United States, this was simply a matter of building bigger. Britain, with its restricted

loading gauge, lacked that option and designers sought other ways of generating more power. Some things, however, were imported from across the Atlantic, principally the 4-4-0 wheel arrangement.

The 4-4-0 became the standard express passenger type on Britain's railways. Its two-axle leading bogie gave stability at the speeds generated by its large-diameter driving wheels, and the whole chassis could support a reasonably sized boiler. It was also the kind of format that allowed designers to pursue locomotive engineering as an art form. British locomotives of the Victorian period were characterized by their clean, flowing lines, ornate liveries and gleaming brasswork. There was the minimum of external 'plumbing' to offend the eye, as appearance was elevated above accessibility.

An American influence, however, continued to be felt. The 4-4-2, or Atlantic, type originated with railroads on the eastern seaboard of the United States. This development of the 4-4-0, with a trailing axle to support a larger firebox, was first adopted in Britain by the Great Northern Railway. The Americans also extended the 4-4-0 into the 4-6-0, using the third set of driving wheels to improve adhesion, which was important as trains grew heavier. Additionally, the longer chassis supported a larger boiler, increasing power output, but the firebox dimensions were still restricted. The 4-6-0 reached Britain in 1894, with the 'Jones Goods' design of the Highland Railway, and went on to become the most numerous of passenger types.

Left: Most British railways adopted the 4-4-0 as their standard passenger locomotive and William Paton Reid's 32-strong K class was built by Scotland's North British Railway as late as 1913–1920. Outshopped from Cowlairs works, Glasgow, in September 1913, No256 Glen Douglas *was preserved as part of the National Collection.*

The pre-eminent express type, however, was a logical combination of the advantages of the 4-4-2 and 4-6-0. The 4-6-2, or Pacific, also originated in the United States, in 1886, but it was a further 36 years before the first production Pacifics were built in Britain.

Other developments were embraced more quickly. One was a type of firebox invented by a Belgian, Alfred Belpaire. He had become concerned with the detrimental effect on performance caused by burning low-grade fuel. If the quality of the fuel could not be improved, its combustion would have to be more productive. In contrast to the universally employed round-top firebox, Belpaire developed a flat-topped design that, in filling all the available space within the width of the locomotive, maximized the steam space between the surface of the inner lining of the firebox and its outer shell. The area available inside the firebox for heating water was also the maximum possible.

Many engineers were attracted by another method of improving efficiency: compounding. This involved the expansion of steam through two stages, first in high pressure and then in a low pressure cylinder (or cylinders). Each charge of steam was therefore used twice, increasing power output by between 10 and 15 per cent. Compounding enjoyed its greatest popularity in Continental Europe, particularly France. In Britain, three main line railways actively pursued compounding: the North Eastern, London & North Western and – most successfully – the Midland Railway.

The most significant technical development of the 1890s, however, was superheating. Almost from the outset, engineers realized that power output could be increased and fuel consumption reduced if the steam produced by the boiler could be heated to even higher temperatures before being used in the cylinders. Through superheating, the energy lost through condensation would be lessened appreciably.

Steam vapour generated in a boiler – 'saturated steam' – still contains moisture that offers resistance to the movement of pistons. However, applying additional heat to the steam at much higher temperatures creates a gas. If the temperature is raised sufficiently, the gas will be maintained above saturation level during its passage through the steampipes and cylinders.

A second benefit from superheating comes from the expansion in the volume of the steam as heat is absorbed. More power therefore can be developed from a given weight of steam, although the quantity is dependent on the superheat temperature. Superheated locomotives can generate up to 25 per cent more power than their 'saturated' equivalents.

The deployment of a satisfactory superheater, however, was contingent on advances in metallurgy and lubrication that would enable cylinders, pistons and pipes to withstand the 'cutting' quality of superheated steam. When these were available, two German engineers – August von Borries and Wilhelm Schmidt – led the way in superheater development. Their ideas were eagerly taken up by British designers, among them the newly appointed Chief Mechanical Engineer of the Great Western Railway, George Jackson Churchward.

Above: Churchward's masterpiece was the 'Star' class 4-cylinder 4-6-0, of which No4003 Lode Star *– seen here at the National Railway Museum, York – is the surviving example. When built in 1907,* Lode Star *was way ahead of its contemporaries.*

Above: The Highland Railway's David Jones introduced the 4-6-0 into Britain with his 'Jones Goods' engines of 1894. Built by Sharp Stewart in Glasgow, all 15 saw LMSR service and the last was not withdrawn until 1940. The first of the class, No103, was set aside for preservation in 1934.

Among a host of noteworthy locomotive engineers working around the turn of the century, Churchward was outstanding. More than any of his contemporaries, he married the best of American and French practice with ideas of his own. Churchward equipped the Great Western Railway with a fleet of locomotives significantly in advance of those on any other British railway. Between 1903 and 1911, he introduced a range of types ranging from 2-6-2 passenger tanks, through 2-6-0 and 4-6-0 mixed traffic and express passenger classes, to 2-8-0 heavy freight locomotives, both of tender and tank engine varieties. The standardization of components such as boilers, cylinders and wheels across the nine classes was unprecedented for a British railway, and Churchward's innovations influenced all subsequent steam locomotive development in Britain.

LANCASHIRE & YORKSHIRE RAILWAY

27 Class 3F 0-6-0

Of the 20,000 or so locomotives in service on Britain's railways around 1900, over one third were six-coupled tender engines. Primarily intended for goods traffic, the 0-6-0 was easily the dominant locomotive type. It included many noteworthy and long-lived designs. One was John Aspinall's Class 27 of 1889, the standard goods engine of the Lancashire & Yorkshire Railway.

The L&YR's huge volume of freight traffic was mainly entrusted to a large fleet of 0-6-0s. Barton Wright's Class 25 of 1887 was one of its more successful constituents and was adopted by his successor, John Aspinall, as the basis for his Class 27. Aspinall opted for a 2-cylinder format with a non-superheated round-top boiler. David Joy's configuration of valve gear was employed. By the time of Aspinall's departure from the L&YR in 1899, over 400 of these simple but powerful machines were in service. More were built under his successors, Henry Hoy and George Hughes, albeit with some modifications. By 1918, the class totalled 484.

It was under Hughes that the class became the subject of an early experiment in superheating. This was the process of increasing the temperature of the steam produced in the boiler so that the minimum amount of energy was lost through condensation. Significant fuel savings resulted. The leading exponent of superheating was a German engineer, Wilhelm Schmidt, and it was a Schmidt device that, in 1905, Hughes had fitted to two new 0-6-0s. Additionally, piston valves supplanted the usual slide valves, although the Joy valve gear was retained.

For some ten months the superheated engines worked alongside their saturated (i.e. non-superheated) classmates. The comparison enabled George Hughes to

inform the L&YR directors of a noteworthy improvement in performance. Not only were the superheated engines capable of hauling heavier loads (about ten per cent greater) but they were showing a saving in coal consumption of some 12.5 per cent. A further six months of trials demonstrated that these figures could be maintained and construction of a further 20 superheated engines was authorized (although it was not until 1909 that they emerged from Horwich works).

The superheated Class 27 0-6-0s retained the boiler pressure of the original (180lb/psi). Although the maximum travel of the valves was reduced, they did benefit from larger steam passages. The area of the exhaust ports, in particular, was increased substantially.

These first superheated examples all had round-topped boilers but, in 1912, a second batch of 20 was constructed with Belpaire fireboxes. This highly efficient design of flat-topped firebox was the work of a Belgian, Alfred Belpaire, and became widely adopted in Europe and North America. It maximized the combustion area within a given space and the water-heating space between the inner and outer firebox wrappers. Like other railway companies, the L&YR was impressed by this Belgian development. A number of earlier, non-superheated examples of the Class 27 were fitted with new boilers incorporating Belpaire fireboxes and extended smokeboxes. Although all the superheated 0-6-0s eventually reverted to, or were converted to saturated operation, they had proved their worth.

Altogether, the class was augmented by a further 60 locomotives between 1900 and 1909, with another ten added in 1917–18. The final five built reverted entirely to

Above: The leading coupled wheelset of the Aspinall 3F 0-6-0, showing axle, crankpin, coupling rod and adjacent footstep. The reversing rod runs behind the wheel splasher.

the original 1889 specification. It is a tribute to the soundness, usefulness and simple practicality of Aspinall's design that some 300 remained in LMS service at the end of World War II. Around 50 were still in British Railways stock as late as the summer of 1960, but just one example survived to be preserved, No52322 (L&YR No1300, LMS No12322). Built at Horwich in 1896, it was withdrawn in 1960 and sold to a Lancashire civil engineering company. Subsequently the locomotive moved to the Steamtown Railway Museum at Carnforth where it was restored to working order. It now lives on the East Lancashire Railway at Bury, near Manchester.

L&YR 27 Class 3F 0-6-0

Built: Horwich works, 1889–1918 (484 built)

Weight: 42 tons 3cwt (locomotive)
    26 tons 2cwt (tender)

Driving wheel diameter: 5ft 1in

Boiler pressure: 180lb/psi

Cylinders: (2) 18in diameter x 26in stroke
    (cylinder diameter on superheated
    locomotives increased to 20in)

Valve gear: Joy (slide valves); (piston valves
    fitted to superheated engines)

Coal capacity: 3 tons 0cwt

Water capacity: 1,800 gallons

Tractive effort: 21,130lb
    (at 85% boiler pressure)

Opposite: Standing in the yard at Steamtown Carnforth on 15 August 1992, preserved Aspinall 3F 0-6-0 No1300 displays the lined black livery applied to Lancashire & Yorkshire goods engines, complete with company crest on the rear wheel splasher. No1300 represents the 27 class as originally built, with short smokebox and round-top firebox.

Above: No1300 seldom ventures away from its current home of the East Lancashire Railway but the summer of 1998 saw it visiting the Chinnor & Princes Risborough Railway, which runs along the foot of the Chiltern Hills. On 5 July 1998, the 1896-built 0-6-0 makes a vigorous start away from the C&PRR's terminus loop at Princes Risborough.

NORTH BRITISH/SOUTH EASTERN & CHATHAM RAILWAY

Six-coupled Goods

Other than sharing the classification 'C', these two designs from railways at the opposite ends of the British Isles have something else in common. Both have been distinguished in ways not normally enjoyed by self-effacing goods engines. In the case of the North British locomotives, it was the attachment of some very distinguished names. For those of the South Eastern & Chatham Railway, it was the application of a livery that would have been elaborate even by prestige express locomotive standards.

Matthew Holmes's C class 0-6-0 was the most numerous design on Scotland's North British Railway. Construction began at its Cowlairs works in Glasgow in 1888 and continued until 1900. Orders for 15 engines apiece were also placed with two Glasgow manufacturers, Neilson's and Sharp Stewart. Fine engineer as he was, Holmes was no innovator and the C class was based firmly on a proven Dugald Drummond model. Holmes had succeeded Drummond in 1882 and went on to become the NBR's longest-serving Locomotive Superintendent, holding the post until June 1903. He introduced the C class to meet the NBR's need for a long-distance freight engine but it also proved its worth on passenger services and this led to many later engines being fitted with Westinghouse train brakes. The locomotives were built with comparatively small boilers and with open cabs that offered crews little protection from the Scottish climate. Following Holmes's retirement, his successors, William Paton Reid and Walter Chalmers, rebuilt the entire 168-strong C class with larger boilers and more sheltered side-window cabs.

It was during Reid's incumbency that the C class enjoyed its moment of glory, with 25 engines requisitioned by the Railway Operating Department for service on the Western Front during World War I. They ferried in supplies and munitions, and pulled the ambulance trains carrying the wounded. In recognition, all 25 were named, either after places associated with the conflict, or personalities. The now-preserved No673 *Maude*, for example, honours Lieutenant General Sir Frederick Stanley Maude KCB.

As was NBR practice, the names were simply painted on to the centre wheel splasher which on occasions led to them 'disappearing' during overhauls, as the works painters neglected to reapply them. By the outbreak of World War II in 1939, withdrawals had reduced the number of named examples to 14. Eleven lasted to become British Railways property, along with a further 112 unnamed C class 0-6-0s, all by now reclassified J36.

Below: North British C class 0-6-0 No673 Maude poses with a breakdown crane at Bo'ness on 24 October 1993. All 168 members of the class were harnessed to 2,500 gallon tenders, although early examples lacked the coal rails sported here by No673's tender. For most of its British Railways career, the 1891-built No673 (BR No65243) was based at Haymarket, Edinburgh. It was retired from Bathgate in July 1966.

As late as June 1967, two – Nos 65288 and 65345 – were still at work. Astonishingly, these engines – built in 1897 and 1900 respectively – were the last working steam locomotives in Scotland.

Construction of the South Eastern & Chatham Railway's C class 0-6-0 began as that of its Scottish counterpart ended, in 1900. As with all locomotive designs bearing the imprint of Harry Wainwright, its humble role was no bar to an ornate livery or abundant use of polished brasswork. However, the operational success of the 108-strong class owed more to Wainwright's colleague, Robert Surtees. The qualities he built into the engines ensured that all but three were still in service at nationalization in 1948.

The C class continued to be reliable, if moderately powered goods engines. Crews liked them because, unlike the majority of tender engines, they were adept at shunting. All were fitted with the SE&CR short, double-handled regulator which was crisply responsive when it came to getting the main steam port open to reach maximum power in the shortest possible time. As with the North British C class, just one of the Wainwright engines has been preserved and can be seen at work on the Bluebell Railway in East Sussex. It also has the distinction of being the sole surviving locomotive built at the SE&CR's Longhedge works at Battersea, south London. Constructed in 1902, No592 worked up to the 1960s.

Left: It is unlikely that Harry Wainwright's C class goods 0-6-0s ever worked Pullman services, but the ornately-liveried No592 does not look out of place at the head of the Bluebell Railway's luxury dining train. The 1902-built locomotive, which ended its days in departmental service as DS239 (it was employed as a yard shunter at Ashford works in Kent), was saved by the C Class Locomotive Preservation Society and arrived on the Bluebell during August 1970.

Six-coupled Goods

	Holmes NBR C Class 0-6-0	Wainwright SE&CR C Class 0-6-0
Built:	Cowlairs works; Neilson & Co; Sharp Stewart, all Glasgow, Scotland, 1888–1900 (168 built)	Longhedge works, Battersea, London, 1900–08 (108 built)
Weight:	41 tons 19cwt (locomotive)) 33 tons 10cwt (tender)	43 tons 16cwt (locomotive) 38 tons 5cwt (tender)
Driving wheel diameter:	5ft 0in	5ft 2in
Boiler pressure:	165lb/psi	160lb/psi
Cylinders:	(2) 18in diameter x 26in stroke	(2) 18½in diameter x 26in stroke
Valve gear:	Stephenson (slide valves)	Stephenson (slide valves)
Coal capacity:	6 tons	4 tons 10cwt
Water capacity:	2,500 gallons	3,300 gallons
Tractive effort:	17,901lb (19,690lb after rebuilding) (at 85% boiler pressure)	19,920lb (at 85% boiler pressure)

MIDLAND RAILWAY

115 Class 4-2-2

What persuaded the locomotive superintendent of the Midland Railway, Samuel Waite Johnson, in 1887 to reintroduce the single-wheeler express locomotive? Twenty-one years had passed since such engines had last been built for the company and, elsewhere, the move towards four-coupled passenger engines was proving irresistible. A key element was the Midland's continuing preference for 'small engines'. Though facing competition to all its major destinations, the Midland stuck to a pattern of lightweight trains and fast timings. It was a policy made for single-wheelers, at least on the undemanding grades south of Derby. Another factor was the invention by the works manager at Derby, Francis Holt, of a steam-powered sanding device. This did wonders for the wheel-on-rail adhesion of large-wheeled locomotives.

But why were single-wheelers built at all? They were a product of fundamental theory and a recognition of the limitations of early locomotives. The speed of any locomotive is regulated by the rate its driving wheels revolve. The greater the diameter of the wheels, the fewer revolutions required to maintain a certain speed. And the fewer the revolutions, the less interaction between valve gear, pistons and cylinders – something that was highly desirable when the science of lubrication was in its infancy. Large driving wheels, between seven and eight feet in diameter, made faster speeds attainable without substantially increasing wear-and-tear on valve gear and cylinders.

However, the single-wheeler always had an Achilles heel: lack of adhesion, or a limited ability to grip the rail when pulling a heavy load. Once the technical constraints

Two classic Midland Railway designs make an unlikely pairing returning from an open day at Tinsley diesel depot, Sheffield, on 15 June 1980. Johnson 'Spinner' No673 pilots Fowler 4F 0-6-0 No4027 on the return trip to the Midland Railway Centre, which was home to these two National Collection locomotives for several years. Although no longer steamable, No4027 remains in the care of the MRC; the 1897-built No673, however, has returned to the National Railway Museum in York.

Above: Looking unrecognizable, given its present, pristine crimson lake livery, the sole survivor of the Midland 'Spinners', No673, awaits its next duty at Birmingham New Street some time in 1926. By the following year it was one of only three survivors from a grand total of 95 single-wheelers spread across four classes.

maintain tight schedules with 350 tons. Speeds up to 90mph were not uncommon and the sight of their huge, whirring driving wheels earned them a lasting nickname: the 'Spinners'.

Thanks to the Midland's practice of building low-powered locomotives and relying on double-heading to cope with its heavier trains, many enjoyed working lives of up to 40 years. The 'Spinners' made ideal pilot engines for the later Johnson/Deeley 4-4-0 classes. During World War I, most were placed in store, but surprisingly pressed into service afterwards as pilots on Nottinghamshire to London coal trains. Nevertheless, by 1927, only three remained. Fortunately one was set aside for preservation.

By rights, the 'Spinners' should have been consigned to the scrapheap well before the 1920s. That they were not was a tribute to their economy and efficiency. Yet the 'big wheel' that was central to the success of the single-wheeler was ultimately the cause of its downfall. To have to allow clearance for an axle and its associated rods and cranks so high above rail level was too great a constraint on building larger diameter (and therefore more powerful) boilers. In Britain, the 'Spinners' ushered out the 'small is beautiful' school of locomotive engineering.

that favoured a single pair of driving wheels were eliminated, it was rendered obsolete for most main line work. On the Midland, though, the combination of dyed-in-the-wool motive power policy and Francis Holt's invention ensured a brief, but glorious, swansong.

Samuel Johnson's first single-wheelers were outshopped from Derby in 1887. Though in terms of locomotive development they were anachronisms, in the specifics of boiler, cylinders, motion and frame design, they reflected contemporary standards. In all, 95 engines were built over a 13-year period. There were variations in cylinder bore, wheelbase length, frame dimensions and tenders, and in the diameter of the driving wheels which grew from 7ft 4in to 7ft 9 1/2 inches. Earlier engines had slide valves, but later ones employed more modern piston valves.

The first two classes of Johnson-designed 4-2-2 were built between 1887 and 1890. They were followed by the Class 179 which was delivered in two batches, in 1893 and 1896. These were the first fitted with piston valves.

However, it was the next generation of single-wheelers that became the most celebrated. With the wheel diameter increased to 7ft 9 1/2in and the cylinder bore to 19 1/2in, 15 of the 115 class were constructed between 1896 and 1899. They were soon acknowledged as one of the highpoints in British locomotive design and styling.

A typical Midland express weighing between 200 and 250 tons suited these engines perfectly. Given a dry rail, they could

Above: Cab interior of the preserved 'Spinner' No673. The backhead is lined with wood, with circular brass frames to the spectacle glasses. Above and to the left of the centrally-placed regulator handle is the vacuum brake gauge and, alongside it, the steam pressure gauge. As is evident, Victorian footplates had the minimum of facilities.

MR 115 Class 4-2-2

Built: Derby works, 1896–99 (15 built)

Weight: 43 tons 14cwt (locomotive)
   21 tons 11cwt (tender)

Driving wheel diameter: 7ft 9 1/2in

Boiler pressure: 170lb/psi

Cylinders: (2) 19 1/2in diameter
   x 26in stroke

Valve gear: Stephenson (piston valves)

Coal capacity: 4 tons

Water capacity: 3,500 gallons*

Tractive effort: 15,280lb (at 85% boiler pressure)

(some engines harnessed to 2,950-gallon tenders)*

GREAT NORTHERN RAILWAY

J13 (J52) Class 3F 0-6-0ST

A railway historian described the six-coupled saddletank as 'a Great Northern institution'. For almost a century, engines of this type were employed on shunting and local goods work by the GNR and its successors. The type originated in 1868 with a design by Patrick Stirling. Although only 16 were built in the ensuing six years, the requirement for them evidently grew as, by 1881, a further 78 were in service. Construction of Stirling's designs continued up to and beyond his death in 1895. However, in 1897, his successor, Henry Ivatt, produced a development of the Stirling original. When engines Nos1201-1210 were outshopped from Doncaster works, they carried a new type of boiler that was larger than its predecessor and sported a steam dome (all the Stirling boilers were domeless). The cab design had been modified, too: it was wider and, unlike the majority of those on the Stirling engines, had a roof.

Construction of the next sequence of engines in what was to become the Great Northern's J13 class was contracted out to Robert Stephenson & Hawthorn of Newcastle-upon-Tyne and delivered between 1898 and 1899. The latter year also saw a further 25 engines built by Sharp Stewart in Glasgow, a batch that included what is now the sole surviving GN saddletank, No1247. Between 1901 and 1909, the class was enlarged by 40 more engines, all constructed at Doncaster. The final 20 emerged from the works with a flared extension, surmounted by coal rails, to the tops of the coal bunkers.

Subsequently, the Ivatt saddletanks remained largely unaltered. Their spring-loaded Ramsbottom safety valves were replaced by the Ross 'pop' type and, in a curious experiment, No1260 was fitted with a mechanical stoker. It retained this device for two years from 1936 to 1938, yet appears not to have undertaken any revenue-earning service during this time.

The majority of the saddletanks were concentrated at six depots on the Great Northern system, all serving major freight-handling centres. There were allocations at King's Cross and Hornsey in London; at New England (Peterborough); and at Doncaster, Ardsley (Leeds) and Bradford. The arrival of the more powerful Gresley J50 tanks saw them displaced from West Yorkshire but the London-based engines, especially, found regular employment throughout the post-Grouping LNER era. Apart from shunting the yards at King's Cross and Ferme Park, they were employed on transfer freights across the capital. The Ivatt saddletanks journeyed to Temple Mills marshalling yard near Stratford and south of the river to Southern Railway yards such as Hither Green. Despite the absence of condensing apparatus to recycle exhaust steam in the tunnels, they were a regular sight on the 'Widened

Lines' of the Metropolitan Railway. The Ivatt saddletanks were reliable, hard-working engines but inevitably diesels arrived to take over their duties. Large numbers were retired in the late 1950s and the last – with one notable exception – went to the breaker's in 1961.

That would have seen the Ivatt saddletanks consigned to the history books were it not for one man's audacity. Captain W.G. (Bill) Smith VRD RNR had spent a childhood in GNR and LNER territory and wanted to ensure the survival of one of the locomotives he admired. However, this was 1959 and the notion of buying an engine from British Railways was unheard of. Nevertheless, Captain Smith made enquiries and received a surprisingly encouraging response. He was taken on a tour of King's Cross depot and, among the ranks of Pacifics, was introduced to the comparatively diminutive (and considerably more manageable) shed pilot, Ivatt saddletank No68846. On 7 May 1959, Bill Smith became the owner of Britain's first privately preserved steam locomotive. For three years, he was allowed to run 'The Old Lady', as the King's Cross enginemen had dubbed it, on the main line. Thereafter, the locomotive worked on preserved railways until, in 1980, Captain Smith donated this 'preservation pioneer' to the National Railway Museum, in whose care it remains.

Above: With the North Sea as a backcloth, Great Northern saddletank No1247 heads away from Weybourne with a North Norfolk Railway service for Holt on 12 September 1993. The 1899-built veteran was participating in a gala marking the centenary of the Midland & Great Northern Joint Railway, of which the NNR was once part.

Opposite: Sunshine brings out the splendour of the lined apple green GNR livery of No1247 as it runs round at Sheringham during its 1993 visit to the North Norfolk Railway. In 1959, the Ivatt saddletank made history by becoming Britain's first privately-preserved locomotive. Since 1980 it has been in the care of the National Railway Museum.

GNR J13 (LNER J52) Class 3F 0-6-0ST

Built: Doncaster works; Robert Stephenson & Hawthorn, Newcastle-upon-Tyne; Sharp Stewart, Glasgow, 1897–1909 (85 built)

Weight: 51 tons 14cwt

Driving wheel diameter: 4ft 8in

Boiler pressure: 170lb/psi

Cylinders: (2) 18in diameter x 26in stroke

Valve gear: Stephenson (piston valves)

Coal capacity: 3 tons

Water capacity: 1,100 gallons

Tractive effort: 21,735lb (at 85% boiler pressure)

Above: Although the J52s ventured south of the Thames on cross-London freights, joint working such as this was unlikely. Complete with a 34B (Hornsey) shedcode, in its British Railways guise of No68846, the last of the Ivatt saddletanks pilots another of preservation's 'loners', the Bluebell Railway's SE&CR H class 0-4-4T No263.

LONDON & SOUTH WESTERN RAILWAY

02, M7 Classes OP/2P 0-4-4T

In the second half of the 19th century the 0-4-4 tank locomotive became a popular choice for that relatively new phenomenon, suburban commuter traffic. The London & South Western Railway, with its intensive services to south-west London and Surrey, relied heavily upon such engines. Of its 0-4-4 classes, the most celebrated and longest-lived were the 02 design of William Adams and the later M7 of his successor, Dugald Drummond.

Adams's first 0-4-4 tank for the L&SWR was the T1 of 1888, an engine whose 5ft 7in diameter coupled wheels and 18in x 26in cylinders marked it out as a sprinter. With its smaller cylinders and 4ft 10in diameter drivers, the 02, which appeared the following year, was more a general purpose design. Twenty 02s were built at the L&SWR's Nine Elms works during 1889, and 30 more ordered the following year. By 1895, 60 were in service, distributed throughout the L&SWR system. From 1897, however, they were displaced increasingly by Drummond's new M7s. The Isle of Wight Central Railway looked at buying some of the redundant 02s and discussions reached the stage where a group of IoWCR directors came to Nine Elms to inspect one of the class. However, the deal foundered and – for the time being, at least – the 02s stayed on the mainland.

Then, in 1914, two examples were tried successfully on push-pull working. This led to a further 21 02s being modified and used on services as contrasting as Bodmin to Padstow and Clapham Junction to Kensington. The class would probably have ended its days in these roles had not the Southern Railway revived the notion of shipping 02s to the Isle of Wight. The 02s were both suitable and available and, despite their years, in better shape than most of the locomotives in use there. Between 1923 and 1936, 21 02s crossed the Solent, to be renumbered with a 'W' prefix and, from 1928, named after towns and resorts on the island.

Above: Aptly, today's Isle of Wight Steam Railway is home to the surviving 02 NoW24 Calbourne. During 1991, the Adams tank celebrated its centenary and on 20 July hauled the inaugural trains over the IoWSR's extension from Havenstreet to Smallbrook Junction.

Above: The National Collection's M7, No245, was built in 1897 at a cost of £1,846. It gave good value for money: mileage upon withdrawal in 1962 was 1,603,998.

Of the original 60 Adams 02s, 48 survived to be nationalized in 1948. Twenty-one of those were on the Isle of Wight and two more were sent to join them in 1949. On the mainland, the last 02 was withdrawn in 1962, but eight of the IoW engines remained active up to the last day of scheduled steam on the island, 31 December 1966.

The 02's bigger cousin, the M7 0-4-4 tank, was Dugald Drummond's first design for the L&SWR after replacing William Adams as Locomotive Superintendent in 1895. The first 25 were built at Nine Elms between March and November 1897 and numbers steadily increased until the 105th and last, No481, was completed in December 1911. Over its 14-year construction span, many detail differences appeared within the M7 class. Examples were fitted with feedwater heating, conical smokebox doors, steam reversers and other devices. The most significant modification, however, was the fitting, from 1912, of push-pull equipment to over a third of the class. At first, a primitive cable-and-pulley device was employed but, when this was shown to be unsafe, it was replaced on 31 engines by a compressed air system.

Except for No126, which had been experimentally fitted with a superheated boiler and enlarged cylinders in 1921 but withdrawn in 1937, all the Drummond M7s passed into British Railways ownership. In L&SWR and Southern Railway days, the M7s had been successful suburban passenger engines. Now they took on a new role as reliable branch-line locomotives, especially in south-west England. By the end of 1963, the majority of the 14 surviving M7s were based at Bournemouth, chiefly to work the Swanage branch, but in the following May all were retired. Two have survived, No245 (built 1897) as part of the National Collection, and No30053 of 1905 which, when not on its travels, is based appropriately enough on the Swanage Railway.

O2, M7 Classes

	L&SWR Adams O2 Class 0-4-4T	L&SWR Drummond M7 Class 0-4-4T
Built:	Nine Elms works, Battersea, London,1889–95 (60 built)	Eastleigh and Nine Elms works, 1897–1911 (105 built)
Weight:	48 tons 8cwt	60 tons 4cwt (as first built)
Driving wheel diameter:	4ft 10in	5ft 7in
Boiler pressure:	160lb/psi	175lb/psi
Cylinders:	(2) 17½in diameter x 24in stroke	(2) 18½in diameter x 26in stroke
Valve gear:	Stephenson	Stephenson
Coal capacity:	1 ton 10cwt	3 tons (later 3 tons 5cwt)
Water capacity:	800 gallons	1,300 gallons
Tractive effort:	17,235lb (at 85% boiler pressure)	19,775lb (at 85% boiler pressure)

M7 No30053 starts away from Swanage with a train for Harman's Cross. This engine spent its last months in BR service at Bournemouth depot and regularly worked on the Swanage branch up to retirement in May 1964. In 1967, it was shipped to the United States, remaining there for some 20 years.

METROPOLITAN RAILWAY

E Class 0-4-4T

Today, when London Underground's Metropolitan Line is home to featureless electric multiple units, it is hard to imagine that the line from Aldgate, in the heart of the city, to Amersham and Aylesbury once boasted a 70-strong fleet of steam locomotives. The world's first underground railway, the Metropolitan, opened for business on 10 January 1863. In its first months of operation, it relied upon locomotives supplied by, first, the Great Western Railway and then the Great Northern. However, such was the popularity of the new service that it was soon able order its own motive power. The delivery of 18 4-4-0 tanks from Beyer Peacock in the summer of 1864 began a long-standing relationship with the Manchester-based engine builders. A further 48 were built between 1866 and 1885.

Although the Beyer Peacock tanks proved ideal for inner suburban workings, the longer runs out into Hertfordshire and Buckinghamshire called for something faster and with a larger coal capacity. In 1891, four 0-4-4 tanks (the design of which clearly owed much to much to their counterparts on the South Eastern Railway) were ordered from Neilsons of Glasgow. These proved first-class machines and were the precursors of the long-lived E class tanks.

The design of the E class 0-4-4T was the work of Thomas Clark who took over as Locomotive Superintendent of the Metropolitan in 1896. Three were built at the company's Neasden workshops and a further four by Hawthorn Leslie. This quartet was numbered 79 to 82, in sequence with two of the Neasden engines, which were given Nos77 and 78. The third Neasden product, however, had the honour of becoming No1. The reason, though, was mundane: it merely replaced the original No1, an A class 4-4-0T that had been wrecked beyond repair in an accident at Baker Street in December 1897. Ironically, the new No1 proved to be the last Metropolitan Railway locomotive constructed 'in-house' at Neasden, in 1898.

On 30 June 1904, garlanded with flowers and foliage and accompanied by much pomp and ceremony, E class tank No1 hauled the first train from Baker Street over the newly opened Uxbridge branch. However, the Metropolitan had already begun electrifying its line out to Rickmansworth and the days of steam-hauled passenger trains were numbered. No further E class tanks were built and, after electric working began in 1905, they were gradually downgraded to secondary duties. At the same time, the condensing apparatus that had allowed them to work over the inner-city lines was removed. Instead, the E class became the mainstay of the branch line between Chalfont & Latimer and Chesham, until displaced by LNER locomotives during World War II. For a time after the war, E class tanks fulfilled the role of stand-by engines at Rickmansworth, covering for motive power failures.

However, three of the class failed to see the outbreak of war. Nos78, 79 and 82 were scrapped by the newly formed London Passenger Transport Board (the forerunner of London Transport) in 1935. The remaining four were retained and renumbered: Nos1, 77, 80 and 81 became L44, L46, L47 and L48 respectively. NoL47 was retired in 1941, but the other three saw in the 1960s. NoL46 was scrapped in 1962 and NoL48 in 1963. By this time, NoL44 had been given the melancholy task of hauling the last scheduled steam-hauled passenger service on London Transport, on 9 September 1961. Its final duty on behalf of LT was to appear at the Metropolitan Railway centenary parade on 23 May 1963.

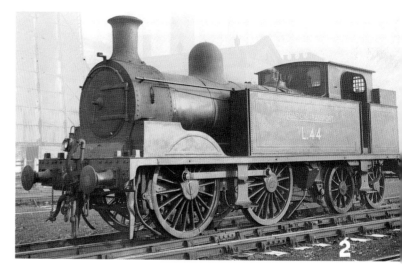

Above: In its London Transport guise as NoL44, the sole survivor of the seven-strong E class stands alongside its birthplace of Neasden works, in north-west London. The final steam locomotive to be constructed there, in 1898, 65 years on, in May 1963, NoL44 became LT's last working steam engine.

By now, efforts were underway to save this last working example of Metropolitan steam and the London Railway Preservation Society became the owners of E class 0-4-4T NoL44 on 20 March 1964. It arrived at the embryo Buckinghamshire Railway Centre at Quainton Road – appropriately an ex-Metropolitan Railway station – in 1970 to begin what proved to be a lengthy overhaul. Restored as Metropolitan No1, it was not steamed again until 1985. In 1989, No1 was back at its old haunts, hauling specials to mark the centenary of the Chesham branch. Although 'Steam on the Met' has since become an annual event, No1 has not put in an appearance since 1990. Its boiler insurance period expired, it remains at Quainton Road awaiting overhaul.

Above: With a wisp of steam at the safety valves, Metropolitan No1 poses at the Buckinghamshire Railway Centre's base of Quainton Road – its home since 1970. A protracted restoration did not see the locomotive turn a wheel until April 1985.

MR E Class 0-4-4T

Built: Neasden works, Metropolitan Railway; Hawthorn Leslie, Newcastle-upon-Tyne, 1898–1901 (7 built)

Weight: 54 tons 10cwt

Driving wheel diameter: 5ft 6in

Boiler pressure: 150lb/psi

Cylinders: (2) 17in diameter* x 26in stroke

Valve gear: Stephenson

Coal capacity: 2 tons 5cwt

Water capacity: 1,300 gallons

Tractive effort: 14,515lb (at 85% boiler pressure)

(* *engines built by Hawthorn Leslie had a cylinder diameter of 17¹/₂ inches*)

Left: Metropolitan No1 leads a colourful rake of engines and rolling stock as it approaches Moor Park with one of London Underground's Amersham to Harrow-on-the-Hill shuttles on 21 July 1990. Following No1 are Great Western pannier tank No9466, an LU battery locomotive (to supply braking power), two support vehicles and an Anglia Region Class 305 electric multiple unit!

LONDON & SOUTH WESTERN RAILWAY

T9 Class 3P 4-4-0

When he came south in 1895 to join the London & South Western Railway, Dugald Drummond had plenty of experience with four-coupled express engines. He had designed successful inside cylinder 4-4-0s for both of his previous employers, Scotland's North British and Caledonian Railways. There seemed no reason why what worked on Scottish metals should not perform equally well on the main line out of Waterloo and on the grades west of Salisbury. In 1898, Drummond's C8 4-4-0 duly appeared, using the boiler of the M7 0-4-4T designed the previous year.

Unfortunately, Drummond had greatly overestimated the steam-producing ability of that boiler. It was sufficient for the shunting, empty stock and branch passenger duties allotted the M7s, but proved inadequate for keeping tight main-line schedules. Within 12 months, another bigger-boilered 4-4-0 was on Drummond's drawing board as he acknowledged the limitations of the C8. His confidence in the new design, the T9 class, was such that 50 were ordered without a single prototype being tested.

Construction was shared between the L&SWR's own workshops at Nine Elms, London, and the Glasgow-based firm of Henry Dübs & Co. Between 1899 and 1900, Nine Elms delivered 20 engines and Dübs the remaining 30. Nine Elms then built a further 15 while Dübs, evidently proud of the workmanship that had gone into its product, built a final example for the Glasgow exhibition of 1901.

The one significant difference between the first 50 locomotives and the last 16 was that the later ones saw one of Drummond's pet theories put into practice. This was the fitting of firebox cross-water tubes. He argued that increasing the surface area available to heat water within

the firebox brought an improvement in the general circulation of the boiler, especially in the water spaces. Any benefit, however, had to be offset against the added cost and complexity of firebox construction. Moreover, the inclusion of the tubes made for complicated maintenance. Despite these disadvantages, cross-water tubes were fitted in all of Drummond's post-1900 express locomotives.

The T9 4-4-0s were still in the front rank of L&SWR passenger engines when, in 1912, Dugald Drummond was succeeded by another Scottish engineer, Robert Urie. The new man was swift to make his presence felt and began updating much of his inheritance. This mainly involved fitting superheaters, but the performance of the T9s – now known to all as 'Greyhounds' – convinced Urie to leave them well alone. In 1922, however, he decided that Drummond's firebox tubes would come out and that superheaters would go in, along with extended smokeboxes and stovepipe chimneys that did little for the T9s' looks. Urie also enlarged the cylinder bore by half-an-inch, to 19in.

Rebuilding to Urie's revised specification continued until 1929. Even allowing for the excellence of the Drummond original, the Urie rebuild benefited from superheating. The modified T9s retained their popularity with crews, too, despite the addition of new 4-6-0s to the Southern's express passenger roster. This was especially true west of Salisbury where the T9's light axleloading, good power-to-weight ratio and ability to negotiate tight curves maintained its usefulness.

All 66 T9s were taken over by British Railways' Southern Region in 1948. Twenty were still on the books in 1959, but by 1961 all had been retired. No120 was to be the only survivor. Withdrawn as British Railways' No30120, the preserved example was repainted in L&SWR livery and used on specials during the early 1960s. It then spent several years on the Mid-Hants Railway in Hampshire where, for a spell, it sported – rather fetchingly – BR lined black. Now wearing Southern malachite green, No120 is currently on loan from the National Railway Museum to the Bluebell Railway in East Sussex. Even at the age of 100, No120 looks capable of giving anything a run for its money. Sadly, it requires major boiler repairs.

Left: Recreating a 1950s scene, T9 4-4-0 No30120 arrives at Medstead and Four Marks with a Mid-Hants Railway service for Alton. The National Collection locomotive, completed at the L&SWR's Nine Elms works in August 1899, went on loan to the MHR in September 1981. It was overhauled and returned to traffic in May 1983.

Above: A Dorset double-header, with No120 heading for Swanage piloted by USA class 0-6-0T No30075 on 19 September 1992. No30075 was not one of the original US Army Transportation Corps 'switchers' bought by the Southern Railway in 1946, but belonged to a batch acquired by Yugoslavian railways. It came to the Swanage Railway in 1992.

Below: The Drummond T9 epitomized the classic four-coupled British express passenger type of the late Victorian era and remained in front-rank service until the arrival of the Urie and Maunsell 4-6-0s during the 1920s. No120 was rebuilt to its present superheated form in 1927.

L&SWR T9 Class 3P 4-4-0

Built: Nine Elms works, London; Dübs & Co, Glasgow, 1899–1901 (66 built)

Weight: 51 tons 18cwt/51 tons 7cwt (locomotive) 44 tons 17cwt (tender)

Driving wheel diameter: 6ft 7in

Boiler pressure: 175lb/psi

Cylinders: (2) 19in diameter x 26in stroke

Valve gear: Stephenson (slide valves)

Coal capacity: 5 tons

Water capacity: 4,000 gallons

Tractive effort: 17,670lb (at 85% boiler pressure)

SOUTH EASTERN & CHATHAM RAILWAY

D Class 3P 4-4-0

There were few more elegant locomotive designs than Harry Wainwright's D class 4-4-0 for the South Eastern & Chatham Railway. However, while Wainwright was undoubtedly responsible for the overall look of these graceful engines, the detail work was undertaken by Robert Surtees, his chief draughtsman at Ashford works. Surtees took his inspiration from the M3 4-4-0 of the London, Chatham & Dover Railway. He adopted its boiler tube arrangement, valve gear, cylinders, bogie design and springing, along with its basic cab and tender layout. All were refined as necessary to produce a locomotive whose performance matched its looks.

Underneath the flowing curves and symmetry of the exterior lay a sturdy and sure-footed machine that responded to hard work. The D class rode well, steamed freely and was economical to operate. Hand-in-hand with the pleasing proportions of the design went the application of the ornate SE&CR livery that seamlessly unified the component parts of the locomotive. This was where Harry Wainwright's skill came into its own. These engines did not look as much assembled, as moulded by a craftsman's hands.

Construction of the initial 20 engines was shared between Ashford works and the Glasgow builder, Sharp Stewart. The first to enter service, in 1901, was a Glasgow product and, by 1907, 51 were in traffic. Of those, 22 were Ashford-built while the rest were supplied

by outside contractors. These included another Glasgow factory, Dübs & Co., Robert Stephenson & Co. of Newcastle-upon-Tyne, and Vulcan Foundry of Newton-le-Willows, Lancashire.

Initially, the D class was put to work on the front-rank Kent coast and Hastings services out of London's Cannon Street. An immediate concern was the incidence of lineside fires attributed to the engines, a consequence of firing with low quality coal. A cure was found when locomotive No247 was experimentally fitted with a different blastpipe and equipped with a spark arrestor. The rest of the class was modified to suit, and given shorter, cast-iron capuchon chimneys.

The last years of Wainwright's reign at Ashford were not happy ones. The management of the SE&CR went through several crises and Wainwright eventually

Above: The coupled wheels and splashers, along with the curved cab sidesheets, of D class 4-4-0 No737 embody the symmetry of Harry Wainwright's masterpiece. This was emphasized by the elaborate lining-out (seven lines in total!), which extended to the boiler bands. The design combined style with engineering excellence, being mechanically robust and sure-footed at speed.

Left: It was not solely its ornate livery or flowing lines that led many to judge the D class the most beautiful of locomotives, but the balance and unity of the design. An impression of lissom elegance was conjured by the virtual absence of squared-off straight lines. The barest minimum of boiler fittings clutter the exterior of No737, which remained in BR service until 1956.

departed, ostensibly because of ill-health, in 1913. His replacement was Richard Maunsell who instigated the rebuilding of 21 D class 4-4-0s with Belpaire fireboxes to produce the more powerful D1. These bigger engines were needed to cope with increasing loads on the Kent Coast line through Chatham, but they lost some of their original flamboyance in the rebuilding process.

By the early 1930s, the largest allocation of D class 4-4-0s was at Gillingham depot in Kent, but they had been relegated to secondary services and local trains. Even the now-preserved No737 had lost its status as the regular engine for Royal Train duty. At the outbreak of World War II in 1939 some of the Ds were placed in store. Then, in 1941, others surprisingly were transferred to Nine Elms depot on the Southern Railway's Western Division where they found themselves on London Waterloo to Salisbury services. A handful were based at Redhill to work the Reading-Tonbridge cross-country line.

In 1948, British Railways inherited 28 Wainwright 4-4-0s. One, No1742, had been destroyed in an air raid and another, No1726, scrapped in 1947. Their final years saw them concentrated at Guildford, in Surrey, and the last of this elegant line, No31075, was withdrawn from there in 1956. Thankfully, No31737 already had been set aside for preservation. After a spell in storage – at Tweedmouth,

in Northumberland, of all the unlikely places – it was refurbished at Ashford in 1959 and returned to its original, resplendent SE&CR guise. Today, this aristocrat among locomotives – Wainwright's 'Coppertop', as it was dubbed – continues to evoke admiration at the National Railway Museum in York.

SE&CR D Class 3P 4-4-0

Built: Ashford works; Sharp Stewart & Co., Dübs & Co. (both Glasgow); Vulcan Foundry, Newton-le-Willows, Lancashire; Robert Stephenson & Co., Newcastle-upon-Tyne, 1901–07 (51 built)

Weight: 50 tons 0cwt (locomotive)
39 tons 2cwt (tender)

Driving wheel diameter: 6ft 8in

Boiler pressure: 175lb/psi

Cylinders: (2) 19in diameter x 26in stroke

Valve gear: Stephenson link motion (piston valves)

Coal capacity: 4 tons 10cwt

Water capacity: 3,300 gallons

Tractive effort: 17,910lb (at 85% boiler pressure)

Above: The D class 4-4-0s still looked smart in the plainer green livery of the Southern Railway, as this profile of No1477 – leaving Bromley with a Kent coast-bound train on 26 August 1934 – shows. By this date, 21 of the class had been rebuilt by Maunsell as D1 4-4-0s and the remaining engines had been downgraded to semi-fast and local services, with the largest allocation at Gillingham in Kent. Built at Ashford works in 1907, No1477 lasted in traffic until 1951.

GREAT NORTHERN RAILWAY

C1, C2 Class 'Atlantic' 4-4-2

The 4-4-2, or Atlantic, type made its first appearance in 1888, in the United States. It was a natural development of the ubiquitous 4-4-0, the additional trailing truck not only supporting a larger firebox but improving the riding. Ten years later, the Great Northern Railway's Henry Ivatt introduced the Atlantic to Britain.

Ivatt had the daunting task of replacing the venerable Patrick Stirling at the head of the GNR's locomotive department. Stirling, who had died in office aged 75, was revered not only for the performance of his locomotives, but their looks. 'Artistry in metal' was one description of his work, and many still consider the legendary 'Stirling Single' (pages 22-23) to be the apotheosis of British locomotive aesthetics.

However, by the turn of the century, these single-wheelers were being taxed by increasing train loadings on the East Coast Main Line. Seeking greater power and adhesion, Ivatt took the American route. He was not alone: his counterpart on the Lancashire & Yorkshire Railway, John Aspinall, was also working on an Atlantic. Possibly to register a British 'first', construction of the first of the Ivatt Atlantics was given a high priority. Numbered No990 and named *Henry Oakley*, after the General Manager of the Great Northern Railway, it was outshopped from Doncaster works in 1898, beating Aspinall's prototype by a few months.

Like Churchward on the Great Western, Ivatt placed great importance on boiler design. On No990, he opted for a large capacity vessel and it was this extra steam-raising capacity that gave the Atlantics the edge over Stirling's single-wheelers. The first production Atlantics entered service in 1900 and proved fast, lively runners – so lively that Ivatt had to caution his drivers to rein in the speed because of stretches of uneven track between London and Doncaster. In their turn, the enginemen would have told Ivatt that the cylinders were no match for the boiler. These first Atlantics had to be worked at undesirable and uneconomic rates to achieve the expected performance – thrashed, in other words.

Considering this, surprise was expressed when, in 1902, Ivatt unveiled his 'large Atlantic'. It had a boiler of (for the time) astonishing proportions. The barrel was 5ft 6in in diameter and the heating surfaces showed a 65 per cent increase over their predecessors, yet the chassis, valve gear and cylinder size were unchanged. That this unbalanced, over-boilered locomotive worked at all is attributable to the new-found efficiency of the cylinders. Ivatt's design of balanced slide valves allowed a free

exhaust, and this was married to an excellent blastpipe and chimney arrangement.

Outwardly, both classes of Atlantics were attractive, exciting engines, and GNR publicity capitalized on their appeal. Behind the scenes, however, Ivatt was making modifications. He introduced 20in diameter cylinders and piston valves on some of the 'large Atlantics', and this improved their performance to a degree. However, upon

Above: The first of the Ivatt C1 class 'large Atlantics', No251, stands on one of the turntable roads at the National Railway Museum, York. Its introduction in 1902 started a fashion for large-boilered Atlantics in Britain, with similar designs appearing on the North Eastern, Great Central, North British and London Brighton & South Coast Railways.

Right: Still in wartime black livery, C1 class 4-4-2 No2815 of 1904 waits to depart from Lincoln on 19 April 1947. It was condemned in October that year.

C1, C2 Class 'Atlantic'

	GNR/LNER C1 Class 4-4-2	GNR/LNER C2 Class 4-4-2
Built:	Doncaster works, 1902–10 (94 built)	Doncaster works, 1898–1903 (22 built)
Weight:	69 tons 12cwt (locomotive) 43 tons 2cwt (tender)	62 tons 0cwt 42 tons 2cwt (tender)
Driving wheel diameter:	6ft 8in	6ft 8in
Boiler pressure:	175lb/psi	175lb/psi
Cylinders:	(2) 18¼in diameter x 24in stroke	(2) 19in (later 20in) diameter x 24in stroke
Valve gear:	Stephenson (slide valves)	Stephenson (slide valves)
Coal capacity:	6 tons 10cwt	6 tons 10cwt
Water capacity:	3,500 gallons	3,500 gallons
Tractive effort:	17,340lb (at 85% boiler pressure)	11,130lb (at 85% boiler pressure)

Above: In 1975, the first British Atlantic, GNR C2 class No990 Henry Oakley, was returned to working order for the first time in over 20 years to take part in celebrations marking the 150th anniversary of the opening of the Stockton & Darlington Railway. Two years later, it paid a visit to the Keighley & Worth Valley and undertook a number of special workings, including this improbable partnership with the K&WVR's ex-steelworks saddletank No57 Samson. The pair are pictured approaching Mytholmes tunnel en route to Haworth and Oxenhope. This was the last occasion No990 appeared in steam. Although rumours of a projected overhaul abounded during the early 1990s, this historic locomotive remains a static exhibit.

taking over from Henry Ivatt in 1911, Nigel Gresley recognized the engines' deficiencies. He ordered the fitting of 32-element superheaters to the 'large Atlantics', a move that not only brought an immediate improvement, but proved unexpectedly prescient. When, during the 1920s, teething troubles affected Gresley's new Pacifics, the Atlantics frequently came to the rescue. They put in some incredible performances striving to maintain the accelerated East Coast schedules.

Finally displaced from the heavier trains, the Ivatt Atlantics found new fame on the LNER's newly launched, lightweight Pullman services but, after World War II, their usefulness diminished. A final run from King's Cross to Doncaster took place on 24 November 1950. At its conclusion, the last working Ivatt Atlantic, No294 (BR No62822), entered Doncaster works for scrapping.

By then, the two prototypes, No251 and No990, had been preserved and, in 1953, they were turned out to head the 'Plant Centenarian' specials marking the centenary of Doncaster works. They were the last main-line appearances of locomotives that, while falling just short of greatness, had no competition when it came to glamour.

MIDLAND RAILWAY

4P Class Compound 4-4-0

As a means of making more efficient use of steam power, the compound principle had been in use since the mid-19th century. However, these were static applications of the technique and not constrained by the confined area and mechanical complexity of the steam locomotive. In France, compounding proved particularly effective, but in Britain results varied widely. The greatest success was enjoyed by designers working for the Midland Railway. Beginning with Samuel Waite Johnson, they overcame the practical obstacles to using compounding in steam locomotives.

Unlike more common 'simple' locomotives, compounds are equipped with both high- and low-pressure cylinders. The former receive a charge of high-pressure steam from the boiler, but do not exhaust it in the normal way. Instead, that steam – now at reduced pressure – is used again in a low-pressure cylinder (or cylinders). Originally compounding was seen as a method of fully utilizing steam that, because of inadequate valve performance, was being exhausted before all its potential power had been extracted.

Samuel Johnson introduced compounding to the Midland Railway in 1902. His design was based on a three-cylinder arrangement employed by the North Eastern Railway some four years earlier. In it, a single high-pressure cylinder fed two at low pressure. The latter pair were located outside the frames and the former between them, where it had to compete for space with three sets of valve gear.

Johnson's successor, Richard Deeley, refined the design, largely through the introduction of superheating. The engines proved ideal for the comparatively short, but tightly timed, trainloads that characterized pre-grouping Midland passenger services. Nevertheless, the decision by the LMSR – which absorbed the Midland in 1923 – to adopt the 'Midland Compound' as its standard express passenger locomotive astonished many observers. It was true that, in comparative trials, the compound had scored over its rival, the L&NWR's 'Prince of Wales' class. However, there is evidence that the choice was more a reflection of Midland dominance within the LMSR hierarchy. If the trials

Above: The second of the Midland compounds is seen in its British Railways guise as No41001, but with 'LMS' still inscribed on its tender. Its BR career lasted less than four years, withdrawal coming in November 1951.

were intended to decide the matter, why had an order for 20 Midland compounds already been placed?

These new engines incorporated modifications proposed by Henry Fowler, Chief Mechanical Engineer of the Midland before the 1923 Grouping. Fowler trimmed the driving wheel diameter by three inches, from 7ft 0in to 6ft 9in, and increased the cylinder diameters by three-quarters of an inch. However, this second alteration only lasted into the first LMSR-built batch. All later production reverted to the original dimensions and the experimentally enlarged locomotives had their cylinders reduced to conform.

Under, first, George Hughes and, from 1925, his successor as LMSR locomotive supremo, Henry Fowler, construction of the compounds continued apace. It only tailed off after 1927, when the LMSR invested in the 'Royal Scot' 4-6-0s. With the somewhat reluctant approval of William Stanier, a final quartet of compounds was built in 1932. In all, 240 were constructed, carrying Nos900-939 and 1000-1199.

The Midland compounds were useful and economical locomotives, but dependent on sympathetic driving and firing. They frequently suffered at the hands of inexperienced crews when operating outside traditional Midland territory. The technique for starting, for example, was not easy to master. In the end, the Achilles heel of the Midland compounds was not their complexity. It was simply the increase in train lengths. The compounds' inability to cope with heavier loads contributed to the uneconomic double-heading that characterized so many of the LMSR's pre-1939 operations. Double-heading remained prevalent right into the British Railways era.

Nevertheless, despite their limitations, the compounds continued to grace ex-LMSR lines until 1961, although the sole survivor, No1000, had been withdrawn for preservation ten years earlier. It enjoyed main-line outings in the 1960s, and in late 1970s and early 1980s, but currently resides out-of-traffic at the National Railway Museum, York.

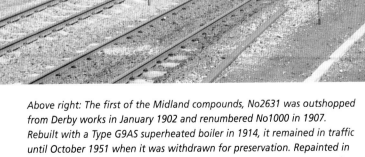

Above right: The first of the Midland compounds, No2631 was outshopped from Derby works in January 1902 and renumbered No1000 in 1907. Rebuilt with a Type G9AS superheated boiler in 1914, it remained in traffic until October 1951 when it was withdrawn for preservation. Repainted in crimson lake livery in 1959, No1000 came out of storage to work specials, one of which took it to Birmingham New Street.

Above: A second overhaul of No1000 was completed in 1975 and it remained on the list of main-line-approved engines until 1984. On 5 May 1980, it partnered 'Jubilee' 4-6-0 No5690 Leander on a Carnforth-Sellafield special, seen here passing Ulverston.

MR 4P Class Compound 4-4-0

Built: Derby works; North British Locomotive Co., Glasgow; Vulcan Foundry, Newton-le-Willows, Lancashire, 1902–32 (240 built)

Weight: 61 tons 14cwt (locomotive)
42 tons 14cwt (tender)

Driving wheel diameter: 7ft 0in
(later reduced to 6ft 9in)

Boiler pressure: 200lb/psi

Cylinders: (3)
High pressure (1) 19in diameter x 26in stroke
Low pressure (2) 21in diameter x 26in stroke

Valve gear: Stephenson

Coal capacity: 5 tons 12cwt

Water capacity: 3,500 gallons

Tractive effort: 23,205lb (at 85% boiler pressure)

GREAT WESTERN RAILWAY

3700 'City' Class 4-4-0

In September 1902, George Jackson Churchward rebuilt 'Atbara' class 4-4-0 No3405 *Mauritius* – then just one year old – with his new Standard No4 boiler. Did he want to put the new steam-raiser through its paces, or did he consider the original 'Atbara' boiler inadequate? Whatever the reason, it was a move that was to influence all subsequent Great Western locomotive design, and much elsewhere. *Mauritius* was the first GW engine to carry a taper boiler and, apart from Churchward's solitary prototype 4-6-0 No100, the most powerful engine in the GW fleet.

After trials with the rebuilt *Mauritius*, Swindon works was instructed to build ten locomotives along similar lines. Though powerful by GW standards, the newcomers were lightweights compared with their contemporaries, the Great Northern Atlantics and North Eastern Railway 4-4-0s. In essence, they were the final development of the four-coupled, double-framed format advocated by Churchward's predecessor, William Dean.

Double frames were inevitably heavier and more expensive to construct than their single counterparts and, by 1903, when the first of the 'Cities' was delivered from Swindon, most railways had discarded them. They did retain one advantage, though. Double frames allowed a considerable increase in the area of bearing surfaces, so reducing the chance of overheated axleboxes when working at high speed. Combining this mechanical robustness with a potent steam-raiser such as the Churchward boiler was always likely to produce a flier.

Not long after the debut of the first production 'City', No3433 *City of Bath*, the class was registering some startling performances. In July 1903, *City of Bath* covered the 240 miles from London to Plymouth at an average of 63.2mph. Its average over the 90 miles between Langley and Bath was 72mph, with a maximum of 81mph at Chippenham.

GWR 3700 'City' Class 4-4-0

Built: Swindon works, 1903 (20 built, including 10 rebuilds of 'Atbara' class 4-4-0s)

Weight: 55 tons 6cwt (locomotive)
36 tons 15cwt (tender)

Driving wheel diameter: 6ft 8½in

Boiler pressure: 200lb/psi

Cylinders: (2) 18in diameter x 26in stroke

Valve gear: Stephenson (originally slide valves; piston valves later fitted to all but one of class)

Coal capacity: 5 tons

Water capacity: 3,500 gallons

Tractive effort: 17,790lb (at 85% boiler pressure)

Above: The record-breaking City of Truro *was among several celebrated Great Western locomotives appearing at an open day at Old Oak Common depot, London, on 18 August 1991.*

Below: Returned to working order for the GW150 events of 1985, City of Truro visited a number of preserved railways, among them the West Somerset. On 25 July 1992, it was seen between Williton and Doniford Beach Halt at the head of a train for Minehead.

The 'Cities' place in railway lore, though, is down to one locomotive and one day – 9 May 1904. The GWR was in competition with the London & South Western Railway for the trans-Atlantic mails traffic from liners docking at Plymouth. Given that the L&SWR route to London was 15 miles shorter, the GWR had to put its faith in speed. That spring day, it was actively seeking to publicize its new service between Plymouth and Paddington. The 'Ocean Mails Express' normally carried no passengers but the GWR made a point of asking railway commentator Charles Rous-Marten on the journey. Clearly, something special had been planned.

Less than an hour out of Plymouth, *City of Truro* was flying through Exeter. There now followed 30 miles of high-speed running, culminating in the five mile descent from Whiteball Tunnel through Wellington in Somerset. *City of Truro* hurtled down Wellington bank in what Rous-Marten described as 'a hurricane descent'. Over one quarter-mile, he claimed to have logged a time of eight-and-four-fifths seconds, corresponding to a speed of 102.3 miles per hour.

Though the 'Cities' were now assured a lasting place in railway history, their working lives were comparatively short. Displaced from top-link expresses by Churchward's new 4-4-2 and 4-6-0 designs, they found employment on secondary routes but the first withdrawals came after just 24 years' service. By 1931, just two remained, *City of Truro* being one of them. Its survival, however, owed little to the GWR whose General Manager, James Milne, declared that he 'did not consider the engine of outstanding importance'. To its great credit, the LNER disagreed and offered to display *City of Truro* in its York museum. Since that time, the record-breaker has been overhauled twice to working order, most recently in 1985 to mark the 150th anniversary of the formation of the GWR. It remains to be seen whether it will be in steam in 2004 to mark the centenary of its record-breaking run.

GREAT WESTERN RAILWAY

2800/2884 Class 8F 2-8-0

Though it was possible to see an innovative mind at work, George Jackson Churchward's first Great Western designs were cautiously transitional. He kept faith with many of the principles of his predecessor, William Dean, and it was not until 1903 that a locomotive emerged that was pure Churchward. It was also the precursor of a new breed of freight locomotives.

Eight-coupled tank and tender engines, notably the Webb 0-8-0s of the L&NWR and the Aspinall 0-8-0s of the Lancashire & Yorkshire Railway, had been around for several decades. Churchward's No97, however, was a first – at least for Britain. The 2-8-0 type had been introduced in the United States of America in 1866. The coal-carrying Lehigh Valley Railroad of Pennsylvania used 2-8-0s to haul 300 ton trains on grades as steep as 1 in 40. For Churchward, ever receptive to new ideas, particularly those originating from North America and France, what worked in Pennsylvania would work in Pontypool.

With South Wales mineral traffic mainly in mind, a heavy freight locomotive was integral to Churchward's range of locomotive types. With its leading pony truck, or guiding wheels, the 2-8-0 offered greater stability and better weight distribution than an 0-8-0. Thirty-seven years after the type made its American debut, the first British 2-8-0, GWR No97, was outshopped from Swindon. Initial results suggested that only the front end needed further development. Nevertheless, the prototype undertook two years of trials before going into production.

Initially, the boiler pressure of the 2-8-0 was set at 200lb/psi, with 18in diameter cylinders. Tractive effort started out at 29,775lb but was increased substantially in the production locomotives. This followed the enlargement of the cylinder diameter (to 18$^{1}/_{2}$ inches), the raising of the steam pressure to 225lb/psi, and the substitution of the 8$^{1}/_{2}$in piston valves by ones of 10in.

The most visible difference between No97 (later renumbered No2800) and the first of the 1905 production batch was the higher pitch of the boiler (8ft 2in as opposed to 7ft 8$^{1}/_{2}$in). At first, the prototype was given a 4,000 gallon tender but, almost without exception, the 2800s were harnessed to the 3,500 gallon variety throughout their working lives. Superheating was incorporated into the class from 1909, with No2808 the

first to be 'retro-fitted'. Other ongoing modifications centred on improving the weight distribution, alternating smokebox lengths and fitting larger diameter chimneys.

The 84 2-8-0s built under Churchward remained the Great Western's principal long-haul freight locomotives throughout the 1920s and 1930s. The only serious problem met with in traffic was with the sealing of the internal steampipes. Beginning in 1934, most of the class had them replaced with the outside kind.

Outside steampipes were incorporated from the outset when Churchward's successor, Charles Collett, enlarged the class. Although 35 years had elapsed since the appearance of No97, little other updating was needed. Construction of Collett's version, designated the 2884 class, began in 1938. They were distinguished by their side window cabs and shorter safety valve bonnets, and by the addition of whistle shields. Changes to the framing also marginally increased the locomotive weight.

Between 1945 and 1947, coal shortages saw 20 of the 2800s converted to oil-burning. The experiment, encouraged by government, was abandoned in 1948, once the extra maintenance costs were calculated and the bill had arrived for the imported oil. That year saw one of the 2-8-0s, No3803, emerge remarkably successfully from trials against more modern freight engines, including the LMS 8F 2-8-0 and the WD 2-8-0 and 2-10-0. It took the appearance in 1954 of the British Railways Standard 9F 2-10-0 to displace the 2800s from their main role of mineral haulage. Nevertheless, there was still work for them right up to the end of steam on the Western Region in 1965. Six decades of service testify to the fundamental excellence of Churchward's original – in every sense – conception. Sixteen surviving 2800s perpetuate that record.

Right: Given that the 2800 class was built for South Wales mineral traffic, it was appropriate that, on 10 September 1985, No2857 had the honour of hauling the first steam-hauled goods on a British main line for 17 years. Contributing to an 'ancient-and-modern'-style demonstration, it is seen approaching Newport station with a rake of wooden-bodied wagons. Behind can be glimpsed the Class 56 diesel-electric which followed on with a train of modern, purpose-built freight vehicles.

GWR 2800/2884 Class 8F 2-8-0

Built: Swindon works, 1903–19
(Collett 2884 class 1938–42) (165 built)

Weight: 75 tons 10cwt
(Collett engines 76 tons 5cwt)
40 tons 0cwt (tender)

Driving wheel diameter: 4ft 7½in

Boiler pressure: 225lb/psi

Cylinders: (2) 18½in diameter x 30in stroke

Valve gear: Stephenson

Coal capacity: 6 tons

Water capacity: 3,500 gallons

Tractive effort: 35,380lb (at 85% boiler pressure)

Above: Nine 2884 class 2-8-0s have been preserved but, to date, only one has been restored, the 1940-built No3822. Acquired by the Great Western Society in 1975, No3822 made its debut in the summer of 1985. While visiting the West Somerset Railway in 1992, No3822 set a new record for the heaviest train worked on a British preserved line (19 vehicles, 650 tons).

Below: With safety valves blowing, No3822 pulls alongside the platform on the main demonstration line at Didcot Railway Centre.

GREAT WESTERN RAILWAY

4500/4575 Class 4MT 2-6-2T

Churchward's 'Small Prairie' design has been described as the ideal branch-line locomotive. Certainly, in terms of power-for-weight, there was little to touch the 4500 class 2-6-2T and it was the clear inspiration for later LMSR and British Railways Standard designs. Built at Swindon in 1905, the prototype for the Great Western Prairies, No115, was allowed less than a year to prove itself before the class went into production. Ten engines were constructed at the workshops in Wolverhampton. Initially, the new locomotives were allocated Nos3101-10 but soon lost those to a new design of 'large Prairie' under construction at Swindon. The Wolverhampton engines were renumbered in the 44XX sequence.

The 4400s were well suited to their role, with the small coupled wheels supplying lively acceleration. Nevertheless, modifications were soon made. The straight-backed bunker acquired a lipped extension to increase coal capacity and other changes were gradually

introduced. The most significant of these was the fitting of superheated boilers, pressed to 180lb/psi. Despite these changes, the 4400s displayed one serious drawback. While their 4ft 1½in driving wheels could deliver acceleration, they also imposed an upper limit on speed, so compromising the class's usefulness. No further examples were built and the 4400 was superseded in 1906 by the 4500 class. This retained the best features of its predecessor but enlarged the scope of the 'small Prairies', principally through the fitting of 4ft 7½in diameter driving wheels. Although these took the working weight to 57 tons, no additional limitations on route availability were incurred. Other lessons learned from experience with the 4400s were incorporated, but Churchward remained unconvinced of the value of superheating in small tank engines. It would be a further eight years before superheaters were fitted from new (with Nos4540-54 of 1914–15). The retrospective addition of superheaters to existing locomotives began in 1913.

Wolverhampton was again given the job of building the 4500 class but the order for Nos4500-19 was the last placed there. The following 20 examples were Swindon-built, and were notable for an increase in boiler pressure, to 200lb/psi, and consequent extension of the tractive effort from 19,120lb to 21,250lb.

Starting with the now-preserved No4555 of 1924, new locomotives were fitted with outside steampipes as standard, improved superheaters and enlarged bunkers that took the coal capacity to 3 tons 14cwt. Nos4555-74 were last of the small Prairies to be built to the original Churchward specification. When the operating department

GWR 4500/4575 Class 4MT 2-6-2T

Built: Swindon and Wolverhampton works, 1906–29 (175 built)

Weight: 57 tons 18cwt(4500)/61 tons 0cwt (4575)

Driving wheel diameter: 4ft 7½in

Boiler pressure: 200lb/psi

Cylinders: (2) 17in diameter x 24in stroke

Valve gear: Stephenson (piston valves)

Coal capacity: 3 tons 14cwt (with enlarged bunker)

Water capacity:
1,000 gallons (4500)/
1,300 gallons (4575)

Tractive effort: 21,250lb
(at 85% boiler pressure)

Right: Swindon-built in 1929, the Great Western Society's No5572 is one of ten surviving 4575 Prairies. Its working life began at Exeter but, by 1933, it had been transferred to Kidderminster. Following spells at Westbury, Bristol and Taunton, No5572 became one of 14 4575 tanks despatched to Cardiff Cathays, where it was equipped for auto-train working. Displaced by diesel multiple units, No5572 returned to the West Country in 1958. It was withdrawn in 1962.

requested more of the same, Churchward's successor, Charles Collett, took the opportunity to increase the water capacity substantially. Larger side tanks, holding 1,300 gallons, were fitted and had sloping top edges so that forward vision from the cab was not impaired. The extended range that this offered was judged to be worth the extra three tons added to the locomotive weight, and the modification warranted a new description, the 4575 class. One hundred locomotives were delivered between 1926 and 1929, taking Nos4575-99 and 5500-74.

In GWR days, the designated livery for the 'small Prairies' was normally unlined green. Under British Railways, the engines were first painted unlined black but subsequently lined out. From the late 1950s, fully lined out brunswick green was applied.

Both the 4500 and 4575 classes were good servants of the GWR and BR's Western Region. The West Country, with its many picturesque branch lines, was their regular haunt but examples were employed in South Wales and the West Midlands, and around Bristol, Gloucester, Machynlleth, Shrewsbury, Taunton and Worcester. A handful even reached the London area, working empty stock into and out of Paddington and freights on the Brentford branch. Withdrawals began in 1950, with No4531, but the 'small Prairies' did not disappear entirely from BR metals for another 14 years. The last to be retired were Nos5508, 5531, 5564 and 5569. Three of the 4500 class have been preserved and all have worked in recent years. Additionally, 11 of the 4575s were saved from scrap but only three have been restored to working order.

Top: With chocolate-and-cream coaches completing an authentic Western Region image, 4500 class Prairie No4566 emerges from the southern portal of Greet tunnel with a Gloucestershire Warwickshire Railway service on 14 October 1995.

Above: On home territory on the Severn Valley Railway, No4566 'brews up' before departure from Kidderminster with a train for Bridgnorth on 29 October 1987. Swindon-built in 1924, No4566 ended its working life in 1961 on the branch lines of Cornwall.

LONDON, TILBURY & SOUTHEND RAILWAY/LAMBTON, HETTON & JOICEY COLLIERY CO.

Two Tank Types

Both locomotives illustrated here entered service in 1909, and both were built by Robert Stephenson & Hawthorn, but that is where the similarity ends. A more striking illustration of the diverse roles performed by Britain's standard gauge tank engines is hard to imagine.

From London's Fenchurch Street terminus, the London, Tilbury & Southend Railway provided an intensive service to destinations along the Thames estuary and to the Essex coast. In maintaining a punctuality record that would be the envy of today's electric services, it was well served both by its operating staff and by its locomotives. The most celebrated of those locomotives were the so-called 'Tilbury tanks', of which No80 *Thundersley* is the sole survivor.

The success of the 'Tilbury tanks' was the result of the combination of a brilliant engineer and a bold manager. After its incorporation in 1852, the LT&SR relied upon the Great Eastern Railway to supply its motive power. By the late 1870s, however, its general manager, Arthur Stride, decided the LT&SR needed locomotives designed to meet its specific needs. It is likely that Stride sought the views of William Adams, who had recently left the GER to take over locomotive matters on the London & South Western. The outcome of this consultation was a series of 4-4-2 tanks built by Sharp Stewart and delivered in 1880. It may be, too, that Adams put in a word for the young man who had been his assistant on the GER, Thomas Whitelegg. As the new 4-4-2 tanks arrived, so did Whitelegg, as Locomotive Foreman.

By 1897, Whitelegg was advising Arthur Stride that more powerful locomotives were needed. Whitelegg's solution was another 4-4-2 tank, but this time with 6ft 6in coupled wheels. Britain's first express passenger tank locomotive, the LT&SR 37 class, was born. It was followed, in 1900, by an enlarged version, the 51 class, and, in 1909, by the celebrated 79 class. All of these 'Tilbury tanks' worked hard for a living. Leaving London, they had to negotiate a number of speed restrictions before opening up east of Barking, where 70mph was regularly attained.

Above: Ex-Lambton, Hetton & Joicey Colliery Company 0-6-2 tank No5 awaits departure from Goathland with a North Yorkshire Moors Railway service for Grosmont on 7 October 1990, not far from the Durham coalfield where it spent its working life.

Right: The last of the 'Tilbury tanks', No80 Thundersley *stands in the exhibition hall of Bressingham Steam Museum. The engines were kept in immaculate condition during LT&SR days and it was not unusual for one to be taken out of service for two or three days simply to have its paintwork touched up!*

Two Tank Types

	LT&SR 79 Class 4-4-2T	LH&JC Co. 0-6-2T
Built:	Robert Stephenson & Hawthorn, Newcastle-upon-Tyne, 1909–30 (39 built, including 35 for LMSR)	Robert Stephenson & Hawthorn, Darlington; Kitson's, Leeds; Hawthorn Leslie, Newcastle-upon-Tyne, 1904–20 (7 built)
Weight:	69 tons 7½cwt	62 tons
Driving wheel diameter:	6ft 6in	4ft 7½in
Boiler pressure:	170lb/psi	165lb/psi
Cylinders:	(2) 19in diameter x 26in stroke	(2) 18½in diameter x 26in stroke
Valve gear:	Stephenson (slide valves)	Stephenson
Coal capacity:	2 tons 10cwt	2 tons
Water capacity:	1,926 gallons	1,500 gallons
Tractive effort:	17,388lb (at 85% boiler pressure)	24,400lb (at 85% boiler pressure)

Above: The success of the Lambton colliery tanks on steeply-graded lines in north-east England was one of the reasons Charles Collett produced a similar 0-6-2 design for the Great Western's Welsh valley lines, the 5600 class. Both types are in tandem here, with LH&JCR No5 piloting GWR No6619 on the climb through autumnal Darnholm on the North Yorkshire Moors Railway.

When the LT&SR was absorbed into the Midland Railway in 1912, its engines began to work further afield. By the 1920s, they were working services out of two other London stations, St Pancras and Broad Street. Some even turned up in the Nottingham and Leicester areas. The LMSR thought highly enough of the 79 class to order a further 35 examples between 1923 and 1930.

No80 *Thundersley* was among the last LT&SR engines built before the Midland take-over. It became Midland Railway No2177, LMS No2148 and, finally, BR No41966. In 1956 – by then the sole survivor from all 80 locomotives built for the LT&SR – *Thundersley* was restored to its original livery to mark the line's centenary and worked a number of specials. In recent years, it has been on display at the Bressingham Steam Museum, near Diss in Norfolk.

While *Thundersley* was powering fast commuter trains in the south-east, some of its 1909-built counterparts were pulling coal trains 250 miles to the north. Robert Stephenson & Hawthorn's Darlington works contributed to a fleet of hard-working inside-cylinder 0-6-2 tanks for one of the north-east's major coal-mining concerns, the Lambton, Hetton and Joicey Colliery Company. Based around Philadelphia, County Durham, a fascinating feature of the LH&JC's extensive operation was that its locomotives had running rights over main lines in the area. This enabled them to work trains from the pitheads to the quayside coal staithes at Sunderland and, once outside colliery limits, these strong engines showed they were no slouches. LH&JC No5 is the sole surviving representative of the Robert Stephenson-constructed engines but has been joined in preservation by a classmate built by Kitson's of Leeds, LH&JC No29.

Steam working over the LH&JC system ceased in February 1969 but, in the ensuing 30 years, both No5 and No29 have been seen hard at work between Grosmont and Pickering on the equally demanding gradients of the North Yorkshire Moors Railway.

GREAT WESTERN RAILWAY

4200/5205 Class 7F/8F 2-8-0T

Short-haul mineral traffic – coal, coke, iron ore and steel – contributed significantly to the Great Western Railway's activities in South Wales. By the early 1900s, there was a growing need for more modern and powerful engines to handle short-haul, pithead-to-port coal traffic. Given the success of his 2800 class 2-8-0 of 1903 (pages 74-75), George Jackson Churchward took the logical step of designing a tank engine equivalent.

GWR 4200/5205 Class 7F/8F 2-8-0T

Built: Swindon works, 1910–40 (205 built, including those rebuilt as 7200 class)

Weight: 81 tons 12cwt (4200)/82 tons 2cwt (5205)

Driving wheel diameter: 4ft 7½in

Boiler pressure: 200lb/psi

Cylinders: (2) 18½in diameter (4200)/19in diameter (5205) x 30in stroke

Valve gear: Stephenson link motion (piston valves)

Coal capacity: 4 tons 2cwt

Water capacity: 1,800 gallons

Tractive effort: 31,450lb (4200)/33,170lb (5205) (at 85% boiler pressure)

The prototype for the 4200 class 2-8-0T, No4201, was built at Swindon in 1910. It shared the coupled wheel diameter and cylinder dimensions of the 2800, but with a reduced working pressure of 200lb/psi. A similar pony truck and cylinder block casting were used, but with the notable difference that the cylinders drove on to the second coupled axle rather than the third. Importantly, given the steep, twisting nature of the Welsh valley lines, 72 tons 10cwt of its 81 tons 12cwt total weight was available for adhesion. Additionally, it was designed to negotiate curves with a radius as sharp as two chains, despite a coupled wheelbase of 20ft.

A consequence of Swindon works' role in munitions manufacture during World War I was that the first series of 2-8-0 tanks, Nos4202-61, took five years to complete, the last not entering traffic until May 1917. Construction restarted in 1919 and a further 24 engines had joined the fleet by August 1920. Twenty more were outshopped between August 1921 and February 1923.

Construction of the 2-8-0 tanks continued under Churchward's successor, Charles Collett, but with sufficient modifications to warrant a new classification. The cylinder diameter was increased by half-an-inch, to 19in, and the boiler was altered to enlarge the total heating surface from 1,566.74 to 1,670.15 square feet. The result was an increase in tractive effort from 31,450lb to 33,170lb. The first of the Collett engines, No5205, emerged in June 1923 and ten were in traffic by that November. Deliveries continued up to April 1926.

In late 1930, the story of the Great Western 2-8-0 tanks took a curious turn. Twenty new engines, Nos5275-94, went straight from the Swindon paint

Left: Outshopped from Swindon in May 1924, 5205 class 2-8-0T No5224 spent its working life in South Wales. It was withdrawn from Cardiff East Dock in April 1963 and joined hundreds of other redundant locomotives in Woodham Brothers' Barry scrapyard. It remained there for 15 years. Privately purchased, No5224 was restored on the Great Central Railway and steamed again on 14 October 1984. One of three surviving 5205 tanks, No5224 is currently undergoing its second overhaul in preservation.

Above: Sometime resident of Severn Tunnel Junction and Aberbeeg sheds, 4200 class 2-8-0T No4277 makes an imposing sight standing in the yard at Toddington, on the Gloucestershire Warwickshire Railway.

Right: The driver reaches to collect the single line token from the signalman as No4277 starts away from Toddington with a morning service for Gotherington on 18 October 1998, second day of the Gloucestershire Warwickshire Railway's gala weekend.

shop into store because there was no work for them. The worldwide economic depression was hitting South Wales badly and rail traffic had declined dramatically. The 2-8-0 tanks had been designed for short-distance work and this was reflected in their relatively small fuel capacities. For them to be of use elsewhere, these capacities would have to be increased and this, simply but ingeniously, is what Collett did. Between 1934 and 1939, Nos5275-94 were rebuilt with extended frames, an additional trailing axle, and enlarged coal bunkers and water tanks to become the 7200 class 2-8-2 tank. It was the largest conventional tank locomotive ever to operate in Britain.

The success of this conversion persuaded Collett to take a further 34 4200 and 5205 tanks out of traffic for rebuilding as 2-8-2Ts. However, there was to be an ironic twist in the tail. By 1940, wartime demands had caused a reversal in the fortunes of the South Wales coal industry and this, coupled to growing imports of iron ore and oil through South Wales ports, meant there was now a shortage of the smaller 2-8-0 tanks. So, while the rebuilding of their classmates continued, ten new 5205 class tanks were quickly constructed.

The demise of the 4200/5205 classes (apart from those rebuilt as the 7200 class) began in February 1959 with the withdrawal of No4224. By the end of 1964, this once 205-strong group of locomotives had been reduced to just 18 survivors. The last in traffic was No5235, which was retired in September 1965, fittingly from a South Wales depot, Ebbw Junction, Newport. Five of the 4200 class, three of 5205 class and three 7200 rebuilds have been preserved but, to date, only three – Nos4277, 5224 and 5239 – have been restored to working order.

GREAT WESTERN RAILWAY

4300 Class 4MT 2-6-0

George Jackson Churchward introduced the 4300 class 2-cylinder Mogul to fill the vacancy for a secondary-duty mixed traffic locomotive in his range of standard types. At its peak the class totalled 342, a figure exceeded within the Great Western fleet only by the 863 of the 5700 class pannier tanks. Churchward's design for the 2-6-0 was essentially a tender version of his 3150 class 2-6-2 tank of 1906. It even employed the same boiler. Little about the design, therefore, had not been tried-and-tested, which allowed Churchward to dispense with prototypes. Twenty engines, ordered straight from the drawing board, appeared in 1911 and a further 20 were outshopped from Swindon in 1913. It was four years before a significant modification was deemed desirable, with the fulcrum of the leading pony truck relocated for better weight distribution.

Further orders were placed in 1921 but – unusually for the GWR – not with Swindon Works. Instead, Robert Stephenson & Company built 35 engines and then supplied the components for a further 15. These were assembled at Swindon. Following the completion of this batch in 1922, three years passed before construction resumed. The final 20 appeared seven years later.

Many of the 4300s were distinguished by a heavy front-end casting ahead of the running plate, fitted as a response to excessive flange wear on the leading driving wheels. Such wear was a consequence of regular operation over sharply curved lines, mainly in Cornwall. The casting transferred weight to the front of the locomotive, forcing the pony truck to apply more side thrust to the main frames. These then absorbed more of the force exerted, deflecting it from the wheels.

However, this remedy came at a price. The GWR used a system of colour coding to identify which of its classes could operate where. The 4-cylinder 4-6-0s, for example, were barred from many secondary routes by their weight (it was generally a question of how great an axleloading the bridges could bear). The additional two tons of the 4300's front-end casting took the modified engines out of the 'blue' category and into the much more restricted 'red'. Altogether, 89 of the class were affected.

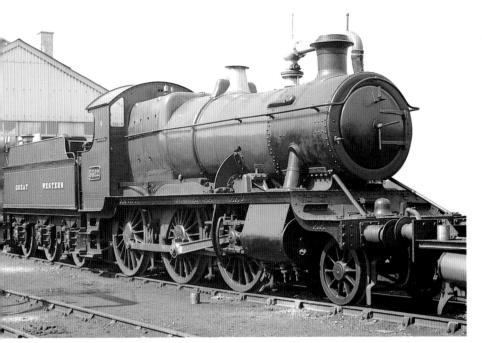

However, this was minor stuff compared to the fate that had befallen many of the class in the 1930s. The 4300s remained intact as a class of 342 until 1936 but in the ensuing three years 100 were withdrawn from traffic. They were 'cannibalized' to provide parts – principally wheels and motion components – for the new 'Manor' and 'Grange' 4-6-0s. It was planned to 'recycle' the entire class but the constraints of wartime permanently halted the scheme. The surviving Churchward Moguls continued to serve both the Great Western and, from 1948, British Railways whose Western Region inherited 241. The major allocations were at depots in the West Midlands; the West Country; South Wales; the Bristol, Gloucester, Worcester and Taunton areas; and on the ex-Cambrian Railway routes in central Wales. The last six 4300s were condemned in 1964, but two have been preserved: No5322 by the Great Western Society at its Didcot Railway Centre in Oxfordshire, and No7325 on the Severn Valley Railway in Shropshire/Worcestershire.

This would not have mattered had there been sufficient 'blue' route locomotives of other types to fulfil requirements. Unfortunately, after World War II, the scrapping of life-expired engines – chiefly 4-4-0s – left the GWR with a deficit in this area. There was no option but to restore a quantity of the 4300s to their original 'blue' status and some 50 engines duly had the front-end casting removed. The process of 'lightening' Churchward Moguls continued until 1958.

Opposite: Amid a rich variety of motive power including Standard 4 2-6-4T No80080, Churchward Mogul No7325 stands on shed at Bridgnorth, on the Severn Valley Railway, on 16 April 1994. During its working life, No7325 was based at Penzance, Old Oak Common (London), Reading and Tyseley (Birmingham). Coincidentally, its BR career ended alongside the other preserved 4300 class engine, No5322, at Pontypool Road.

Below: No7325 started life as No9303, one of a batch of 20 Moguls constructed at Swindon during 1932. It was not renumbered until June 1958, when its front-end casting was removed. Lined green paintwork became the official livery for the 4300 class in February 1959.

GWR 4300 Class 4MT 2-6-0

Built: Swindon works; Robert Stephenson & Company, Newcastle-upon-Tyne, 1911–32 (342 built)

Weight: 63 tons 17cwt (locomotive)
40 tons 0cwt (tender)

Driving wheel diameter: 5ft 8in

Boiler pressure: 200lb/psi

Cylinders: (2) 18½in diameter x 30in stroke

Valve gear: Stephenson (piston valves)

Coal capacity: 6 tons

Water capacity: 3,500 gallons

Tractive effort: 25,670lb (at 85% boiler pressure)

GREAT CENTRAL RAILWAY

8K (04) Class 8F 2-8-0

The first of the 8K class was outshopped from the Great Central Railway's Gorton workshops in 1911. It was essentially a superheated version of an earlier 0-8-0, the 8A class, with the addition of a leading pony truck. This both supported the greater front end weight and gave a smoother ride. The 8K was introduced in anticipation of increased traffic stemming from the GCR's vast new docks complex at Immingham on Humberside and, by June 1914, 126 were in traffic. Robust and straightforward, the 2-8-0s steamed well and proved outstandingly reliable, qualities that commended the design to the wartime Ministry of Munitions.

By 1916, two years into World War I, the Ministry had requisitioned some 600 engines from Britain's railway companies. With no end to the conflict in sight, it decided to build locomotives rather than borrow them. The Robinson 8K was a proven design, and had some influential backing: the Great Central's General Manager, Sir Sam Fay, had become the government's Director of War Transport.

Deliveries of the new engines, which were handed over to the Railway Operating Division (ROD) of the Royal Engineers, began in August 1917. Gorton works built only a handful of the 344 ordered, the bulk of the work being handled by four private builders. The placing of further orders as late as October 1918, just weeks before the

Armistice, was more a policy decision to keep wartime production lines active. As a consequence, by the end of 1919, the government was the owner of 521 unemployed locomotives, only 305 of which had ever performed their intended role overseas. Its first attempt to sell them was only modestly successful, which was not surprising as it was asking £12,000 for second-hand engines that had cost between £6,000 and £8,000 to construct. The next scheme to offload the remaining 468 engines met with a more enthusiastic response. They were advertised for hire and a host of companies, from Scotland's Caledonian Railway to the South Eastern & Chatham, took up the offer.

Then, in 1921, the hire agreements were abruptly terminated and the locomotives recalled. If this was intended to force companies into buying the engines, the ploy failed, and they languished in dumps around the country. By 1923, with its asset fast devaluing, the government reluctantly settled for whatever prices it could obtain. The bulk of the ex-ROD locomotives was bought by the Great Western and London & North Western Railways, and by the London & North Eastern Railway, which had absorbed the Great Central.

The 421 ex-GC and ROD Robinson 2-8-0s that came into LNER ownership enjoyed long careers. Under Robinson, the 8K had undergone little modification. There were superheater experiments, and some trials using a

Below: Now in traffic on today's Great Central Railway is the sole British-based example of the Robinson 8K 2-8-0, No102 (BR No63601), which was outshopped from Gorton works in January 1912. Withdrawn in June 1963, it was photographed in York shed yard two years earlier on 5 October 1961. The 36C shedcode indicates a Frodingham (Scunthorpe) engine.

Above: In characteristically grimy condition, an O4 2-8-0 brings a southbound rake of coal wagons through the Holmewood area, mid-way between Sheffield and Nottingham, on 29 September 1959.

GCR 8K (O4) Class 8F 2-8-0

(Weights and dimensions refer to 8K class as built)

Built: Gorton works, Manchester; Kitson & Co., Leeds; Nasmyth, Wilson & Co., Manchester; North British Locomotive Co., Glasgow, 1911–19 (666 built)

Weight: 73 tons 4cwt (locomotive)
48 tons 6cwt (tender)

Driving wheel diameter: 4ft 8in

Boiler pressure: 180lb/psi

Cylinders: (2) 21in diameter x 26in stroke

Valve gear: Stephenson (piston valves)

Coal capacity: 6 tons

Water capacity: 4,000 gallons

Tractive effort: 31,326lb (at 85% boiler pressure)

new type of fuel. However, this was nothing compared to the various degrees of rebuilding undertaken by the LNER. The changes mainly centred on replacing the Belpaire boilers with the LNER round-top variety, altering the cab design, and cutting down the boiler mountings to bring them within the LNER loading gauge. As a consequence, there were no less than eight sub-divisions of the O4, as the LNER had reclassified the 8K.

In 1941, 92 of the Robinson 2-8-0s were again requisitioned for war service. This time, however, there was a drawback: the LNER's modifications had robbed the class of vital uniformity. The War Department switched its allegiance to the LMSR's 8F 2-8-0, but not before a

number of the Robinson engines had been despatched to the Middle East.

After World War II, the home-based Robinson 2-8-0s were generally confined to former GCR routes, although five went to the north-east to work Tyne Dock to Consett iron ore trains. Withdrawals began in 1958 and were completed in 1966, with the notable exception of No63601 (GCR No102) which was set aside for the national collection. Four years ago, the locomotive was placed in the care of today's Great Central Railway, in Leicestershire. Its restoration to working order has coincided with the centenary of the opening of the original GCR's London extension in 1899.

Below: Pictured at Leicester Central depot on 9 May 1962, O4/3 No63656 was visiting from Staveley shed (41H). This was originally one of the Robinson 2-8-0s ordered by the ROD and built by Kitson's in June 1918. Between 1919 and 1922, it was loaned to the Great Western and did not become part of LNER stock until March 1924.

MIDLAND RAILWAY

4F Class 0-6-0

The six-coupled goods engine had been the mainstay of the Midland Railway's freight operations for several decades before Henry Fowler concluded that the basic design evolved by his predecessors, Samuel Waite Johnson and Richard Deeley, needed updating. It did, after all, date back to 1863. In the autumn of 1911, the prototypes for the Fowler 4F 0-6-0, Nos3835 and 3836, emerged for Derby works. The most radical improvement over the existing Midland 0-6-0s was the inclusion of superheaters. No3835 was equipped with the type invented by the German engineer, Wilhelm Schmidt; No3836 sported a version of the double-pass superheater developed by the Great Western at Swindon. Both were incorporated into the Midland's new Type G7S boiler.

Midland orthodoxy dictated the use of inside cylinders, with inside admission piston valves operated by Stephenson link motion through rocking shafts. A coupled wheel diameter of 5ft 3in was selected, with the wheelsets spaced to what had become the Derby standard of 8ft and 8ft 6in. It was in the wheelsets that a longstanding Midland design weakness was perpetuated: the use of undersized axleboxes, resulting in inadequate axle bearing surfaces.

The prototype 4Fs were allocated to Saltley shed in Birmingham and used on both passenger and goods work. In the summer of 1912, comparative tests were undertaken with two saturated (i.e., non-superheated) Deeley 0-6-0s to measure coal and water consumption. Southbound, the locomotives were attached to loaded trains of around 600 tons and, on the return, hauled rakes of 50 or 100 empty wagons. Problems immediately occurred with the joints between the superheater elements and superheater headers on both engines. In addition, after only two runs, No3836 had to be fitted with new valves and liners. Nevertheless, results showed the locomotive with the Schmidt superheater, No3835, to be the most economical, with worthwhile savings in both coal and water consumption.

Given the success of the superheated 0-6-0s, it is surprising that five years passed

Right: Pictured at Arley at the head of a Severn Valley Kidderminster-Bridgnorth service, the only currently operational 4F 0-6-0 ended its BR days at Gloucester, in June 1965. It went for scrap but was rescued by the North Staffordshire Railway Company in 1977. Following the completion of its restoration in 1992, the 4F became one of preservation's most-travelled engines. It has recently worn its BR identity as No44422.

Right: Backing off shed at Bridgnorth during a visit to the Severn Valley Railway on 25 September 1993 is Fowler 4F 0-6-0 No4422. Outshopped from Derby in October 1927, No4422 spent its early years in the Leicester district but, by 1940, had begun a 25-year association with the Somerset and Dorset route.

MR 4F Class 0-6-0

Built: Crewe, Derby, Horwich, St Rollox (Glasgow) works; Andrew Barclay, Kilmarnock; Armstrong Whitworth, Newcastle-upon-Tyne; Kerr Stuart, Stoke-on-Trent; the North British Locomotive Company, Glasgow, 1911–41 (772 built)

Weight: 48 tons 15cwt (locomotive)
41 tons 4cwt (tender)

Driving wheel diameter: 5ft 3in

Boiler pressure: 175lb/psi

Cylinders: (2) 20in diameter x 26in stroke

Valve gear: Stephenson link motion (piston valves)

Coal capacity: 4 tons

Water capacity: 3,500 gallons

Tractive effort: 24,555lb (at 85% boiler pressure)

before the Midland went into production. Doubtless the delay was due in part to the outbreak of war in 1914, and to the fact that the company already had a stock of no less than 1,495 0-6-0 tender engines – around 50 per cent of its fleet. The question remains why the prosperous Midland made do for so long with huge numbers of undersized and underpowered 0-6-0s that frequently had to double-head on even modestly sized trains.

A batch of 15 Fowler 4F 0-6-0s, beginning with No3837, appeared in 1917 and construction continued steadily up to the Grouping in 1923, when 197 were in traffic. The prevailing Midland influence within the newly formed LMSR then ensured that, with only minor modifications, the design was adopted as the standard freight locomotive. More were built every year up to 1928. Even more extraordinary than the decision to continue building these engines was that no attempt appears to have been made to correct their fundamental deficiencies.

With the introduction of the Stanier 8F 2-8-0 in the mid-1930s, it would have been reasonable to assume that the LMSR's reliance on the 4F 0-6-0 would end. Yet, in 1937, the great modernizer, William Stanier, bowed to pressure from the operating department and authorized the construction of a further 45 examples. It took the number of 4Fs built by the LMSR to 575 and the class total to 772, all of which joined the British Railways list in 1948. They put in many more years' useful, if unspectacular, service, mainly in ex-Midland territory.

Withdrawals began in 1954, with No43862, and the last to be retired was No44525, in 1966. Four have been preserved, including the first 4F built for the LMSR, No4027, as part of the National Collection. It, along with two others of the surviving quartet, Nos43924 and 44422, has worked in preservation but the fourth, No44123, is still undergoing restoration. Currently, only No44422 is operational but is due for overhaul in 2000.

SOMERSET & DORSET JOINT RAILWAY

7F Class 2-8-0

In 1876, the Midland Railway and London & South Western Railway combined forces to rescue the financially ailing Somerset & Dorset Railway. In the new scheme of things, the Midland took responsibility for locomotives and rolling stock. Unfortunately, its 'small engine' policy did not suit the line's long, and often severe gradients. The Midland's medium-power 0-6-0s limited the loads that could be hauled and invariably required a second, banking engine. This added significantly to running costs, especially on the mineral traffic originating from the mines and quarries of the Mendip Hills.

The Locomotive Superintendent of the Somerset & Dorset Joint Railway (as the combined enterprise was known), M.H. Ryan, argued for a locomotive tailored to the Bath to Bournemouth route. In 1907, two designs for 0-8-0s were submitted but ruled out on weight grounds. However, in 1914, Ryan's wish was granted. The Chief Mechanical Engineer of the Midland, Henry Fowler, asked his senior draughtsman at Derby, James Clayton, to come up with a locomotive that could take heavy mineral trains over the Mendips unassisted.

Clayton relished being given a free hand in the design. He broke with Midland tradition and produced a big, powerful outside cylinder 2-8-0. It was unlike any other Derby-designed locomotive.

By including a leading pony truck, Clayton redistributed the weight and overcame the objections that had ruled out the earlier 0-8-0 proposals. He used the Type G9AS superheated boiler fitted to the Midland's compound 4-4-0s, with a Belpaire firebox and circular smokebox. Walschaerts valve gear was employed, with the cylinders inclined at 1 in 12 to avoid fouling platform faces. Conscious that the locomotives would be descending steep gradients with heavy loads, Clayton took a 'belt-and-braces' approach to braking and included three steam brake cylinders on the engine and a further one on the tender.

Below: Wearing its S&DJR guise, Fowler 7F 2-8-0 No88 arrives at Williton, on the West Somerset Railway with a service for Bishops Lydeard on 20 June 1993. As BR No53808, this locomotive languished in the scrap line for six years before it was rescued in 1970 and restored by the Somerset and Dorset Trust.

S&DJR 7F Class 2-8-0

Built: Derby works, 1914; Robert Stephenson & Hawthorn, Darlington, 1925 (11 built)

Weight: 64 tons 15cwt (locomotive) (with G9AS boiler) 44 tons 4cwt (tender)

Driving wheel diameter: 4ft 7½in

Boiler pressure: 190lb/psi

Cylinders: (2) 21in diameter x 28in stroke

Valve gear: Walschaerts

Coal capacity: 5 tons 10cwt

Water capacity: 3,500 gallons

Tractive effort: 35,932lb (at 85% boiler pressure)

Above: Evoking memories of the Somerset and Dorset, when both classes of locomotive graced the line, 7F 2-8-0 No53809 pilots BR Standard 9F 2-10-0 No92203 across the viaduct at Summerseat with an East Lancashire Railway Bury-Rawtenstall service on 21 August 1993.

Given the many ways in which the design departed from usual Midland practice, it was curious that the undersized 'Derby standard' axleboxes were retained. As a consequence, the S&D 2-8-0 was as prone to 'hot boxes' as most Midland classes, although the later fitting of mechanical lubricators went some way to alleviating the problem.

The first of the S&DJR 2-8-0s, No80, entered traffic in March 1914. That year, Derby delivered a further five and they quickly proved their worth. Their eight-coupled wheelbase made for a sure-footed locomotive and the power available was of a different order from the resident 0-6-0s. A tractive effort of 35,932lb compared to 24,555lb told its own story.

The Midland's operating department did conduct trials with the S&D 2-8-0s on, for example, Nottingham-London coal trains but, for whatever reason, they were unable to replicate the performances put in over the Mendip Hills. One drawback was a prodigious appetite for coal – around 87lb per mile – and the engines did not respond well if fired on second-rate fuel.

In 1925, the LMSR added to the number of S&D 2-8-0s by ordering five further examples from Robert Stephenson & Hawthorn. For some reason, these were fitted with larger boilers (Type G9BS) and, as a consequence, differed in other details from their predecessors. They gradually acquired the smaller G9AS boilers, but it was a process that took until 1955.

By this time, vacuum brake gear had been fitted to all 11, allowing them to work passenger trains. By the late 1950s, however, the 2-8-0s were being displaced by an influx of BR Standard types, especially 9F 2-10-0s (the only engines that could compete on the Mendip freight hauls). The 1914-built locomotives were retired between 1959 and 1962, but the 1925 examples lasted until 1963–64. Two have survived: No88 (BR No53808) on the West Somerset Railway, and No89 (BR No53809) at the Midland Railway Centre in Derbyshire.

GREAT EASTERN RAILWAY

L77 (N7) Class 3MT 0-6-2T

The Great Eastern Railway maintained the most intensive suburban service in Britain. On an average weekday in the period 1910–14, there were over 1,200 movements into and out of its London terminus of Liverpool Street. It was a slick operation, and one undertaken with manual signalling and a fleet of modestly powered locomotives. Chief among these were James Holden's diminutive, but nippy 0-6-0Ts that daily climbed the 1 in 70 of Bethnal Green bank with packed ten-coach commuter trains.

As loadings increased, however, the GER's Locomotive Superintendent, Alfred Hill, began work on a larger and more powerful suburban tank engine. Two prototypes for his L77 class, Nos1000 and 1001, were built in 1914. The latter incorporated a superheater, the first Great Eastern locomotive to benefit from the device. Both proved ideal for their intended role but, with the outbreak of war in Europe that year, further construction was put on hold. It was not until 1921 that the class was enlarged and then modestly. By the Grouping in 1923, when the Great Eastern became part of the LNER, only 14 were in service.

However, the Chief Mechanical Engineer of the new company, Nigel Gresley, was quick to see the potential of the design. This was just as well since track, signalling and operational improvements had allowed the Liverpool Street west side suburban service to be greatly intensified. There had been a 75 per cent increase in services during the weekday morning peak.

Under Gresley, 122 more N7 (as the L77 was reclassified by the LNER) tanks were constructed between 1923 and 1928. Superheaters were now fitted as standard, as was the Westinghouse compressed air brake. This had always been vital to the efficiency of the GER's suburban operation, with its requirement for rapid acceleration away from the many, closely spaced station stops. However, the N7 departed from the usual GER practice in using Walschaerts rather than Stephenson valve gear in conjunction with its inside cylinders. The first production batch of GER-built engines had been fitted with Belpaire fireboxes, but later examples received the round-top fireboxes that the LNER had decreed as standard. In turn, the GER-built examples were re-boilered with round-top fireboxes as renewals fell due.

Surprisingly few (only 10) of the new N7s were built at the one-time Great Eastern works at Stratford, in east London. The now-preserved No69621 was one of them and, in 1924, the last locomotive built there. The majority of the new engines were constructed at other LNER workshops, with Gorton contributing 40 and Doncaster 32. The private manufacturers, Robert Stephenson & Hawthorn and Beardmore's each supplied 20.

The N7 was the ideal inner-suburban tank locomotive. A weight of 61 tons 16cwt, with 49 tons 5cwt of that available for adhesion, gave it a significant advantage over, for example, the Holden 2-4-2 tanks. It was able to maintain timings on the Enfield and Chingford runs which were not all that far off today's electric multiple units. When given their head on longer trips out to Hertford or Bishop's Stortford, 60mph sprints along the flatlands of the Lea Valley with 250 tons in tow were far from rare.

Left: Front end of the Hill L77 suburban tank showing the Westinghouse air brake pump which was a vital element in the slick operation of the Great Eastern Railway's intensive services to east and north-east London. Air braking allowed brisk getaways from the many station stops. The L77's two cylinders and Walschaerts valve gear are located between the frames.

Below: The survivor from the once 134-strong N7 tanks, No69621, was also the last locomotive to be built at the Great Eastern Railway's workshops at Stratford in east London. It entered traffic, as LNER No999, in 1924. It was one of 122 N7s constructed between 1923 and 1928, the majority by private manufacturers. No69621 proudly declaims its Stratford links with the 30A shedplate on the smokebox door.

The N7s were not confined to north-east London. Examples could be found in East Anglia and they became the mainstays of the Luton to Dunstable branch in Hertfordshire. Others were employed on the ex-Great Central line between London Marylebone and Aylesbury. They hauled LNER services over the Metropolitan line to Watford, and engines fitted with push-pull apparatus worked the Chesham branch prior to its take-over by London Transport. They ended their days, though, on the Liverpool Street lines, working right up to electrification in 1960. By the winter of 1961, only 25 of the once 134-strong class were still in service. The last eight were withdrawn in September 1962. Undoubtedly the most celebrated member of the class was No69614 which, as Liverpool Street's station pilot, was always turned out in pristine condition by Stratford depot. It failed to survive, but classmate No69621 (GER No999) was privately preserved and is normally based at the East Anglian Railway Museum at Chappel & Wakes Colne in Essex.

GER L77 (N7) Class 3MT 0-6-2T

Built: Doncaster, Gorton , Stratford works; Robert Stephenson & Hawthorn, Newcastle-upon-Tyne; William Beardmore & Son, Glasgow, 1914–28 (134 built)

Weight: 61 tons 16cwt – 64 tons 17cwt, depending on boiler and firebox type

Driving wheel diameter: 4ft 10in

Boiler pressure: 180lb/psi

Cylinders: (2) 18in diameter x 24in stroke

Valve gear: Walschaerts (inside) (piston valves)

Coal capacity: 3 tons 5cwt

Water capacity: 1,600 gallons

Tractive effort: 20,512lb (at 85% boiler pressure)

NORTH EASTERN RAILWAY

T3 (Q7) Class 8F 0-8-0

Like his counterpart Nigel Gresley of the Great Northern, the North Eastern Railway's Vincent Raven was a convert to the 3-cylinder configuration. Towards the end of World War I, when the NER concluded that it needed a bigger and more powerful mineral engine, Raven argued for a 3-cylinder design. He maintained that the smooth starting torque achievable with three cylinders would be ideally suited to the NER's heavy hauls of coal, ore and limestone. Engines would be less prone to wheelslip when handling such loads.

The detail work on the new freight locomotive was entrusted to the Assistant Chief Mechanical Engineer, A.C. Stamer. What appeared on Stamer's drawing board was an 0-8-0 akin to the Raven 2-cylinder T2 of 1913. However, the newcomer – designed to work 1,400 ton loads unassisted on gradients of 1 in 200 – would be considerably stronger. The cylinders were in three castings, the two for

the outside consisting of the cylinders only, and a central unit made up of the inside cylinder and a common steam chest. Each piston valve was worked by its own independent set of Stephenson valve gear positioned between the frames. All three cylinders drove on to the second axle.

An order for the new T3 was placed in 1918 but limited to five engines. Clearly, the NER reasoned that its need for such powerful locomotives was limited. There was, for example, a practical problem that Gresley was later to meet with his P1 2-8-2s for the LNER. These locomotives could unquestionably handle long, heavy trains. Unfortunately, the sidings and passing loops were too short to accommodate them.

The first of the T3s, No901, was outshopped from Darlington in November 1919. A month later, the NER organized a test train over the Newcastle to Carlisle line. The load consisted of 60 loaded coal wagons, a brake van

and the company's dynamometer car, which had been included to record the locomotive's performance. No901 had 1,402 tons in tow but handled the load with ease, registering both high power and steady acceleration. There were no problems starting on a 1 in 298 grade and, on the return, with a reduced load of 787 tons, the 0-8-0 was untroubled by gradients as severe as 1 in 107.

Despite their prowess, the original quintet of T3s was not augmented by the North Eastern Railway, a move that would have pleased footplate crews who disliked having lubricate and maintain the centre cylinder and valve gear, or 'middle engine' as it was known. Instead, the enlargement of the class came under London & North Eastern Railway auspices. It authorized the construction of ten additional T3s (or Q7s, in the LNER scheme of things) and these emerged from Darlington during 1924.

Surprisingly, two of the new locomotives were first allocated to York, and a further four to Hull. The remaining four gravitated to their natural habitat: Tyne Dock depot near South Shields. It was there, eventually, that all 15 T3s/Q7s congregated. Here they performed the role they were destined for, one of the toughest jobs on any British railway. This was to haul 700 ton rakes of iron ore hoppers to the steelworks at Consett, 1,000ft above sea level. On the steepest sections, as severe as 1 in 35 in places, one 0-8-0 pulled while another pushed. They remained

masters of this task until the arrival of the BR Standard 9F 2-10-0s (pages 190-191) in the 1950s.

Their usefulness diminished, British Railways retired all 15 of its Q7s in November and December 1962. There was no justification for retaining such a small number of non-standard engines. However, as it represented the final development of NER freight power, the prototype T3 No901 (BR No63460) was selected to become part of the National Collection. In 1979, No901 was entrusted to the North Eastern Locomotive Preservation Group and taken to the North Yorkshire Moors Railway. After NELPG had returned No901 to working order in 1990, this mighty machine was once more to be seen storming up a steep bank, only this time between Grosmont and Goathland at the head of NYMR passenger trains.

NER T3 (Q7) Class 8F 0-8-0

Built: Darlington works, 1919 and 1924 (15 built)

Weight: 71 tons 12cwt (locomotive)
44 tons 2cwt (tender)

Driving wheel diameter: 4ft 7¼in

Boiler pressure: 180lb/psi

Cylinders: (3) 18½in diameter x 26in stroke

Valve gear: Stephenson (piston valves)

Coal capacity: 5 tons 10cwt

Water capacity: 4,125 gallons

Tractive effort: 36,963lb (at 85% boiler pressure)

Left: Raven T3 (Q7) 3-cylinder 0-8-0 No901 stands under the coaling plant at Grosmont, on the North Yorkshire Moors Railway on 3 August 1991. It is the survivor from a class of 15, all of which were withdrawn from Tyne Dock shed (52H) between 26 November and 17 December 1962.

Above: The overhaul of No901 was completed in time for the NYMR's 1990 autumn gala. For an engine which once handled 700-ton iron ore trains on 1 in 35 gradients, the loading of the 3.45pm Grosmont-Goathland local, passing Esk Valley on 6 October 1990, was a modest running-in turn!

Speed and Power

1920–1940

L&SWR S15 class • GNR/LNER N2 class

GWR 4073 'Castle' • LNER A1/A3 Pacifics

LMSR 3F class 0-6-0T

SR N15 'King Arthur', LN 'Lord Nelson' classes

West Coast Moguls • GWR 6000 'King'

LMSR 'Royal Scot' • GWR 4900 'Hall'

SR U class Mogul • GWR 5700 pannier tank

SR V 'Schools' • LMSR 'Princess Royal' Pacific

LMSR 5XP 'Jubilee' • LMSR 5P5F 'Black Five'

LMSR 8F class • LNER A4 Pacific • LNER V2 class

LNER K4 class Mogul • GWR 7800 'Manor'

LMSR 'Princess Coronation' Pacific

1920–1940

Speed and Power

Britain's railways had been under government control throughout World War I and, after the Armistice of 1918, remained so for a further three years. During this period, the benefits of a unified rail network were widely acknowledged. Previous rivalries had cost companies dear through uneconomic duplication of services and many were far from viable. The Railways Act of 1921 proposed the 'grouping' of these 120 existing concerns into just four – the 'Big Four', as they became known. The Act came into force on 1 January 1923, and with it came into being the London Midland & Scottish Railway, the London & North Eastern Railway and the Southern Railway. Only the Great Western retained its pre-grouping name. It was by far the largest railway operator in Wales and the West Country and, unlike the LMSR, LNER and SR, absorbed only relatively minor constituents.

The effect of the 'Grouping' on locomotive development was significant. The dominant influence in the LMSR became the Midland Railway and this resulted in a decade of near-stagnation as the Derby-based hierarchy pursued the Midland's 'small engine' policy. The Southern appointed the competent and well-qualified Richard Maunsell to control motive power matters, but Maunsell was often frustrated in his efforts to modernize and standardize the SR's ageing locomotive fleet. Increasingly, the Southern's electrification programme absorbed much of its investment in new stock.

The Great Western had to do little more than maintain the status quo. Churchward's 4-cylinder and 2-cylinder 4-6-0s, introduced between 1902 and 1906, had

inaugurated two decades during which the GWR assembled a fleet of modern steam locomotives without parallel in Britain. It continued to build locomotives to the Churchward precepts – his successor, Charles Collett, was not one to change a successful formula – and it exploited its technical lead to the full.

The GWR's pre-eminence, however, was under threat. At the helm on the London & North Eastern Railway was Nigel Gresley. In 1922, as Locomotive Superintendent of the Great Northern Railway, Gresley had begun building Britain's first production series of Pacifics, his 3-cylinder A1 class. In many respects, the 4-6-2, or Pacific, type was the ideal express passenger locomotive. The leading four-wheel bogie supplied guidance and stability at speed; the six driving wheels delivered that speed, along with adhesion and power; and the trailing truck supported a large firebox that helped generate the power. The first British Pacific – Churchward's 4-cylinder No111 *The Great Bear* of 1908 – had failed to live up to expectations. In contrast, Gresley's design was the first of a new breed of high-power, fast-running and – by British standards – 'big engines'.

Its appearance was timely. During the 1920s, railways first began to feel the effect of competition from road transport. Some decided faster speeds were the best means of countering that competition yet, before World War I, few regular scheduled services averaged more than 50mph. There were exceptions, and these usually occurred when railway companies were in direct competition. The 'Races to the North' of 1895, when east and west coast companies dramatically accelerated their overnight Anglo-Scottish services, were an example.

However, in 1923, the GWR rescheduled an afternoon train from Cheltenham, in Gloucestershire, to London. Over the 77 miles between Swindon and Paddington, the train was scheduled for an average speed of 61.8mph, making it the fastest timetabled service in Britain. When that was increased to 66.2 mph in 1929, the *Cheltenham Flyer,* as it was now called, became the fastest train in the world.

During 1931, the *Flyer* was further accelerated to an average of 71.4mph, the world's first 70 mph-plus schedule. Its 'Castle' class engines, though, were more than equal to the task, and were also instrumental in turning Gresley's Pacifics into record-breakers. The lessons learned from comparative trials during 1925 led to a transformation in the performance of the LNER engines and allowed the introduction of high-speed services along the east coast, and between London and Yorkshire. The culmination came in 1935–37 with 'Silver Jubilee' and 'Coronation' expresses hauled by the streamlined A4 Pacifics.

These were engines that could maintain 80mph averages on reasonably level track and reach maximum

Above: Introduced in 1934, the 5XP 'Jubilee' 4-6-0s were a component of William Stanier's plan to modernize and restock the LMSR's fleet. Intended for secondary passenger work, 191 were built. Here, No5593 Kolhapur *masquerades as the first of the class, No5552* Silver Jubilee.

Right: The Great Eastern Railway's S69, or '1500' class was introduced in 1911 and 67 were in service by 1921. A further ten – including the preserved No8572 – were built by Beyer Peacock of Manchester in 1928. Withdrawn from Norwich in 1961, No8572 is the sole remaining example of the inside-cylinder British 4-6-0.

Below: 12-cylinder power! Three examples of Great Western 4-cylinder express passenger locomotives parade at the Birmingham Railway Museum, Tyseley, on 14 October 1989. Newly-restored 'King' No6024 King Edward I *leads 'Castles' No5080* Defiant *and No7029* Clun Castle.

speeds around 100mph on a regular basis. The first authenticated 100mph was attained by Gresley Pacific No4472 *Flying Scotsman* in 1934 and, in 1938, one of its streamlined successors, No4468 *Mallard*, reached what is still a world record speed of 126mph.

Many elements of the design contributed to these performances. The kind of improved front-end arrangement of valves and cylinders that originated with Churchward not only helped produce 'flyers' but also enhanced the performance of freight locomotives. High tractive effort was combined with high speeds. However, from the mid-1920s, increasing fuel costs highlighted the need for greater fuel efficiency and the work of the French engineer, André Chapelon, was vitally important here. His techniques of eliminating pressure losses caused by tortuous or constricted steampipes and inadequate steamchests were shown to increase power and efficiency by up to 40 per cent. Chapelon's principles were first adopted by Gresley, and later by William Stanier on the LMSR and Oliver Bulleid of the Southern Railway. It was no coincidence that the record-breaking *Mallard* was equipped with the Chapelon-developed Kylchap exhaust system.

At first, the LNER's west coast rival, the London Midland & Scottish Railway, had little to compete with the Gresley Pacifics on the London to Scotland run. That situation altered in 1927 with the debut of the 'Royal Scot' 4-6-0s, but the

real challenge was mounted after 1932. That was the year William Stanier arrived from Swindon to become Chief Mechanical Engineer of the LMSR. His brief was to restock the largest of the 'Big Four' with a standard range of modern locomotives. The result was a series of outstanding designs such as the Class 5 4-6-0, 8F 2-8-0, 4MT 2-6-4T and the 'Princess Coronation' Pacific. Not to be left out, Maunsell updated the Southern's express passenger fleet with some fine locomotives, among them the 'King Arthur' and 'Lord Nelson' 4-6-0s and, arguably his masterpiece, the 'Schools', the last 4-4-0 to be built in Britain.

A feature of all of these designs was their use of Walschaerts valve gear, patented as far back as 1844 by a Belgian, Egide Walschaerts. Its adoption in Britain, with its long commitment to inside-cylinder locomotives, was slow but, by 1920 – apart from small tank locomotives – Walschaerts gear was widely employed in new construction. As a consequence, the appearance of the last of the LNER B12 class 4-6-0s in 1928 also marked the end for inside-cylinder passenger express locomotives. The transmission of higher power outputs in inside cylinder engines resulted in crank axle stresses and increased maintenance. Designers now settled on two outside cylinders for most roles.

The exceptions were usually in the express passenger category. Altogether, some 1,900 3-cylinder and 4-cylinder locomotives ran in Britain (800 3-cylinder Gresley engines on the LNER alone), but they represented only 10 per cent of the total. Apart from on the LNER, 2-cylinder designs were preferred for all but the heaviest passenger duties. Freight was entrusted to 2-cylinder 0-6-0s, 0-8-0s and 2-8-0s, with the LNER's 3-cylinder Q7 0-8-0 and V2 class fast freight 2-6-2 notable exceptions. Both the GWR and LMSR built mixed-traffic 2-cylinder 4-6-0s in large numbers, a pattern that was to continue into the 1940s.

By 1939, even before the outbreak of war, the emphasis was shifting towards simplicity, flexibility and ease of maintenance. War only accelerated the process.

SOUTHERN RAILWAY

S15 Class 6F 4-6-0

The S15 4-6-0 had its origins in 1912, when the ever-pragmatic Robert Urie replaced Dugald Drummond as head of locomotive matters on the London & South Western Railway. The Drummond inheritance included 26 complex 4-cylinder 4-6-0s built to four designs, none especially successful. Urie's response was to produce a far more robust and straightforward machine, the H15 of 1913. It was the first true mixed traffic 2-cylinder 4-6-0 in Britain to employ outside Walschaerts valve gear. Recently recruited from the North British Locomotive Co., Urie's Chief Draughtsman, Thomas Finlayson, was well versed in building big-cylindered 4-6-0s for export to India and southern Africa.

Unfortunately, like several Urie designs, the H15s were unreliable steamers and, initially, only 11 were built. A restricted steam flow at the front end (the cylinders and exhaust arrangement) meant they struggled to attain speeds much above 55mph.

Undeterred, Urie pressed ahead with two new 4-6-0 designs during World War I. Many components were duplicated between them, principally the boiler, cylinders and valve gear. The main difference was in driving wheel diameter. The one intended for express passenger work had 6ft 7in wheels and would be the forerunner of the famous 'King Arthur' class (pages 110-111); the other, classified S15, was fitted with 5ft 7in drivers and intended for fast freight duties.

Built at Eastleigh, the first of these new goods engines entered traffic in February 1920. By May 1921, 16 were in service, all but one shared between the London area depots at Nine Elms and Strawberry Hill. The exception was No496, which went to Salisbury. In 1922, the opening of the L&SWR's giant marshalling yard at Feltham saw the Strawberry Hill engines transferred to the newly-built motive power depot adjacent to the yard. It was the beginning of a 40-year association.

Urie's successor, and first Chief Mechanical Engineer of the newly created Southern Railway, Richard Maunsell, authorized – possibly with some reluctance – the building of ten more H15 4-6-0s. However, he delayed further construction of the S15 until comparative trials had taken place. It was put through its paces alongside one of Maunsell's mixed-traffic 2-6-0s for the South Eastern & Chatham Railway and a similar 2-6-0 from the London Brighton & South Coast Railway. Both in maintaining schedules and fuel economy, the S15 was clearly the superior freight engine. Maunsell decided to build more of the class, but not before he had undertaken a radical revision of the front-end layout. The boiler pressure was increased from 180lb to 200lb/psi and the cylinder

Left: With cylinder cocks blowing, one of two surviving examples of the 20 Urie-designed S15 4-6-0s, No30506, comes off shed at Ropley, on the Mid-Hants Railway. As L&SWR No506, this locomotive was completed in October 1920 at a cost of £9,567. Apart from two months on loan to Exmouth Junction in 1927, from mid-1923 until withdrawal in January 1964, No506 was based at Feltham depot in south-west London.

Right: In 1923, the S15s became the most powerful and capable heavy goods engines inherited by the Southern Railway. This persuaded its CME, Richard Maunsell, to produce his own version. The Maunsell Society's No847, seen here at the head of the Bluebell Railway's Pullman rake, was both the last S15, and the last 4-6-0 built by the Southern. It entered service in December 1936.

SR S15 Class 6F 4-6-0

Built: Eastleigh works, 1920–21 (Urie engines); 1927–36 (Maunsell engines) (45 built)

Weight: 79 tons 16cwt (Urie); 79 tons 5cwt* (Maunsell) (locomotive)
56 tons 8cwt (8-wheel double-bogie tender)

Driving wheel diameter: 5ft 7in

Boiler pressure: 180lb/psi (Urie engines); 200lb/psi (Maunsell engines)

Cylinders: 21in diameter x 28in stroke (Urie); 20½in diameter x 28in stroke(Maunsell)

Valve gear: Walschaerts (piston valves)

Coal capacity: 5 tons 0cwt (8-wheel double-bogie tender)

Water capacity: 5,000 gallons (8-wheel double-bogie tender)

Tractive effort: 28,198lb (Urie); 29,860lb (Maunsell) (at 85% boiler pressure)

(* *Maunsell engines Nos823-837 weighed 80 tons 14cwt*)

Above: Wearing 1930s lined green livery, and with an 'E' prefix (for Eastleigh) to its number, Maunsell S15 No828 storms away from Harmans Cross while working on the Swanage Railway on 20 August 1998. Built at a cost of £6,585, No828 entered service in July 1927 and spent its entire working life at Salisbury. It had run 1,287,124 miles when withdrawn in January 1964. Restoration was completed in 1993.

diameter reduced by half-an-inch to 21½ inches. Additionally, the valve travel was lengthened and larger, outside steampipes fitted.

The benefits of these modifications became evident in the improved performances of the first batch of Maunsell S15s over their Urie equivalents. Nos823-837 were delivered from Eastleigh during 1927 and 1928, and a further 10, Nos838-847, authorized in 1931. This, however, coincided with a downturn in the freight business – a consequence of the worldwide economic depression – and the construction of these last S15 4-6-0s was not completed until 1936.

Both the Urie and Maunsell S15s spent most of their working lives on the Southern's Western Division. Eventually, all the Urie engines were concentrated at Feltham and, with a few exceptions, remained there until withdrawal. Alongside Feltham, the Maunsell S15s were allocated to Exmouth Junction, Hither Green (which, like Feltham, served another major freight yard) and Salisbury. Sent new to Wiltshire's cathedral city in 1927, four locomotives – Nos828, 829, 831 and 832 – remained at Salisbury all their working lives up to withdrawal in 1963–64. Nos833-37 were originally allocated to Brighton and harnessed to shorter six-wheel tenders to suit the Central Division turntables.

The S15s were retired between 1962 and 1965, with all the Urie engines having given over 40 years' service. However, it was a Maunsell example, No30837, that returned to Feltham in January 1966 to work a farewell railtour. Two of the Urie design have been preserved, Nos30499 and 30506, both of the Mid-Hants Railway (although the former is undergoing restoration off-site). Of the five Maunsell survivors, three have been restored to running order and two, the Eastleigh-based No828 and the North Yorkshire Moors Railway's No30841, have worked on the main line.

LONDON & NORTH EASTERN RAILWAY

N2 Class 3P2F 0-6-2T

Over the years, services to Great Northern Railway's suburban hinterland were entrusted to everything from small Stirling and Ivatt 0-4-4 tanks to the massive L1 2-6-4Ts of Edward Thompson. However, it is the Gresley N2 that remains synonymous with suburban services out of London's King's Cross. It had its origins in Henry Ivatt's N1 tank of 1907. This was a nippy enough machine but, by 1919, it was clear that something more powerful was required to cope with increasing peak-time trainloads. Initially, the Doncaster drawing office came up with schemes for 3-cylinder 2-6-2 and 2-6-4 tanks. These were ruled out by the civil engineer – not, as was usual, because they were too heavy, but for being too long. There was insufficient clearance for such engines at the GNR's cramped City of London terminus at Moorgate.

This left the GNR's Nigel Gresley with little option but to update and enlarge the Ivatt N1. Though superficially similar to the N1, the new N2 was technically its superior, largely through the incorporation of superheating, larger cylinders and the use of piston valves. The high-pitched boiler (needed to provide adequate clearance for the piston valves above the cylinders) and squat boiler mountings (dictated by loading gauge constraints over the King's Cross to Moorgate section) lent the N2 an imposing profile.

The only prototype work undertaken for the design was the fitting of a superheater to an Ivatt N1 to test its likely effectiveness. The Great Northern promptly ordered 60 N2s and, by Christmas 1920, the first had been delivered. Doncaster works built just ten, but the North British Locomotive Company turned out 50 in the remarkable time of five months. All were fitted with condensing apparatus. This returned spent steam from the cylinders to the side tanks where, as the name implies, it was condensed to water.

After the 1923 Grouping, the LNER adopted the N2 as a 'group standard' class and ordered a further 47 engines for delivery between 1925 and 1929. Doncaster works constructed only six, but these were notable for being fitted with both vacuum and Westinghouse air brakes for use in Scotland. However, it was in the King's Cross 'Met Link' that the N2s gained their reputation. This involved some 45 engines each of which was rostered – as far as was practicable – to just two of the 90 footplate crews in the 'Link'. Allocating crews their 'own' engine inspired great pride in the N2s' appearance and performance.

The fast peak-hour services that ran non-stop between Finsbury Park and Hatfield saw the Gresley tanks regularly attain 60-70mph. They could accelerate to 50mph or more within one and a half miles of a start, and were well able to maintain a 30mph average when taking 200 tons up the 1 in 60 of the Highgate branch, or the two and a half miles of 1 in 59/63 on the climb to High Barnet.

The Gresley N2 needed its hill-climbing capabilities. Leaving King's Cross, the hard work began immediately, through the tunnels and up Holloway bank. For crews working through from Moorgate, there was the challenge of the intermediate stop at the old platform 16 at King's Cross. This was located on a gradient of 1 in 37 and a curve of 7 chains radius. Restarting a heavy train was a test of skill. The key was to allow the handbrake to be slowly released while watching the rotation of the coupling rods. When they reached the point of maximum tractive effort, the regulator was fully opened and – with luck – the driving wheels took hold.

All 107 Gresley N2s passed into British Railways ownership and, for over a decade, remained in charge of King's Cross suburban duties. The first withdrawals occurred in 1956 and the last were disposed of in 1962. Thanks to the efforts of the Gresley Society, one of the North British-built engines, No69523 (LNER No4744), survived to represent this most famous of Gresley tank classes in preservation. It normally works on the less taxing gradients of the Great Central Railway in Leicestershire.

Left: The preserved N2, No69523, was one of a batch of 50 built by the North British Locomotive Company. Retired from New England, Peterborough, in September 1962, it was acquired by the Gresley Society the following October.

25

69523

DEPOT

LNER N2 Class 3P2F 0-6-2T

Built: Doncaster works; Beyer Peacock
& Co., Manchester; Hawthorn Leslie
& Co., Newcastle-upon-Tyne; North
British Locomotive Co., Glasgow;
Yorkshire Engine Co., Sheffield,
1920–29 (107 built)

Weight: 70 tons 5cwt/72 tons 10cwt
(N2/4 class)

Driving wheel diameter: 5ft 8in

Boiler pressure: 170lb/psi

Cylinders: (2) 19in diameter x 26in stroke

Valve gear: Stephenson (piston valves)

Coal capacity: 4 tons

Water capacity: 2,000 gallons

Tractive effort: 19,945lb
(at 85% boiler pressure)

Above: Making a foray away from the Great Central Railway, No69523 went on loan to the Chinnor & Princes Risborough Railway during 1997. In dappled sunlight, and with one of the smokebox destination boards worn in LNER and BR days, the N2 approaches Chinnor on 1 June with the last arrival of the day.

Inset: Driver's side of the N2, showing the running plate, splasher, lubricator and – alongside the smokebox – the condensing apparatus that recycled exhaust steam.

GREAT WESTERN RAILWAY

4073 'Castle' Class 7P 4-6-0

The performances of the Great Western Railway's 'Castle' class 4-6-0s have become the stuff of legend. For over 40 years, these engines were the mainstay of the GWR's and, from 1948, British Railways' Western Region express passenger services. Their duties took them to the holiday resorts of the West Country, to the ports of Bristol and Plymouth, to the industrial centres of South Wales and the West Midlands, and to the cathedral cities of Gloucester, Exeter, Hereford and Worcester.

Several of the GWR's crack expresses were entrusted to 'Castles', including the 'Cheltenham Flyer'. During the 1920s and early 1930s, this was the fastest scheduled service in the world. By 1929, this was allowed just 70 minutes for the 77.3 miles from Swindon to Paddington, an average speed of 66.2 miles per hour. Even in their twilight years, 'Castles' were recorded at speeds of more than 100 miles per hour at the head of enthusiast specials.

Although they made their much-publicized debut in 1923 (the GWR was never a company to squander a public relations opportunity), strictly speaking the 'Castle' had originated 20 years earlier. That was when the first of the GWR 4-cylinder classes, the 'Star', had been rolled out of Swindon. The 'Star' was the work of George Jackson Churchward, the engineer whose radical (at least for Britain's railways) ideas transformed Great Western motive power policy and influenced the thinking of every successive British locomotive designer.

Over two decades the 'Stars' proved their worth, but by the time of Churchward's retirement in 1922 there was a pressing need for a more powerful machine. This was particularly acute on the holiday routes to Devon and Cornwall where train loadings were reflecting the brighter postwar mood. The task of producing a successor to the 'Star' fell to Churchward's heir, Charles Collett.

Unlike Churchward, Collett was no revolutionary (although, in his defence, it is worth recalling that even some of Churchward's key innovations were derived from American and French experience). Collett had little time in which to produce the GWR's new express locomotive. His scope for change was also limited by the axleweight restrictions in force on the West of England main line between London and Plymouth. Collett took the pragmatic

Above: At the head of one of 1985's GW150 specials, 'Castle' No5051 Drysllwyn Castle, piloting 'Hall' class 4-6-0 No4930 Hagley Hall, bursts out of Parson and Clerk tunnel near Dawlish, on the south Devon main line, on 7 July. Built in May 1936 and retired in May 1963, No5051 spent its working life based in South Wales.

Left: Double-chimney 'Castle' No7029 Clun Castle *stands on the turntable at its home of the Birmingham Railway Museum on 14 October 1989. Built under British Railways auspices in May 1950, No7029 accumulated a mileage of 618,073 before withdrawal in 1965. It has added considerably to that total in preservation.*

Below: 'Castle' No5080 Defiant, *at the head of a chocolate-and-cream rake, dashes through the Warwickshire countryside near Henley-in-Arden with a special from Stratford-upon-Avon to Birmingham on 15 April 1990. In 1941,* Defiant *(originally* Ogmore Castle*) became one of 12 'Castles' renamed after famous World War II aircraft.*

GWR 4073 'Castle' Class *7P* 4-6-0

Built: Swindon works, 1923–50 (171 built, including six rebuilds from 'Star' class engines)

Weight: 79 tons 17cwt* (locomotive)
40 tons 0cwt** (tender)

Driving wheel diameter: 6ft 8½in

Boiler pressure: 225lb/psi

Cylinders: (4) 16in diameter x 26in stroke

Valve gear: Inside Walschaerts valve gear with rocking shafts to outside motion (piston valves)

Coal capacity: 6 tons

Water capacity: 3,500 gallons**

Tractive effort: 31,625lb (at 85% boiler pressure)

(* locomotives with 4-row superheaters weighed 80 tons 15cwt)

(** capacity and weight refer to tenders originally attached. Some engines fitted with 4,000 gallon tenders)

course and opted to produce a larger, more powerful version of the 'Star'.

Fitting a bigger boiler and enlarged cylinders on the 'Star' chassis gave him the extra output within the constraints imposed by the Civil Engineer. Yet the 'Castles' still mustered a tractive effort of 31,635lb. By that measure, it took the laurel as the most powerful locomotive on any British railway. The GWR's publicity department trumpeted the fact when, at the British Empire Exhibition of 1924, the prototype, No4073 *Caerphilly Castle*, was displayed alongside the new pride-and-joy of the LNER, Gresley A1 Pacific No4472 *Flying Scotsman*.

The gauntlet had been thrown down and a series of exchange trials followed between one of the LNER Pacifics and a 'Castle'. These left no one in any doubt, least of all the LNER's Nigel Gresley, of the Great Western engine's superiority. It was not solely the haulage capacity that impressed him, or its appetite for sustained high speed running, but its remarkable economy. Here was one of the all-time classics of British locomotive design, and the lessons it taught the LNER did not go unheeded.

Today, eight 'Castles' live on in preservation, including *Caerphilly Castle*. Four others have hauled main-line excursions in Britain and a fifth, No4079 *Pendennis Castle*, has seen action in its present homeland of Western Australia. The final two await restoration.

GREAT NORTHERN RAILWAY/LONDON & NORTH EASTERN RAILWAY

A1/A3 Class 7P6F 4-6-2

The Great Northern Railway's first A1 Pacific, No1470, created quite a stir. It not only impressed with its size – massive by British standards – but its sleek, modern lines. The A1 was the most striking example to date of Nigel Gresley's 'big engine' policy. He argued that it was preferable to build engines that had ample capacity for their tasks, with higher construction costs offset by long-term operating economies.

Gresley was also an advocate of balancing the reciprocating forces in a locomotive, and No1470 had the requisite 3-cylinder layout. All three cylinders drove on to the centre coupled axle, with Walschaerts gear driving the valves of the outside cylinders. To minimize the possibility of this inside gear over-riding at high speed, Gresley opted for short- rather than long-travel valves. It was a decision he was to regret. Likewise, setting the steam pressure at 180lb/psi appeared adequate, and the initial performances of No1470 and a second prototype, No1471, seemed to bear this out. On a test run, No1471 averaged 70mph with a load of no less than 610 tons. An order was placed for ten more A1s but by the time the first was outshopped from Doncaster in February 1923, the Great Northern Railway had been absorbed into one of the post-Grouping 'Big Four' companies, the London & North Eastern. Gresley became Chief Mechanical Engineer of the new concern.

Even as the LNER was ordering more Pacifics, Gresley was being advised that their coal consumption was too high and that the valve settings needed re-working. He rejected the notion and, during 1924 and 1925, Doncaster works and the North British Locomotive Co. each produced 20 engines to the original specification. However, 1925 also saw the beginning of the transformation of the A1 Pacific from a good engine into a great one. The LNER and the Great Western Railway had agreed to an exchange trial and the performance of GW 'Castle' class 4-6-0 No4079 *Pendennis Castle* on the East Coast was revelatory. Not only did the smaller engine maintain the Pacific schedules, it consumed 10 per cent less coal in the process. Doncaster promptly embarked on a redesign of the A1 valve gear.

On test in March 1927, the reduction in coal consumption recorded by modified A1, No2555 *Centenary*, was calculated as equivalent to a one-and-a-half ton saving on the London to Newcastle run. The new long-lap, long-travel valve gear was immediately adopted for new construction and existing engines were altered as they were overhauled. Simultaneously, Gresley accepted that a higher steam pressure was needed and all new locomotives received boilers pressed to 220lb/psi and with larger superheaters. This warranted a new classification, and they became the A3 class. The original

A1s received A3 boilers as their own fell due for renewal, though the change took until December 1948.

The Pacifics' improved coal consumption allowed the LNER to introduce non-stop running between London and Edinburgh, at 392.75 miles the longest non-stop journey in the world. The 10.00am from King's Cross – the famous 'Flying Scotsman' – was inaugurated on 1 May 1928, hauled, appropriately, by the first production A1, No4472 *Flying Scotsman*. It hit the headlines again on 30 November 1934 when it achieved the first authenticated 100mph by a steam locomotive. The following year, classmate No2750 *Papyrus* touched 108mph on a high-speed trial between London and Newcastle, still the world record for a non-streamlined locomotive.

After World War II, the A1/A3 Pacifics remained the mainstay of east coast express passenger services. In 1957 – 20 years after A3 No2751 *Humorist* had demonstrated the dramatic effects of the device – they were given a new lease of life by the fitting of Kylchap double blastpipes and chimneys. Equally belatedly, it took until 1958 for the problem of drifting smoke to be rectified with the fitting of trough-style smoke deflectors. That year, the first A3 was withdrawn, but most were retired between 1962 and 1964. The last, No60052 *Prince Palatine,* was condemned in January 1966. By then, the most famous member of the class, *Flying Scotsman,* had been privately purchased from British Railways to begin a new, and equally eventful life in preservation.

Right: A3 Pacific No60103 Flying Scotsman draws away from Castor, on the Nene Valley Railway, during a driver experience course in 1994. The locomotive carries its later British Railways guise, complete with trough-style smoke deflectors. The smokebox shedplate indicates King's Cross (34A), home depot to Scotsman for six years prior to withdrawal in January 1963.

Left: During the 1990s, several British preserved railways enjoyed the services of arguably the most famous locomotive in the world, Flying Scotsman. In 1993, it was the turn of the Gloucestershire Warwickshire Railway and, on 17 October, the 1923-built Gresley Pacific was captured making a smart departure from Winchcombe with a service for Far Stanley.

Below: During 1986, Flying Scotsman enjoyed a third spell on ex-Great Central metals, being based at Marylebone (London) to work specials to Stratford-upon-Avon. Previously, it had been allocated to Gorton (Manchester) in 1944 and was at Leicester Central between 1950 and 1953. As LNER No4472, it makes a fine sight crossing the West Coast Main Line at South Hampstead. After a lengthy and costly overhaul, Scotsman returned to main-line work during 1999.

GNR/LNER A1/A3 Class 7P6F 4-6-2

Built (Rebuilt): Doncaster works; North British Locomotive Co., Glasgow, 1922–35 (1927–48) (79 built)

Weight: 92 tons 9cwt (A1); 96 tons 5cwt (A3) (locomotive)
56 tons 6cwt (GNR tender); 57 tons 18cwt (LNER non-corridor tender); 62 tons 8cwt (corridor tender); 60 tons 7cwt (streamlined non-corridor tender)

Driving wheel diameter: 6ft 8in

Boiler pressure: 180lb/psi (A1); 220lb/psi (A3)

Cylinders: (3) 20in diameter x 26in stroke (A1); 19in diameter x 26in stroke (A3)

Valve gear: Walschaerts (piston valves); Gresley-Holcroft conjugated gear to inside cylinder

Coal capacity: 8 tons (corridor tender 9 tons)

Water capacity: 5,000 gallons

Tractive effort: 29,835lb (A1); 32,909lb (A3) (at 85% boiler pressure)

LONDON MIDLAND & SCOTTISH RAILWAY

3F Class 0-6-0T

Between 1874 and 1876, Neilson's of Glasgow and Vulcan Foundry supplied the Midland Railway with 40 six-coupled shunting tanks to a design of Samuel Waite Johnson. They not only became the standard Midland shunter, but the basis of a design that was still in general use 90 years later. By 1899, 280 of these 0-6-0 tanks had been delivered, with Derby works joining the two existing outside contractors. That year, Johnson produced an enlarged version, 60 of which were ordered from Vulcan Foundry. Under the direction the Midland's Chief Mechanical Engineer, Henry Fowler, this second series was later rebuilt with Belpaire fireboxes and an improved driving cab, and these rebuilds became the blueprint for the LMSR's 3F tank of 1924.

It is easy to see why the LMSR settled on the Midland design. It was proven, and straightforward to maintain and operate. Few modifications were deemed necessary and the non-superheated Belpaire boiler was retained, along with two inside cylinders. Along with the basic steam and handbrakes, most of the 3F tanks were equipped with steam-heating apparatus to allow them to work local or branch passenger trains and empty coaching stock. The wheelbase followed the standard Midland axle spacing for six-coupled engines of 8ft and 8ft 6in. Seven locomotives were equipped for push-pull working on the Swansea-Brynammen line.

The most prominent feature of the 3F tank, however, was its large steam dome. This housed a vertical regulator valve and incorporated two pilot slots. These opened in advance of the two main ports, reducing the pressure on the main valve. A number of pipes were also fitted vertically within the dome, supplying steam to cab backhead fittings such as the injectors, blower valve, vacuum ejectors, steam brake and sanding gear.

A total of 422 3F tanks were built over a six-year period between 1924 and 1930, with orders shared between five private builders and the ex-Lancashire & Yorkshire Railway works at Horwich. The work they undertook – shunting, trip freights, station pilots, banking, local passenger – was not the stuff of locomotive legend, although the sight of three 3F tanks banking on the Lickey Incline between Bristol and Birmingham was never less than memorable! The greatest adventures were enjoyed by eight locomotives that, in 1940, were transferred to the War Department and, after the 1944 Normandy invasion, saw service in France. Only five returned from this escapade; the others were presumed destroyed, although

Below: No47279 – one of ten preserved 3F tanks – shunts the sidings at Swithland, on the Great Central Railway, on 24 June 1995. The locomotive, a 1924 product of Vulcan Foundry (LMSR No7119) was on loan from the Keighley & Worth Valley Railway. The 60A (Inverness) shedplate is misleading. No47279 spent most of its days around Bedford and Wellingborough; its most northerly posting was Workington.

Above: *3F tank No7298 approaches Rawtenstall with an East Lancashire Railway service from Bury on 9 August 1993. Outshopped by the Hunslet Engine Company of Leeds in October 1924, No7298 had spells at Camden (London), Northampton and Bletchley before withdrawal from Sutton Oak, near Liverpool, in December 1966.*

their exact fate remains uncertain. Two other 3F tanks entered the history books in 1944 and 1945 when they were altered to 5ft 3in gauge and sent to work on the Northern Counties Committee (NCC) lines in Northern Ireland, which were operated by the LMSR.

From the crew's point of view, the Belpaire boiler of the 3F tank steamed as well as any main-line model. They were also comfortable engines and a pleasure to drive. The response of the controls during engine movements was rapid. However, although doors allowed the lower half of the cab to be enclosed, the upper half could feel exposed if standing in wind and rain between shunting operations. Normally, a tarpaulin clipped to the cabside beading alleviated the discomfort.

For almost 40 years, the Fowler 3F tanks were a vital component of LMSR and British Railways operations. The first withdrawal, apart from the WD engines lost in France, came in 1959 with No47331 and, by 1964, half the class had been scrapped. 1966 saw no less than 76 go to the breakers, but the final five lasted into 1967. One, No47445, continued in service with the National Coal Board. The last on BR's books was No47629.

Ten of the Fowler 3F tanks have been preserved, appropriately enough four of them at the Midland Railway Centre at Butterley in Derbyshire. Six of the survivors have been at work in recent years, with the Severn Valley Railway's No47383 the most travelled. It has visited, among others, the Gloucestershire Warwickshire Railway and the North Norfolk Railway, continuing the class's long-standing reputation for useful, if unspectacular, service.

LMSR 3F Class 0-6-0T

Built: Horwich works; Bagnall & Co, Stafford; Beardmore's, Glasgow; Hunslet Engine Company, Leeds; North British Locomotive Co., Glasgow; Vulcan Foundry, Newton-le-Willows, Lancashire, 1924–30 (422 built)

Weight: 49 tons 10cwt

Driving wheel diameter: 4ft 7in

Boiler pressure: 160lb/psi

Cylinders: (2) 18in diameter x 26in stroke

Valve gear: Stephenson link motion (piston valves)

Coal capacity: 2 tons 5cwt

Water capacity: 1,200 gallons

Tractive effort: 20,835lb (at 85% boiler pressure)

Above: *3F tank No47383 started life based at the ex-North London Railway depot at Devons Road, Bow, in October 1926. For some 25 years from 1936, it was allocated to Chester and this was followed by brief spells at Carlisle, Rose Grove (Burnley) and Newton Heath (Manchester) before ending its BR career at Westhouses, Derbyshire, in 1967.*

SOUTHERN RAILWAY

'King Arthur' & 'Lord Nelson' Classes

Appointed Chief Mechanical Engineer of the Southern Railway in 1923, Richard Maunsell's inheritance was an unenviable one: 2,285 locomotives spread across 125 classes and with an average age of 28. He evolved a long-term plan to standardize on nine types of locomotive, among them a 4-cylinder express passenger 4-6-0. However, the Southern's need for new express power was too urgent to await its development.

Maunsell's short-term solution was to produce an improved version of the N15 4-6-0 already working on the Western Division. This 1918 design by Robert Urie for the L&SWR had shown potential but consistently failed to deliver. Regardless of the crews' efforts, steam pressure fell steadily during journeys of any length. Testing revealed that fitting the larger chimney and blastpipe employed on another Urie 4-6-0, the H15, brought a significant improvement. This, and Maunsell's other modifications to the draughting and the steam circuit, transformed the 20 N15s into free-steaming, fast-running machines. Meanwhile, the Southern's publicity manager, John Elliot, had the splendid idea of naming the class after the characters and places in the Arthurian legend. These tales were inseparably associated with the counties of Somerset and Cornwall, which the Southern served.

In 1925, ten new locomotives were delivered from Eastleigh works, using the tenders, bogies and other fittings from a batch of Drummond-designed 4-6-0s which had been earmarked for rebuilding. Additionally, 30 wholly new locomotives were ordered from the North

British Locomotive Company and built in record time between May and October 1925.

The 'Arthurs' put in outstanding work on the London-Salisbury-Exeter route. They also enjoyed immediate success on the Eastern Section, allowing loadings on the London to Dover boat trains to be increased from 300 to 425 tons. The success of the 2-cylinder 'King Arthurs' gave Maunsell time to develop his original idea for a 4-cylinder 4-6-0. This would meet the operating department's demand for 55mph averages on 500-ton trains, but it would require ingenuity to remain within the stipulated 21-ton axleloading. The design became an exercise in weight-saving, involving everything from the use of high-tensile steels for the coupling and connecting rods to the machining of any excess metal from the moving parts. The newcomer came in at 77 tons 2cwt,7 cwt under the limit, yet the increase in tractive effort was dramatic: 33,510lb compared to the 23,900lb of the 'Arthurs'.

In truth, there were not many duties on the Southern that called for such a powerful machine, evident in the fact that only 16 were built out of an original order for 31. Again, the choice of names was inspired: famous British seafarers. The first of the 'LN' class, No850 *Lord Nelson*, left Eastleigh works in August 1926 with the tag of 'Britain's most powerful locomotive' (which, measured by tractive effort, it was). Despite the prototype undertaking almost two years of trials before production was authorized, performances continually failed to live up to expectations. The huge (33sq ft) grate required skilful firing

Left: During the early 1980s, No850 Lord Nelson *put in many outstanding performances in the unfamiliar territory of the northern fells. It worked several specials over the Settle and Carlisle line and is seen here awaiting departure from the Garsdale water stop with a southbound train. Prominent is the large chimney casting concealing the Lemaitre multiple-jet exhaust added by Oliver Bulleid. After many years out-of-traffic, the National Railway Museum has authorized a group based at Eastleigh works to undertake an overhaul of the 1926-built 4-6-0 to main-line standard.*

Above: Freshly repainted by a team of enthusiasts in BR livery, the National Collection's 'King Arthur' No30777 Sir Lamiel poses in the depot yard at Stewarts Lane, Battersea, on 4 November 1994. Built by the North British Locomotive Company in June 1925, No30777 enjoyed spells on both the Western and Eastern Sections of the Southern Railway and, subsequently, the Southern Region. Withdrawn from Basingstoke shed in October 1961, the locomotive was later entrusted to the Humberside Locomotive Preservation Group. By 1982, its volunteers had overhauled the 'Arthur' to main-line order and the engine enjoyed further main-line work during the 1990s. It is currently undergoing its latest overhaul.

SR 'King Arthur' and 'Lord Nelson' Classes

	Maunsell N15 'King Arthur'	'Lord Nelson'
Built:	Eastleigh works; North British Locomotive Co., Glasgow, 1925–27 (44 built)*	Eastleigh works, 1926/1928–29 (16 built)
Weight:	80 tons 19cwt (locomotive) 57 tons 11cwt** (tender)	83 tons 10cwt (locomotive) 56 tons 14cwt (tender)
Driving wheel diameter:	6ft 7in	6ft 7in
Boiler pressure:	200lb/psi	220lb/psi
Cylinders:	(2) 20½in diameter x 28in stroke	(4) 16½in diameter x 26in stroke
Valve gear:	Walschaerts (piston valves)	Walschaerts (separate drive to all cylinders) (piston valves)
Coal capacity:	5 tons**	5 tons
Water capacity:	5,000 gallons**	5,000 gallons
Tractive effort:	23,900lb (at 85% boiler pressure)	33,510lb (at 85% boiler pressure)

(* an additional 30 locomotives in the class consisted of 20 modified Urie N15s and ten engines assembled using components from Drummond G14 4-6-0s – see text)

(** 14 locomotives attached to smaller 6-wheel tenders to allow them to be turned on the narrower turntables of the Central Section [ex-LB&SCR] lines)

and, to ensure they were handled by crews accustomed to their idiosyncrasies, the 'LNs' were always based at just four depots: Nine Elms and Stewarts Lane in London, Eastleigh and Bournemouth.

Several of the 'Nelsons' were subjected to modifications, but the only one to make a significant difference – the fitting of a Kylchap double blastpipe and chimney to No862 *Lord Collingwood* in 1937 – was not pursued, probably on cost grounds. The greatest improvement in the performance of the 'Nelsons' was made by Maunsell's successor, Oliver Bulleid, who fitted

the class with the Lemaitre five-jet multiple blastpipe and larger piston valves.

Withdrawals of the 'Lord Nelsons' took place in 1961–62, but the scrapping of the first of the modified Urie N15s, No30754 *The Green Knight*, came in January 1953. Nevertheless, the last working Maunsell 'Arthur' outlived the 'Nelsons' by one month. No30770 *Sir Prianius* was retired from Basingstoke shed in November 1962. By this time, happily both its classmate, No30777 *Sir Lamiel*, and No30850 *Lord Nelson*, had become part of the National Collection.

LONDON MIDLAND & SCOTTISH RAILWAY

West Coast Moguls

The 2-6-0 or 'Mogul' type originated in the United States during the 1850s but it was not until 1878 that the first British-built example appeared, on the Great Eastern Railway. Subsequently, both the Great Western and the Great Central bought 2-6-0s from America's Baldwin Locomotive Works. Among British engineers, Churchward, on the GWR, and Maunsell, on the SE&CR, produced outstanding 2-6-0 designs. Another was drawn up by the first Chief Mechanical Engineer of the LMSR, George Hughes. The detail work was undertaken by Hughes's old team at Horwich works, and many characteristics were pure Lancashire & Yorkshire. Other aspects, though, owed more to American practice. It had large, 11in diameter piston valves and 21in diameter cylinders whose steeply inclined angle required the raising of the front portion of the running board. As a result, the boiler appeared to 'squat' between the frames, a look that earned the sobriquet of 'Crab'. The large capacity cylinders were needed because Hughes refused to contemplate a boiler pressure above 180lb/psi. Long-travel, long-lap Walschaerts valve gear was employed, and substantial coupled axleboxes provided.

Construction did not get underway until 1926, by which time George Hughes had retired to be replaced by ex-Midland man, Henry Fowler. The basic parallel-boiler format was left unaltered, but Fowler insisted on the use of a number of Midland fittings, such as the vacuum-controlled steam brake and clack valves. Most significantly, Fowler scrapped the L&YR tender blueprint and had the new 2-6-0s harnessed to 3,500-gallon Midland tenders, regardless of the fact that these were considerably narrower than the locomotives.

In spite of Fowler's tinkering, the 'Horwich Mogul' was an efficient and successful machine with 245 built up to 1932. Following the 'cannibalizing' of 100 of the Churchward Moguls on the Great Western, the 'Crabs' became the largest class of 2-6-0s on Britain's railways. Their qualities were doubtless appreciated by Fowler's successor, William Stanier, who also agreed there was a need for more mixed traffic 2-6-0s. However, the model for what would become Stanier's first design for the LMSR was not the 'Horwich Mogul' but its older, Swindon-built equivalent.

For Stanier, this was an early opportunity to examine how the Swindon principles stood up to LMSR conditions. As with the Hughes/Fowler Mogul, the detail design was handed to the Horwich drawing office, with instructions to employ a domeless taper boiler, trapezoidal Belpaire firebox, long-travel piston valves, near-horizontal cylinders, streamlined steam passages and a jumper-top blastpipe. In the Churchward tradition, the boiler had a modest superheating temperature combined with a high working pressure of 225lb/psi.

The first of the Stanier Moguls, No13245, emerged from Crewe on 21 October 1933, attached to a six-wheel Fowler tender (Stanier's tender design had yet to be completed). A further 39 were outshopped by March 1934, at which point construction ceased to make way for the new Class 5 4-6-0. At first, the allocations of the 40 Stanier Moguls were tidily organized, with consecutively numbered batches going to each of the four divisions of the LMSR. Nos13245-54 were allocated to the Northern Division, Nos13255-66 to the ex-Midland lines, Nos13267-79 to the Western Division, and Nos13280-84 to the central area.

The northern-based engines operated out of Carlisle Kingmoor depot and regularly worked into Scotland over the ex-Caledonian main line. It was not long, however, before the engines were concentrated on the ex-L&NWR metals of the Western Division, with the largest allocations at Crewe South, Mold Junction and Nuneaton. They were regarded principally as freight locomotives, but pressed into passenger service when required.

The first of the Hughes/Fowler Moguls was retired in 1961 and, two years on, the axe began to fall on its cousins. The last Stanier Mogul, No42963, was withdrawn in 1966, but some of the Horwich design soldiered on into 1967. Only one of the Stanier engines was saved, No42968, which returned to traffic on the Severn Valley Railway in 1991. Three 'Crabs' survive, including the first of the class, No13000 (as LMSR No2700) in the National Collection. A second, No42765, was restored to working order on the East Lancashire Railway, but little is heard of the still-unrestored No42859.

Above: On display at Swindon on 10 April 1990 is the first of the Hughes/Fowler ('Horwich') Moguls, No2700. From this angle, it is easy to see where the nickname of 'Crab' originated.

LMSR West Coast Moguls

	Hughes/Fowler 5MT 2-6-0	Stanier 5MT 2-6-0
Built:	Crewe and Horwich works, 1926–32 (245 built)	Crewe works, 1933–34 (40 built)
Weight:	66 tons 0cwt (locomotive) 42 tons 4cwt (tender)	69 tons 2cwt (locomotive) 42 tons 4cwt (tender)
Driving wheel diameter:	5ft 6in	5ft 6in
Boiler pressure:	180lb/psi	225lb/psi
Cylinders:	(2) 21in diameter x 26in stroke	(2) 18in diameter x 28in stroke
Valve gear:	Walschaerts (piston valves)	Walschaerts (piston valves)
Coal capacity:	5 tons	5 tons
Water capacity:	3,500 gallons	3,500 gallons
Tractive effort:	26,580lb (at 85% boiler pressure)	26,288lb (at 85% boiler pressure)

Above: Stanier Mogul No2968 starts away from the Bewdley outer home signal with a Kidderminster-Bridgnorth service on 21 April 1991. No2968 began its working life at Willesden, London, and after periods at depots in the Birmingham and Liverpool areas, in 1942 began a 19-year association with the freight engine shed at Crewe South. The locomotive was withdrawn from Springs Branch, Wigan, in 1966. It was acquired for preservation by the Stanier Mogul Fund in 1973.

Right: With its Belpaire firebox, taper boiler and top feed in evidence, No2968 'brews up' on shed at Bridgnorth, on the Severn Valley Railway. Restoration of the Stanier Mogul began in 1975 and the locomotive moved under its own power for the first time in 24 years on 12 November 1990. In recent years, No2968 has put in some remarkable main-line runs.

GREAT WESTERN RAILWAY

6000 'King' Class 8P 4-6-0

It is now 70 years since the final batch of the 30-strong 'Kings' emerged from Swindon Works. From the outset, the Great Western's publicity department went into overdrive promoting the exploits of the class. To this day, the 'Kings' command a loyalty and admiration that would gladden the heart of any real-life monarch.

Magnificent locomotives as they were, the 'Kings' not only represented the GWR's individuality but also its isolation. Churchward's successor, Charles Collett, was largely content to build on the work of his old chief, which was fine as long as it kept the GWR ahead of the field. By 1926, when the detail design work was underway on the new 4-6-0, that was no longer the case. Several new and potentially productive ideas on improving locomotive performance were ignored. As with the 'Castle' class of 1923, the blueprint for the 'King' remained Churchward's 4-cylinder 'Star' of 1907.

Some commentators have concluded that the 'Kings' were an expensive publicity stunt. The GWR claimed that heavier loadings (i.e. longer trains) demanded more haulage power. Yet it was not until 1930, three years after the first 'Kings' had entered service, that the platforms at Paddington were extended to accommodate these trains. The accusation is that the image-conscious general manager, Felix Pole, wanted to reclaim the spurious 'most powerful locomotive in Britain' title lost to the Southern's 'Lord Nelson' class in 1926. Moreover, he wanted to do it comprehensively. A tractive effort of over 40,000lb was the target, and that meant a bigger boiler and consequently a locomotive heavier than the previous holder of the record, the GWR 'Castle'. To accommodate it, track improvements and bridge strengthening had to be undertaken to raise the main-line axleloading to 22 tons 10cwt. Even then, the 'Kings' were confined to the London-Taunton-Plymouth, London-Bristol and London-Birmingham-Wolverhampton runs. It was not until the British Railways era that they were allowed between Bristol and Shrewsbury and through the Severn Tunnel into South Wales.

The first of 4-cylinder 'Kings', No6000 *King George V*, entered service on 29 June 1927. Within a few weeks, it was on its way to the United States of America to take part in the centenary celebrations of the Baltimore & Ohio Railroad. It impressed its hosts both with its looks and with its performance, taking a 543-ton train from Washington DC to Philadelphia at speeds up to 74mph. To commemorate the visit, the B&O struck medallions for the cabsides and the typically American brass bell that still adorns No6000's front bufferbeam.

Less than two months after the triumph of *King George V*'s debut came near-disaster. No6003 *King George IV* was derailed at speed, luckily without serious consequences.

Ironically, the culprit was the one truly novel aspect of the design: the plate-frame front bogie with its four independently sprung wheels. Modifications to the springing resolved the problem and the 'Kings' were able to retake their place at the head of the GWR's crack expresses, such as the 'Cornish Riviera Express' and the 'The Bristolian'.

However, during and after World War II, the 'Kings' were denied the high-grade Welsh coal on which they thrived. As with many pedigree locomotives, their performances suffered. With no sign of fuel quality improving, the alternative was to get the best from what was available. A higher superheat temperature and better draughting were obvious first steps and, in the 1950s, all 30 were fitted with double chimneys and blastpipes and

Above: The first of the 'Kings', No6000 King George V, *displays the bell donated to the locomotive during its visit to the United States. Also visible is the unusual design of plate-frame bogie responsible for early stability problems, and the double chimney fitted in 1956. Apart from spells at Bristol Bath Road and Plymouth Laira, No6000 spent most of its working life at Old Oak Common, London. Five years of storage followed retirement in December 1962, but for the ensuing 23 years No6000 was in the care of the Bulmer Cider Company of Hereford. In 1971, No6000 became the first locomotive to break BR's ban on main-line steam.*

Above: The last of the 30 'Kings', No6029, emerged from Swindon in August 1930. Until May 1936, it carried the name King Stephen *but was then renamed following the accession of King Edward VIII. Notwithstanding the subsequent abdication, it retained that name until withdrawal in July 1962. The abdication of Edward VIII necessitated a further renaming: the name* King Henry II *was removed from No6028 in January 1937 and replaced by plates reading* King George VI.

Right: Since the present era of main-line steam was inaugurated by King George V *in 1971, it was fitting that the 25th anniversary was marked by one of its classmates, No6024* King Edward I, *seen leaving Hereford on 2 October 1996. After entering traffic in June 1930, No6024 spent much of its working life at Newton Abbot and Plymouth. It was reallocated to Old Oak Common in 1954 and retired from Cardiff Canton in June 1962. No6024 returned to steam in 1989.*

GWR 6000 'King' Class 8P 4-6-0

Built: Swindon works, 1927–30 (30 built)

Weight: 89 tons 0cwt (locomotive)
　　46 tons 14cwt (tender)

Driving wheel diameter: 6ft 6in

Boiler pressure: 250lb/psi

Cylinders: (4) 16¼in diameter x 28in stroke

Valve gear: Inside Walschaerts valve gear with rocking shafts to outside cylinders (9in piston valves)

Coal capacity: 6 tons

Water capacity: 4,000 gallons

Tractive effort: 40,300lb (at 85% boiler pressure)

four-row superheaters. In this condition, they remained on front-rank duties until the early 1960s, enjoying a memorable final fling on the Western Region's Birmingham and Wolverhampton services. These had been intensified during electrification of the London Midland Region's West Midlands route.

　　Three of the 'Kings' live on. No6000 *King George V* is on display at its birthplace of Swindon and No6024 *King Edward I* can be seen in main-line action. No6023 *King Edward II*, once thought to be beyond restoration, has been rescued and is in the final stages of rebuilding at Didcot Railway Centre in Oxfordshire.

LONDON MIDLAND & SCOTTISH RAILWAY

'Royal Scot' Class 7P 4-6-0

By 1926, Nigel Gresley's LNER Pacifics were leaving the LMSR's express locomotives trailing on prestige Anglo-Scottish services. The West Coast route had nothing to match them. All that the LMSR's Chief Mechanical Engineer, Sir Henry Fowler, could propose was to pursue development of a 4-cylinder compound Pacific originated by his predecessor, George Hughes.

The prospect did not fill the LMSR management with confidence. Without consulting Fowler, it arranged for a Great Western 'Castle' class 4-6-0 to undergo trials on the West Coast Main Line. In both performance and economy, the 'Castle' was superior to anything the LMSR possessed. Committed to accelerating its Anglo-Scottish expresses from the summer of 1927, the LMSR attempted to place an order for 50 'Castles' with the GWR's Swindon works. It was declined, ostensibly because the less generous LMSR loading gauge would have required a re-design.

Again bypassing Fowler, the LMSR's motive power superintendent, James Anderson, decided that what was needed – and quickly – was a 3-cylinder, large-boilered 4-6-0 with the benefits of high-degree superheat and long-travel valve gear. Since no LMSR workshop had the capacity to undertake the task in the stipulated time, it was handed to the North British Locomotive Company of Glasgow. It is said that an approach to the GWR for the loan of a set of 'Castle' drawings went unanswered. The Southern Railway, however, was more co-operative in sharing the secrets of its new 'Lord Nelson' 4-6-0 (pages 110-111) with the Derby drawing office.

NBL did well to deliver the first of the class by July 1927 and completed the 50 locomotives by November. Considering the circumstances of their construction, the new 4-6-0s proved remarkably free from teething troubles. The LMSR was back in the business of high-speed travel between London and Scotland. On 26 September 1927, it inaugurated the 'Royal Scot' service, which was scheduled to run non-stop from Euston to Carlisle with a 15-coach load amounting to 420 tons tare.

In October 1927, the doyen of the class, No6100, was named after the train service with which it was now

Right: Rebuilt 'Royal Scot' No46122 Royal Ulster Rifleman *brings a West Coast express through Newbold, three miles north of Rugby. No46122 was built by the North British Locomotive Company in October 1927 and rebuilt in September 1945. It was condemned in October 1964 from Annesley depot after a BR career that included Longsight (Manchester), Camden (London) and Bushbury (Birmingham) sheds.*

LMSR 'Royal Scot' Class 7P 4-6-0

(Alterations through rebuilding in brackets)

Built (Rebuilt): Derby works; North British Locomotive Company, Glasgow, 1927–30 (1943–55) (71 built)

Weight: 84 tons 18cwt (83 tons 0cwt) (locomotive)
42 tons 14cwt (59 tons 11cwt) (tender)

Driving wheel diameter: 6ft 9in

Boiler pressure: 250lb/psi

Cylinders: (3) 18in diameter x 26in stroke

Valve gear: Walschaerts (piston valves)

Coal capacity: 5 tons 10cwt (9 tons 0cwt)

Water capacity: 3,500 gallons (4,000 gallons)

Tractive effort: 33,150lb (at 85% boiler pressure)

Above: A plaque on the leading splasher of No6100 Royal Scot *commemorates the locomotive's 11,194-mile tour of North America in 1933. Upon its return, the locomotive returned to Camden depot in London. Withdrawn in 1962,* Royal Scot *was bought by Butlin's holiday camps and displayed at Skegness until 1971, when it was moved to its present home of the Bressingham Steam Museum in Norfolk.*

Left: No6115 Scots Guardsman *was a Longsight (Manchester) engine for many years and notably 'starred' in the 1936 documentary 'Night Mail'. In 1947, No6115 became the final 'Scot' to be rebuilt by the LMSR and, by 1966, was the last in BR service, escaping the 1962 'purge' of 3-cylinder motive power. As the first 'Scot' to be fitted with the distinctive curved smoke deflectors, it correctly carries the LMSR post-war livery of black lined out with maroon and straw yellow.*

associated, *Royal Scot.* The remainder received an assortment of names, half resurrected from long-gone L&NWR engines and the rest honouring regiments of the British army. Eventually, with three exceptions, the whole class took regimental names.

The success of the 'Scots' persuaded the LMSR to place an order for a further 20 engines, this time with Derby works. The first was delivered, on schedule, in May 1930. However, all the engines were being plagued by one problem: hot axleboxes. It was this that William Stanier addressed immediately on joining the LMSR in 1932. It was the first of a series of modifications that transformed an already fine locomotive into arguably the finest express passenger 4-6-0 ever to run in Britain. The high regard in which the 'Scots' were held was demonstrated in 1933 when *Royal Scot* became the LMSR's exhibit at the Century of Progress exhibition in Chicago.

The fame attached to this first of the 'Scots' contrasted with notoriety of the last of the class, No6170. This had begun life in 1929 as an experimental high-pressure locomotive, No6399 *Fury.* The name was apt: in February 1930, one of the firetubes burst, killing one person on the footplate and seriously injuring another. The engine was placed in store and remained there until 1934 when Stanier took the chassis and fitted it with his newly developed Type 2 taper boiler. Renumbered No6170 and named *British Legion*, the engine became the basis for the rebuilding of all the 'Royal Scots'. Taper boilers, double chimneys and blastpipes, new smokeboxes and new leading bogies left the cab as the only significant surviving component from the original parallel-boiler design. On test, the rebuilt 'Scots' delivered the highest power output per engine-ton of any British 4-6-0, outclassing the Great Western 'King' in drawbar horsepower.

Rebuilding began in 1943 but was not completed until 1955. Withdrawals began seven years later, with *Royal Scot* one of the first. However, it was subsequently preserved, as was the last to be retired (in 1966), No46115 *Scots Guardsman.* Neither is presently operational, although *Scots Guardsman* is undergoing a protracted overhaul.

GREAT WESTERN RAILWAY

4900 'Hall' Class 5MT 4-6-0

The 'Castles' and 'Kings' may have been the most celebrated of the Great Western 4-6-0s, but the 'Halls' made the more significant contribution to the general development of British steam traction. They were the first true mixed traffic locomotives, and as such precursors of the Stanier 'Black Five', Thompson B1 and BR Standard 5MT 4-6-0.

The notion of a locomotive that was as adept at hauling heavy freights as express passenger trains was a novel one in the 1920s. Ever the visionary, George Jackson Churchward anticipated the need for just a such a locomotive but his proposal was defeated by axleloading restrictions. As a result, by the time Charles Collett replaced Churchward in January 1922, the latter's excellent, but limited 4300 class 2-6-0s (pages 82-83) were being stretched by the demands of the motive power department.

One suggestion was to rebuild a quantity of the 4300s as 4-6-0s but Collett instead chose to modify another Churchward type, the 'Saint' 4-6-0 of 1902. The locomotive selected for conversion was No2925 *Saint Martin*. The

main modification was the exchange of its 6ft 8½in driving wheels for ones of 6ft 0in diameter. Additionally, the cylinders were realigned in relation to the driving axle and a more modern, 'Castle'-type cab was fitted.

The rebuilt *Saint Martin* emerged from Swindon in 1924 and, renumbered No4900, embarked on three years of trials. During that period, Collett introduced other modifications. The pitch of the taper boiler was altered and outside steampipes were added. Satisfied with No4900's performance, he placed an order with Swindon works and the first of the new 2-cylinder 'Halls' entered service in 1928. They differed little from the prototype. The bogie wheel diameter had been reduced by two inches, from 3ft 2in to 3ft 0in and the valve setting amended to give an increased travel of 7¼in. The overall weight of the locomotive had increased by 2½ tons to 75 tons, but a tractive effort of 27,275lb compared favourably with the 24,935lb of the 'Saint'.

In what amounted to another 'trial run', the first 14 were despatched to the arduous proving ground of the Cornish main line. However, they were so successful here

Above: Having brought in a railtour from Shrewsbury on 26 February 1983, No4930 Hagley Hall *stands in the centre road at Hereford. Outshopped in May 1929, No4930 ended its days at Swindon shed in November 1963. Acquired by the Severn Valley Railway, No4930 was steamed again in 1979 but currently awaits overhaul.*

Left: *Typically of the mixed-traffic 'Halls', 1931-built No5900* Hinderton Hall *spent its 32-year working life at a wide variety of locations ranging from Worcester to Carmarthen, Westbury and Wolverhampton. It was retired from St Philip's Marsh (Bristol) in November 1963 and subsequently acquired by the Didcot-based Great Western Society.*

Below: *No4920* Dumbleton Hall *is the oldest of the surviving 'Halls', entering traffic in March 1929. It worked at the extremes of the GW system, being based at Old Oak Common, London, Carmarthen, South Wales and Truro in Cornwall. When retired in December 1965, it was a Bristol (Barrow Road) engine.*

and elsewhere on the GW system that, by the time the first production batch of 80 had been completed in 1930, a further 178 were on order. By 1935, 150 were in service and the 259th and last 'Hall', No6958 *Oxburgh Hall*, was delivered in 1943. By this time, Collett had been replaced by F.W. Hawksworth who produced a modified version of the class (pages 158-159) that remained in production until 1950. One of Hawksworth's motivations in changing the design was to equip it better for coping with the widely varying quality of coal available during World War II. If anything, the situation worsened after the war, leading to serious consideration being given to oil-firing. Beginning in 1946 with No5955 *Garth Hall*, the GWR converted 11 of the class to burn oil. Within four years, however, all had reverted to coal.

All but one of the original Collett 'Halls' entered service with British Railways Western Region in 1948. The exception was No4911 *Bowden Hall* which received a direct hit during a bombing raid on the Plymouth area in April 1941 and was broken up. Official withdrawals began in 1959 with the prototype *Saint Martin*. Its accumulated mileage, both in its original and rebuilt forms, was a remarkable 2,092,500 miles.

The 4900 class was rendered extinct in the final year of Western Region steam, 1965. Surprisingly, for such a seminal design, not a single example was selected for the National Collection. Eleven, however, were saved by various railways and societies. The Great Western Society at Didcot, Oxfordshire, has two, No5900 *Hinderton Hall* and No4942 *Maindy Hall*. In an ironic twist, the latter is being rebuilt to represent the original 'Saint' class, none of which has survived. No5900 is one of four 'Halls' to have been used for main-line railtours in recent years, the others being the Severn Valley's No4930 *Hagley Hall*, the Birmingham Railway Museum's No4965 *Rood Ashton Hall* (now correctly identified after many years masquerading as No4983 *Albert Hall*) and the Carnforth-based No5972 *Olton Hall*. No4920 *Dumbleton Hall* has also returned to working order, but five other 'Halls' await the completion of restoration work.

4900 'Hall' Class 5MT 4-6-0

Built: Swindon works, 1928–1943 (258 built, excluding rebuilt prototype)

Weight: 75 tons 0cwt (locomotive) 46 tons 14cwt (tender)

Driving wheel diameter: 6ft 0in

Boiler pressure: 225lb/psi

Cylinders: (2) 18½in diameter x 30in stroke

Valve gear: Stephenson (piston valves)

Coal capacity: 6 tons

Water capacity: 4,000 gallons

Tractive effort: 27,275lb (at 85% boiler pressure)

SOUTHERN RAILWAY

U Class 4P3F 2-6-0

When Richard Maunsell arrived in 1913 to take over motive power matters on the South Eastern & Chatham Railway, engines of the American-inspired 2-6-0 wheel arrangement were proving their usefulness on at least three British railways. The SE&CR needed similar, modern mixed traffic locomotives and work on a 2-cylinder 2-6-0 began in 1914. A Great Western influence was apparent in the use of a taper boiler, with top feed and long travel valves, but the superheating was of the high-, rather than low-temperature variety.

Unfortunately, the onset of war meant that the prototype, No810, was not completed until 1917 and a further two years elapsed before the impoverished SE&CR went into production. Altogether, 80 of these N class Moguls were built, the last in 1934. With the intention of increasing tractive effort without adding to the axleloading, a 3-cylinder variant of the class, the N1, was introduced in

1922. It was not particularly successful and construction ended with just six engines. However, another 'spin-off' from the N was to have an important bearing on the emergence of the most successful of Maunsell's 2-6-0s, the U class. This was the K class 2-6-4 passenger tank which used the boiler and front end of the N, but exchanged the latter's 5ft 6in diameter driving wheels for ones of 6ft 0in.

Having developed the K class tank out of the N class Mogul, the wheel came full circle when the K gave birth to its tender engine equivalent, the U class. At the same time, it was proposed to double the number of K class tanks from 20 to 40. That plan ended following the events of 24 August 1927. The K class tanks, or 'Rivers' as they had been dubbed, had a reputation for bad riding. There had been three derailments involving the class in the first months of 1927 before, that August evening, NoA800 *River Cray* left the tracks at high speed near Sevenoaks. Thirteen passengers died and the Southern Railway's immediate response was to withdraw the entire class for investigation.

Suspicion centred not just on the locomotives, but on the condition of the ex-SE&CR track. This had been laid and maintained on a tight budget and, during tests undertaken on the better-laid lines of the LNER, the K class engines behaved impeccably. It was concluded that the irregularities of the ex-SE&CR track had induced such a

Above: The yard at Ropley, on the Mid-Hants Railway, plays host to U class No31625 and the sole survivor of its N class predecessors, No31874 (here masquerading as one-time Guildford engine No31873).

Right: Soon after the completion of its restoration, U class No31625 climbs away from Ropley with a morning service for Alton on 26 October 1996. Built at Ashford in March 1929, in 1947 No31625 was one of two Us converted to oil-firing. It reverted to coal after only a year.

SR U Class 4P3F 2-6-0

Built (Rebuilt): Ashford, Brighton and Eastleigh works, 1928–31 (50 built, including 20 rebuilds from K class 2-6-4Ts)

Weight: 62 tons 6cwt (locomotive) 42 tons 8cwt (tender)

Driving wheel diameter: 6ft 0in

Boiler pressure: 200lb/psi

Cylinders: (2) 19in diameter x 28in stroke

Valve gear: Walschaerts (piston valves)

Coal capacity: 5 tons 0cwt

Water capacity: 4,000 gallons

Tractive effort: 23,866lb (at 85% boiler pressure)

Above: Prior to the Sevenoaks disaster of 1927, Brighton-built No1618 would have been outshopped as K class tank River Hamble. Instead it has become one of two U class Moguls on the Bluebell Railway, the other being No31638. As BR No31618, the engine was retired from Guildford shed in January 1964, reaching the Bluebell in 1977.

Right: U class Mogul No31806 was outshopped from Brighton in October 1926 as K class 2-6-4T NoA806 River Torridge but returned there for rebuilding as a 2-6-0 in 1928. Before World War II, it regularly worked passenger services out of London's Waterloo. Withdrawn in January 1964, No31806 came to the Mid-Hants Railway where its restoration was completed in May 1983.

'wash' of water in the side tanks of NoA800 that the resultant swaying and rolling became uncontrolled.

Although the Kent main lines were promptly upgraded, the Southern decided to take no further risks with the K class tanks. All were rebuilt between March and August 1928 as 2-6-0s and incorporated into the new U class. The speed of the process meant that the first rebuilt U, NoA805, preceded the first of the new engines into traffic by some three months. Nevertheless, by April 1929, 19 of the new engines had been completed. By May 1931, the U class, including the 20 rebuilt tank locomotives, numbered 50.

Subsequently, the U class underwent few modifications. Smoke deflectors were fitted from 1933 onwards, and two engines were converted briefly to oil-firing. As with the N class, Maunsell decided to produce a 3-cylinder version. One of the K class rebuilds, No890, became the prototype

for the U1 and entered service in June 1928. However, an order for 20 further engines was delayed until 1931.

The U class Moguls were reliable and economical engines and capable of exceeding their official maximum of 70mph. They were employed throughout the Southern system but were noted especially for their exploits on the ex-London & South Western lines west of Exeter, and on the cross-country North Downs line linking Reading, Guildford, Redhill and Tonbridge. It was from Guildford depot in November 1962 that No31630 became the first to be withdrawn. The U class was rendered extinct – officially, at least – with the retirement of Nos31630 and 31791, also of Guildford, in June 1966. Four were subsequently preserved: Nos1618 and 31638 on the Bluebell Railway, and Nos31806 (the only survivor from the K class rebuilds) and 31625 on the Mid-Hants Railway. Only the last of this quartet, No31625, is currently serviceable.

GREAT WESTERN RAILWAY

5700 Class 3F 0-6-0PT

Three features distinguished Great Western locomotives from virtually all others. They were copper-capped chimneys, brass safety valve bonnets and pannier tanks – oblong water carriers bolted to each side of the boiler. The reasons for using them in preference to the more common side- and saddletanks were twofold. First, the introduction of square-topped Belpaire fireboxes on GW engines made it difficult to accommodate saddletanks. Second, unlike the sidetank, which was mounted on the running board, the pannier allowed ready access to the inside valve gear and cylinders for inspection and maintenance.

The pannier tank originated with Churchward, in 1898, yet, in his later scheme for a series of new, standard locomotive classes, no provision was made for a purpose-built shunting engine. Churchward probably concluded that the GWR had sufficient small tank locomotives. Hundreds had been built during the 1890s and early 1900s and more were inherited when the GWR absorbed minor railways in South Wales. However, by the time Charles Collett replaced Churchward, many of these locomotives were approaching their expiry date. In 1929, 123 of the 1901 class of 1891 remained in service, as did 140 of the 2021 class from 1897. The 2700 class of 1896 still mustered a complete complement of 100, and it was on this engine that Collett based his design for the new, standard GW tank, the 5700.

The main differences between the 5700 and its predecessor were an increase in boiler pressure from 180lb to 200lb/psi and the inclusion of a Belpaire firebox.

Above: Steam returned to London's District Line on 6 June 1993 as 5700 class NoL99 worked shuttles between West Kensington, pictured, and Ealing Broadway. Built by Kerr Stuart in 1930, NoL99 began life as GWR No7715, entering London Transport service in 1963. Retired in 1970, it is now resident at the Buckinghamshire Railway Centre.

Left: Great Western-designed but built by British Railways (Swindon 1949), No9681 awaits departure from Norchard, on the Dean Forest Railway, for Lydney. This example of the 5700 panniers spent its working life in Wales, north and south.

A larger bunker was fitted, together with an enclosed cab, and the valve settings were improved. None of these modifications, however, merited prototype testing and 100 were ordered off the drawing board. Their construction was divided between Swindon works and the North British Locomotive Co. As a contribution to a government scheme to create employment during the economic depression of the early 1930s, five other outside contractors then shared orders for a further 200 engines.

Deliveries from Swindon works resumed in 1933 and continued uninterrupted for a further 17 years, by which time the 5700 panniers numbered 863. It was the second most numerous class ever built in Britain. Adding the later Hawksworth classes took the total of GWR-designed pannier tanks to over 1,200. In all this time, the most significant change in the 5700 was the fitting of 11 engines (Nos9700-9710) with condensing equipment and feedwater heaters. This allowed them to work eastwards from Paddington through the tunnels of London's Metropolitan Line. Later examples also received larger cabs, giving crews greater protection from the elements.

The 5700s were versatile, free-running and surprisingly strong machines, attributes that frequently saw them entrusted with loads at odds with their size. The power generated at low speeds was remarkable, and they were equally at home on branch line or local goods, shunting and handling empty coaching stock. Apart from a few areas barred to the 5700 by its axleloading, the pannier tanks were distributed throughout the GWR system. By 1954, only five depots in BR's Western Region did not have a quota of the class. A handful of engines ventured away from the WR, undertaking banking work on the Southern's Folkestone Harbour branch and pilot duties at London's Waterloo. Some surplus 5700s were sold to the National Coal Board and, in 1956, London Transport began acquiring them to replace life-expired ex-Metropolitan Railway locomotives on shunting work. They also hauled late-night engineers' trains and delivered loads to LT's rubbish tip at Watford.

Up to 1963, a total of 14 pannier tanks saw service with London Transport and the final three – NosL90, L94 and L95 – remained at work until 1971, six years after the retirement of the last Western Region 5700. This trio now numbers among the 16 survivors, and the 5700 continues to prove its worth on preserved lines. A dozen have seen service in recent times.

Left: The Severn Valley Railway's No5764 coasts into Arley. This 1929 Swindon product spent its working life in the London area, being sold to London Transport in 1960 and becoming NoL95. It was one of three remaining LT panniers when bought by the SVR in 1971.

Below left: No5764 pilots classmate No5775, on loan from the Keighley & Worth Valley Railway, out of Bridgnorth. These engines would have last worked together in London Transport service. No5775 was sold to LT in 1963, becoming its NoL89, after almost 40 years in Wales.

GWR 5700 Class 3F 0-6-0PT

Built: Swindon works; Armstrong Whitworth, Newcastle-upon-Tyne; W.G. Bagnall, Stafford; Beyer Peacock, Manchester; Kerr Stuart, Stoke-on-Trent; North British Locomotive Co., Glasgow; Yorkshire Engine Co., Sheffield, 1929–1950 (863 built)

Weight: 47 tons 10cwt (locomotives with condensing apparatus, 50 tons 15cwt; locomotives with enlarged cabs, 49 tons 0cwt)

Driving wheel diameter: 4ft 7½in

Boiler pressure: 200lb/psi

Cylinders: (2) 17½in diameter x 24in stroke

Valve gear: Stephenson (slide valves)

Coal capacity: 3 tons 6cwt

Water capacity: 1,200 gallons

Tractive effort: 22,515lb (at 85% boiler pressure)

SOUTHERN RAILWAY

V ('Schools') Class 5P 4-4-0

The nature of the line between Tonbridge in Kent and Hastings, on the Sussex coast had always presented problems. Its twisting, turning track and exceptionally narrow-bore tunnels ruled out the larger express passenger locomotives that its train loadings called for. In reconciling these factors, Richard Maunsell produced his masterpiece, the 'Schools' class. If ever there was a 'horse for the course', it was this last and most powerful of the many designs of four-coupled express passenger engines built for Britain's railways.

The 'Schools', or V class, 4-4-0 was tailored to the Hastings line. The short frame length gave the necessary reduction in 'throw-over' on sharp curves, and its curved profile fitted within the width restrictions. Two large outside cylinders, however, could not be accommodated and, to achieve a comparable power output, Maunsell opted for a 3-cylinder layout, with the middle cylinder located between the frames. At 25,130lb, the tractive effort of the 'Schools' exceeded that of the 'King Arthur' 4-6-0s.

An inevitable consequence of building such a compact, but powerful machine was a high axleloading (21 tons) and this required the upgrading of the Tonbridge-Hastings route. The necessary trackwork was still underway when, between March and July 1930, the first ten 'Schools' were outshopped from Eastleigh. They were allocated temporarily to other main lines in Kent and Hampshire and promptly turned in remarkable performances. In the opinion of many footplatemen, the 'Schools' was the finest locomotive produced by the Southern Railway up to that point. The only drawback to the 4-4-0 was the need for careful starting to avoid the wheelslip that such a power-to-weight ratio invariably provoked.

Given its favourable reception, Maunsell concluded that the 'Schools' could be used more widely and extended construction beyond those required for the Hastings duties. In all, 40 were built up to July 1935, with one batch allocated to the Western Section. Here, they were first rostered for the London Waterloo to Portsmouth services. On the fastest timings, with 11-coach loads, the 4-4-0s were allowed 90 minutes for the 74-mile run. Following the electrification of the Portsmouth 'direct' line via Guildford and Haslemere, the 'Schools' were switched to the Bournemouth expresses.

The naming of what, officially, was the V class was another masterstroke by the Southern's publicity department. The railway's territory embraced a large number of private and public schools in southern England, from Winchester to Lancing, Charterhouse and King's

SR V ('Schools') Class 5P 4-4-0

Built: Eastleigh works, 1930–35 (40 built)

Weight: 67 tons 2cwt (locomotive)
    42 tons 8cwt (tender)

Driving wheel diameter: 6ft 7in

Boiler pressure: 220lb/psi

Cylinders: (3) 16½in diameter x 26in stroke
    (piston valves)

Valve gear: Walschaerts (piston valves)

Coal capacity: 5 tons

Water capacity: 4,000 gallons

Tractive effort: 25,130lb (at 85% boiler pressure)

Right: Outshopped in 1934, No928 Stowe was one of the second batch of 'Schools' and first based at Fratton to work London-Portsmouth expresses. Following the Portsmouth line electrification, it moved to Bournemouth in 1937 to work London-Weymouth services. No928 holds the record for the highest authenticated speed achieved by a 'Schools': 95mph between Dorchester and Wareham in 1938. Stowe spent much of its later career at Bricklayers Arms in London.

Below: The Southern Railway declared the 'Schools' to be the most powerful 4-4-0 in Europe but, on a damp 7 October 1990, No30926 Repton required rear-end assistance from Raven Q7 class 0-8-0 No901 to avoid stalling on the 1 in 49 through Darnholm with a North Yorkshire Moors Railway service from Grosmont to Pickering.

Right: At nationalization in 1948, the majority of the 'Schools' were on the Southern's Eastern Section, among them No30925 Cheltenham. By October 1958 it was at Bricklayers Arms. Withdrawn from Basingstoke in 1962, Cheltenham joined the National Collection and took part in the 1980 Rainhill cavalcade. It currently resides at York.

Canterbury. As a consequence, the Southern carried many passengers to-and-from these seats of learning and each school gained its 'own' locomotive. Wherever feasible, new engines were first sent to whichever stations were nearest the schools they honoured. There, a naming ceremony would be undertaken, with the pupils invited to climb aboard 'their' engine. The extension of the class saw schools outside the south, among them Malvern, Rugby and Shrewsbury, included in the series.

By 1947, all but three of the 40 'Schools' had congregated at depots along the Hastings line, their original destination. The exceptions were Nos928-930 which were allocated to Brighton to work cross-country trains to Cardiff and Plymouth as far as Salisbury. After nationalization, all were based on the Eastern Section, with the largest contingents at Bricklayers Arms (London) and St Leonards, near Hastings. The remainder was split between Dover and Ramsgate.

The electrification of the Kent coast routes, and the introduction of diesel multiple units on the Hastings services, led to a number of 'Schools' returning to the Central and Western Sections and they ended their days at depots as far apart as Redhill, Nine Elms and Basingstoke. Withdrawals began with Nos30919 and 30932 in January 1961 and concluded in December 1962, when all 19 survivors were condemned. One, No925 *Cheltenham*, was selected for the National Collection, and two others were privately preserved: No30926 *Repton*, now based on the North Yorkshire Moors Railway after 25 years spent in North America, and No928 *Stowe* which is on the more familiar territory of the Bluebell Railway in East Sussex.

LONDON MIDLAND & SCOTTISH RAILWAY

'Princess Royal' Class 8P 4-6-2

Outshopped from Crewe in June 1933, No6200 *The Princess Royal* was the first Stanier-designed locomotive to enter service on the London Midland & Scottish Railway. Its appearance marked the start of a momentous era, both for its designer, and for high-speed running on the West Coast Main Line.

When William Stanier was appointed Chief Mechanical Engineer of the LMSR in 1932, the principal services between London and Glasgow were entrusted to 'Royal Scot' 4-6-0s. With 70 of these in service, there was no pressing need to add to the stock of express passenger motive power. Nevertheless, the 'Scots' were being pushed to their limits. Stanier concluded the task demanded something with power in reserve when handling 500-ton Anglo-Scottish expresses. It should also have the capacity to cover the entire 401 miles to Glasgow, eliminating time-consuming engine changes at Carlisle.

In July 1932, the building of three prototypes was approved and it was no surprise that Stanier drew on his experience with Great Western designs. The 4-cylinder 'King' class 4-6-0 was an obvious inspiration: Stanier adopted its cylinder dimensions, driving wheel diameter, valve events and boiler pressure. Where he departed from the GW design was in the boiler and firebox, both of which were much larger. The size of these components ruled out

a 4-6-0 arrangement and the prototypes became 4-6-2s, with a trailing truck supporting the rear of the locomotive.

In West Coast terms, this first LMSR Pacific, No6200, was a giant. However, its inaugural run between London Euston and Glasgow on 22 September 1933 was, it must be admitted, less than impressive. One Swindon tenet – the use of low-degree superheat – was unsuited to the exceptionally large boiler. Adding this to a steam circuit that restricted the gas flow at certain points left No6200 embarrassingly shy of steam. By the time work was underway to remedy this deficiency, a second prototype had entered traffic, No6201 *Princess Elizabeth* being outshopped from Crewe in November 1933.

Normally, William Stanier was averse to exotic experiments but the third of the planned prototypes used a new, and promising, method of locomotive propulsion. In Sweden, the performance of a turbine-driven 2-8-0 had created great interest. Significant savings in fuel and maintenance costs were claimed for the Ljungström turbine. Using turbines supplied by Metropolitan Vickers, the 'Turbomotive', as No6202 soon became known, was constructed at Crewe in 1935. Measured against some other British locomotive experiments, it was remarkably successful. But for World War II, a quantity of turbine-driven engines may have been produced. Instead, No6202

Above: A rare encounter between the two preserved 'Princess Royal' Pacifics at Carnforth on 30 June 1991 allowed comparison between the second of the prototypes, No6201 Princess Elizabeth *and the first of the production series, No46203* Princess Margaret Rose. *Nos46203-12 had shorter slidebars, with the motion plate set closer to the front of the locomotive to support them. There are also detail differences in other components, such as the expansion links.*

Above: Wearing the 'Royal Scot' headboard and a 5A (Crewe North) shedplate, No6201 Princess Elizabeth *strides away from Hereford en route to Gloucester and Worcester on 13 June 1993. This was the last occasion that the 1933-built Pacific appeared on the main line.*

Below: In contrast to No6201, above, No46203 Princess Margaret Rose *is depicted on its inaugural main-line run in preservation, storming away from Derby on 2 June 1990. A low angle emphasizes the size of the Stanier boiler.*

suffered from the problems that afflict any 'one-off', chiefly long waits for spare parts. No6202's best year was 1936, when it ran 73,268 miles.

When, in 1950, its turbines needed replacing, BR decided to rebuild the locomotive as a more-or-less conventional member of the 'Princess Royal' class, No46202 *Princess Anne*. Tragically, only four months out of Crewe, the locomotive was wrecked beyond repair in the Harrow-and-Wealdstone disaster of October 1952. Its classmates enjoyed longer lives, although boiler performance had continued to concern Stanier and his team. Further production was delayed until the summer of 1935 when an additional ten engines, plus the 'Turbomotive', were delivered. However, proof that the steaming problems had been resolved was emphatically demonstrated by a record-breaking run between Euston and Glasgow undertaken by No6201 on 16 November 1936. At the head of a seven-coach train, it covered the 401 miles in an unprecedented five hours, 53 minutes and 38 seconds.

The introduction of the more powerful 'Princess Coronation' Pacifics in 1937 took the spotlight away from the 'Princess Royals'. During their remaining years they were based mainly at Camden (London), Crewe North, Edge Hill (Liverpool) and Carlisle Kingmoor depots. The arrival of Type 4 diesels on the West Coast Main Line saw the 'Princesses' spending periods in store during the 1950s. Although regularly reinstated to cover for summer motive power shortages, all (apart from No46202) were withdrawn between October 1961 and November 1962. Two have been preserved, the record-breaking No6201 *Princess Elizabeth* and the first of the production engines, No46203 *Princess Margaret Rose*. Both are currently undergoing overhauls.

LMSR 'Princess Royal' Class 8P 4-6-2

Built: Crewe works, 1933 and 1935 (13 built)

Weight: 104 tons 10cwt (locomotive)
56 tons 7cwt (tender)

Driving wheel diameter: 6ft 6in

Boiler pressure: 250lb/psi

Cylinders: (4) 28in stroke x 16¼in diameter

Valve gear: Walschaerts (piston valves)

Coal capacity: 10 tons

Water capacity: 4,000 gallons

Tractive effort: 40,285lb (at 85% boiler pressure)

LONDON MIDLAND & SCOTTISH RAILWAY

'Jubilee' Class 5XP 4-6-0

The first 'Jubilee' class locomotives appeared in 1934 and were simply classified 5XPs. The following year, however, the LMS hierarchy selected the class to commemorate the Silver Jubilee of King George V and Queen Mary. As they entered traffic, the locomotives were named after dominions and dependencies of the British Empire, heroes of the Royal Navy and famous ships of the line. Sadly, these distinguished names were attached to, initially, less-than-distinguished engines.

The theory behind William Stanier's design was apparently sound enough. Combining the best feature of the existing 'Patriot' class – its chassis – with the key elements of the recently introduced 2-cylinder mixed traffic 4-6-0 – the 'Black Five' – seemed a sure-fire recipe for a first-rate express passenger engine. Unlike the 'Princess Royal' Pacifics of 1933, there was nothing radical about the 5XP, although its 3-cylinder layout was a departure. The building of prototypes and subsequent trials was thought unnecessary. This was just as well since the need for the 5XPs was so urgent that the first 79 were ordered straight off the drawing board.

Stanier had joined the LMS as its chief mechanical engineer in 1932. His remit was nothing less than the restocking of its ageing and largely underpowered main-line fleet. A graduate of the Great Western school, Stanier saw no reason why

the Swindon formula could not be applied to LMS practice. He was right, but a miscalculation compromised the performance of the 5XPs.

The problem was the use of low-degree superheating, a Swindon trademark that worked perfectly well when accompanied by a free-flowing steam circuit and good draughting for the fire. However, the draughting arrangement of the 5XP was ill-proportioned. The GWR method for optimizing chimney and blastpipe dimensions had been based on the draughting needed by its 4-cylinder 'Castles' and 'Kings', not the six-beats-per-revolution of a 3-cylinder locomotive. The Swindon engines employed a blastpipe device known as a 'jumper top'. Its job was to reduce wear, especially on boiler stays. Put simply, it lifted in response to a fierce blast, temporarily increasing the diameter of the blastpipe and reducing the velocity of the exhaust. However, with the three cylinders of the 5XP producing less exhaust than a 4-cylinder 'Castle', the draughting was insufficient to overcome the jumper top's deadening effect.

Below: Built by the North British Locomotive Company, 'Jubilee' No45596 Bahamas entered service at Crewe North shed in January 1935. Equipped with a double chimney and blastpipe in 1961, Bahamas lasted in traffic until July 1966, when it was withdrawn from Stockport Edgeley. By that point, the Bahamas Locomotive Society had raised the funds to buy the 'Jubilee' from British Railways.

LMSR 'Jubilee' Class 5XP 4-6-0

Built: Crewe and Derby works; North British
Locomotive Company, Glasgow, 1934–36 (191 built)

Weight: 79 tons 11cwt (locomotive)
54 tons 15cwt* (tender)

Driving wheel diameter: 6ft 9in

Boiler pressure: 250lb/psi

Cylinders: (3) 17in diameter x 26in stroke

Valve gear: Walschaerts (3 sets with divided drive)
(piston valves)

Coal capacity: 9 tons*

Water capacity: 4,000 gallons*

Tractive effort: 26,610lb (at 85% boiler pressure)

(figures refer to Stanier tender; some locomotives
were attached to smaller 3,500-gallon Fowler
tenders)*

Above: 'Jubilee' at speed: No5593 Kolhapur *sweeps down the bank at Eardington, on the Severn Valley Railway, on 20 September 1986. Built in 1934, Kolhapur was one of a trio of Leeds Holbeck 'Jubilees' that lasted in traffic until autumn 1967. By then, it had been bought for preservation and in the ensuing three decades became a regular performer on both main and preserved lines.*

Largely because the LMS lacked scientific testing facilities, it took an inordinate time to discover why its new 3-cylinder 4-6-0 was a poor steamer. By the time No5665 emerged from Crewe with a redesigned boiler incorporating a 24-element superheater and reduced blastpipe diameter, 113 were in service.

In 1937, the 'Jubilees' put past problems behind them with the performances of No5660 *Rooke*. Trials were conducted to see if services on the Bristol-Leeds and Leeds-Glasgow lines could be accelerated. With a load of over 300 tons, No5660 proved the point, with averages of 55mph and 56mph respectively. Both runs included some fearsome climbs. The 'Jubilees' remained associated with these routes throughout the remainder of their careers. They also performed superbly on the Midland main line between London St Pancras and Manchester and over the 'hill-and-dale' road in southern Scotland, through Ayrshire to Girvan and Stranraer.

All 191 entered British Railways stock in 1948 and, three years later, their power classification was revised to 6P. The first to be withdrawn was No45637 *Windward Islands*, damaged beyond repair in the Harrow disaster of 1952. Scrapping proper began in 1960 but it was not until 1967 that the final three were retired from Leeds Holbeck depot. They were the last working Stanier-designed express passenger locomotives. Four 'Jubilees' have been privately preserved.

Above: In April 1935, 5XP No5642 exchanged identities with the doyen of the class, No5552, and was turned out in a special gloss black livery with chromium-plated brightwork. It was named in honour of the Silver Jubilee of King George V.

LONDON MIDLAND & SCOTTISH RAILWAY

5P5F (5MT) Class 4-6-0

The Stanier 5MT 4-6-0 – known to all as the 'Black Five' – was one of the most numerous British locomotive classes. Between 1934 and 1951, 842 of these 2-cylinder mixed traffic engines were built. This total was exceeded only by the 957 DX class 0-6-0s of the London & North Western, the 863 5700 class pannier tanks of the GWR and – if overseas-based examples are included – the 852 of another Stanier design, the 8F 2-8-0.

Inspired by the success of the Great Western's 'Hall' 4-6-0s (pages 118-119), William Stanier gave the design of a similarly-powered 'maid of all work' the highest priority upon joining the LMSR from Swindon in 1932. It was exactly the kind of 'standard' locomotive that the LMSR needed, with its vast route mileage, wide variety of traffic and miscellany of ageing pre-grouping classes. The need was so great that the first orders were placed straight off the drawing board, with Crewe works and Vulcan Foundry sharing the work.

Unlike the 3-cylinder 'Jubilees', whose hasty construction allowed serious design flaws to go unchecked, in the main the Class 5 4-6-0 was a success from the start. Although, unlike the 'Jubilee', steaming was never a problem, the boiler nevertheless required a period of refinement. Unsurprisingly, given Stanier's GWR background, it initially followed the Swindon mantra of low-degree superheat and had a superheater consisting of just 14 elements. It was also domeless, with the regulator housed in the smokebox. Experience on the road saw the superheater elements gradually increased to 28, and the smokebox regulator replaced by the less troublesome dome type.

The weight and length of the Class 5 gave it virtually unrestricted access to the entire LMSR system. It could deal with loose-coupled goods and fitted (i.e. fully vacuum-braked) freights as well as it handled semi-fast and even express passenger services. The free-steaming qualities of the design, allied to Stanier's careful attention to valve settings, comfortably allowed speeds of around 90mph.

The first of the 'Black Fives' to be delivered was actually the 21st in the numerical sequence. No5020 was outshopped from Vulcan Foundry in August 1934, resulting in some red faces at Crewe, which failed to turn out the class leader, No5000, until the following year. Besides the 75 engines originally ordered, the LMSR was responsible for the largest single locomotive-building contract ever placed by a British railway company when it ordered a further 227 engines from Armstrong Whitworth on Tyneside. By December 1938, there were 472 Class 5s in traffic.

Above: Wearing its early post-nationalization identity, 'Black Five' NoM5337 starts away from Ramsbottom with an East Lancashire Railway service for Rawtenstall on 25 October 1997. NoM5337 was built by Armstrong Whitworth in April 1937 and withdrawn in February 1965.

LMSR 5P5F (5MT) Class 4-6-0

Built: Crewe, Derby and Horwich works; Armstrong Whitworth & Co., Newcastle-upon-Tyne; Vulcan Foundry, Newton-le-Willows, Lancashire, 1934–51 (842 built)

Weight: 72 tons 2cwt to 75 tons 6cwt (locomotive) 53 tons 3cwt to 54 tons 2cwt (tender) (weights varied with various modifications)

Driving wheel diameter: 6ft 0in

Boiler pressure: 225lb/psi

Cylinders: (2) 18½in diameter x 28in stroke

Valve gear: Walschaerts* (piston valves)

Coal capacity: 9 tons

Water capacity: 4,000 gallons

Tractive effort: 25,455lb (at 85% boiler pressure)

(* *certain engines fitted with Stephenson link motion or British Caprotti poppet valve gear*)

Wartime restrictions saw construction of the class halted until April 1943 but, thereafter, the LMSR workshops at Crewe, Derby and Horwich turned out batches every year until 1951. Stanier's immediate successor, Charles Fairburn, left the design largely unaltered but his replacement, George Ivatt, had other ideas. Ivatt produced no less than 11 experimental versions of the Class 5. The modifications chiefly centred on replacing the Walschaerts valve gear with the Caprotti variety and assessing the value of roller bearings, both of Skefco and Timken manufacture. Additionally, some engines were fitted with double blastpipes and chimneys; one received a steel firebox and another, the now-preserved No44767, was equipped with outside Stephenson's link motion valve

gear. These later locomotives also incorporated devices that were to become obligatory on the BR Standard designs: self-cleaning smokeboxes, rocking grates and self-emptying ashpans. Moreover, the 'Black Five' became the basis for Robert Riddles's BR 5MT 4-6-0 (pages 178-179).

The first of the class to be withdrawn was No45401, in 1961. Seven years later, on 4 August 1968, No45212 had the melancholy honour of hauling the last steam-hauled timetabled passenger train on British Railways. One week later, the final three 'Black Fives' – Nos44781, 44871 and 45110 – worked the '15-guinea' specials that ushered out BR steam. However, 18 of what Stanier himself described as a 'deuce of a good engine' have survived, and only five of those have failed to see service in preservation.

Left: No5000 should have been the first of the Stanier 5P5F 4-6-0s to enter traffic but Crewe was beaten to the post by Vulcan Foundry, which outshopped No5020 in August 1934. No5000 did not join it in traffic until February 1935. It remained in the north-west all its working life and saw service at depots such as Crewe (North and South), Rugby, Carlisle Upperby, Carnforth, Holyhead and Chester. No5000 was retired from Lostock Hall, Preston, in October 1967 and was selected to represent this most numerous of British 4-6-0 types in the National Collection. In 1979, No5000 returned to the main line but in recent years has been on static display at the National Railway Museum.

Right: With its gleaming paintwork and burnished Walschaerts valve gear, rods and tyres, No5305 has often been judged the best kept of the preserved 'Black Fives'. Responsible for the immaculate turn-out have been the members of the Humberside Locomotive Preservation Group, custodians of the locomotive since its acquisition in 1968 from BR by scrap merchants, Drapers of Hull. For a period, as here, the locomotive was named after the founder of the company. During the 1980s, No5305 was one of seven 'Black Fives' to see main-line action, both in England and Scotland. It is currently undergoing overhaul on the Keighley & Worth Valley Railway.

LONDON MIDLAND & SCOTTISH RAILWAY

8F Class 2-8-0

Since its inception in 1923, the LMSR had struggled to equip itself with a modern heavy goods locomotive. Given the volume of freight the railway carried, its dependence on ageing 0-8-0s and underpowered 0-6-0s was astonishing. Even its newest classes, the Fowler 7F 0-8-0 of 1929 and the articulated Beyer-Garratt 2-6-6-2Ts of 1927, were irretrievably flawed. William Stanier's solution was an eight-coupled design that combined proven precepts (largely Churchward's) and the best features of his mixed-traffic 5MT 4-6-0 of 1934. Introduced in 1935, the new locomotive – originally classified 7F – was an immediate success. A considerable increase in drawbar horsepower over other LMSR freight classes allowed substantially heavier trains and higher speeds. Importantly, the 2-8-0s rode well at speed and, when called upon in emergencies to haul passenger trains, proved capable of 60mph-plus. They could handle partially vacuum-braked freights at up to 50mph. Much was attributable to the well proportioned, free-steaming boiler but the mechanical side of the design was similarly outstanding. They were the kind of trouble-free, easy-to-maintain engines that the LMSR desperately needed.

Given this, it was surprising that, by 1939, only 126 of what by then was the 8F 2-8-0, had been built. However, World War II saw that relatively modest total transformed. In the manner of the Great Central's Robinson 8K 2-8-0 in World War I (pages 84-85), the Stanier 8F became Britain's 'engine of war', both at home and overseas. The War Department had 208 constructed by Beyer Peacock and the North British Locomotive Co., and requisitioned a

further 51 from the LMSR. Few, if any, locomotives experienced more varied lives. Some never turned a wheel: they were lost at sea when the ships carrying them were torpedoed. The majority, though, ended up converted to oil-firing and working throughout the Middle East. Perhaps their most famous exploits, though, came on the vital supply route linking the Persian Gulf with the Caspian Sea, which took the 8Fs into the Soviet Union.

In Britain, the Railway Executive Committee decided that a wartime shortage of freight engines at home should also be filled by the LMSR design, given its wide route availability. As a consequence, 8Fs were built to government contracts by Great Western, LNER and Southern Railway workshops and subsequently were used on all the 'Big Four' systems. The LNER even ordered a further 68 for its own use, classifying them O6.

By 1946, 852 8Fs had been built, making it the most numerous Stanier design and the fourth largest class of engines ever produced in Britain. There would have been even more had the War Department not decided, in 1943, that the 8F had become too expensive and time-consuming to build and devised more basic versions, the 'Austerity' 2-8-0 and 2-10-0 (pages 154-155).

Following nationalization in 1948, all British-based 8Fs were taken into the stock of the London Midland Region. Additionally, 39 engines returned from overseas. Many, however, remained abroad and saw service with railways in Egypt, Iran, Iraq, Israel, Lebanon and even Italy. Some Turkish-based 8Fs – appropriately nicknamed 'Churchills' – remained at work in the 1980s. How many 8Fs survived is

Above: A transatlantic encounter at Toddington, on the Gloucestershire Warwickshire Railway. Stanier 8F No48305 – on loan from the Great Central Railway – is framed by the tender of an American counterpart, S160 2-8-0 No3278, visiting from the Mid-Hants Railway.

Above: Stanier 8F No48151 poses at Steamtown Carnforth on 9 March 1991. Crewe-built, No48151 entered service in September 1942 and was withdrawn in January 1968. Restoration was completed in 1987 and it remains approved for main-line working.

Left: Much-travelled No8233 plods through Oldbury, on the Severn Valley Railway, with a mixed goods. Built in 1940, it became one of 42 8Fs sent to the Trans-Iranian Railway connecting the Persian Gulf and the Caspian Sea. Later employed in the Suez Canal Zone, No8233 did not return to Britain until 1952. Purchased by British Railways in 1957, it remained at work until the last day of BR steam, in August 1968, since when the locomotive has been owned and maintained by the Stanier 8F Locomotive Society.

LMSR 8F Class 2-8-0

Built: Ashford, Brighton, Crewe, Darlington, Doncaster, Eastleigh, Horwich and Swindon works; Beyer-Peacock, Manchester; North British Locomotive Co., Glasgow; Vulcan Foundry, Newton-le-Willows, Lancashire, 1935–46 (852 built)

Weight: 72 tons 2cwt (locomotive)
53 tons 13cwt (tender)

Driving wheel diameter: 4ft 8½in

Boiler pressure: 225lb/psi

Cylinders: (2) 18½in diameter x 28in stroke

Valve gear: Walschaerts (piston valves)

Coal capacity: 9 tons 0cwt

Water capacity:
4,000 gallons

Tractive effort: 32,438lb
(at 85% boiler pressure)

conjecture, but by 1957 British Railways' stock stood at 666. Only the Southern Region had none on its books and they could be seen as far north as Perth, as far west as Plymouth and as far east as Norwich. Even though maintenance standards declined, they remained extremely efficient and reliable, with an average mileage of between 40,000 and 48,000 miles between valve and piston examinations.

In 1960, after a derailment, No48616 became the first 8F to be condemned. Withdrawals proper began in 1962 with No48009, but around 150 survived into the last year of BR steam, 1968. The 8F had the melancholy honour of soldiering on until the final day, 4 August, when Nos48318 and 48773 were retired from Rose Grove depot in Lancashire. Seven ex-British Railways 8Fs – including the much-travelled No48773 – survive in preservation and an eighth example has been repatriated from Turkey.

Right: During World War II, 8Fs were built at several non-LMSR works, including Swindon, from where No48431 emerged in 1944. Apart from a spell at Royston, in Yorkshire, the locomotive remained on ex-GWR territory and was withdrawn from Bath (Green Park) in May 1964. In 1972, the 8F – seen climbing out of Keighley with a train for Oxenhope on 18 October 1992 – arrived on the Keighley & Worth Valley Railway where its restoration was completed within three years.

LONDON & NORTH EASTERN RAILWAY

A4 Class 8P6F 4-6-2

Record-breaking, like streamlining, was in vogue during the 1930s. Competition thrived and records regularly changed hands between Britain, Germany and the United States. One record, however, and one locomotive remains supreme: the 126mph attained by Gresley A4 Pacific No4468 *Mallard* on 3 July 1938.

During a visit to Germany during 1933, Nigel Gresley had been impressed by the streamlined 'Flying Hamburger' diesel train. Consideration was given to buying similar units for an accelerated London-Newcastle service. Then, on 3 March 1935, the performance of A3 Pacific No2750 *Papyrus* proved that the envisaged four-hour timing was achievable with steam traction. Three weeks later, the LNER approved the building of streamlined train sets, and the locomotives to haul them. By early September, the first, No2509 *Silver Link*, was ready. That month, on a press run to publicize the new 'Silver Jubilee' service, it broke the British speed record with 112.5mph.

For its first two weeks of operation, the train was hauled exclusively by No2509, which covered 5,366 miles in the process. It was then joined at King's Cross depot by two more silver-liveried A4s, while a third – No2511 *Silver King* – was based at Gateshead.

The success, both of the A4s and the 'Silver Jubilee', persuaded the LNER to introduce two other streamlined trains, the 'Coronation' and the 'West Riding Limited'. Garter blue was the chosen livery for these services, and for the seven new A4s rostered to work them. In addition, a quantity of A4s was ordered for general service and

received the normal LNER lined green. The 21st A4 constructed, No4498, also happened to be the 100th Gresley Pacific. On 26 November 1937, it was named *Sir Nigel Gresley* after its designer.

There was a certain irony in this. Gresley is said to have described the streamliners as a 'publicity stunt', yet appears to have favoured streamlining as a means of reducing air resistance and, therefore, getting more out of every ton of coal consumed. The key to the A4s' performance, however, was internal, not external. Though direct descendants of the 3-cylinder A1 Pacifics of 1922 (pages 106-107), they benefited from experience with their predecessors, and from work done elsewhere, especially by the French engineer, André Chapelon. He had demonstrated the value of allowing steam to flow freely, and the steam passages of the A4 were streamlined and enlarged, from the regulator valve to the blastpipe. In March 1938, a new A4 became the first to be equipped with a device developed by Chapelon and a Finnish colleague, M.M. Kylala, the Kylchap double blastpipe and double chimney. That locomotive was No4468 *Mallard*.

Gresley had been concerned about the braking capacity of the A4 and, in conjunction with the Westinghouse company, had undertaken some high-speed braking trials. Ostensibly, the runs with *Mallard* on 3 July 1938 were a continuation of those trials, but the LMS had recently snatched the British speed record and the LNER wanted to reclaim it. On the descent of Stoke bank, south of Grantham, driver, Joe Duddington, and fireman, Tommy

Left: A4 No4488 (BR No60009) entered traffic in 1937 and, like others of the class, was to have been named after a bird (the osprey). Instead it was among five A4s that honoured dominions of the British Empire, becoming Union of South Africa. No60009 was always Scottish-based, first at Haymarket (Edinburgh) and then Aberdeen Ferryhill. In 1963, 'No9' hauled the final scheduled steam-hauled service out of King's Cross and then became the last steam locomotive overhauled at Doncaster. Bought privately in 1966, No60009 is nearing the completion of its latest overhaul to main-line standard.

Bray, both of Doncaster depot, accelerated *Mallard* to 125mph – more than two miles a minute. For each of those minutes, the driving wheels went through over 500 revolutions and, at Milepost 90, the accompanying dynamometer car recorded a world record 126mph.

Wartime gave the A4s an opportunity to demonstrate that speed was not their only asset. Like the A3 Pacifics and V2 2-6-2s, they hauled huge loads the length of the east coast. After the war, despite the appearance of new Peppercorn Pacifics, the A4s remained in charge of prestige Anglo-Scottish expresses such as 'The

Elizabethan' and 'The Talisman'. Appropriately, *Mallard* was at the head of the last steam-hauled 'Elizabethan' on 9 September 1961.

The first A4 to be withdrawn (apart from No4499, wrecked during the bombing of York depot in 1942) was *Silver Link* itself, in December 1962. Others, though, enjoyed a 'Scottish swansong' working over the Glasgow-Aberdeen line and on the Waverley route between Carlisle and Edinburgh. The final three A4s were retired in September 1966, but six have been preserved, four in Britain and two in North America.

Left: The record-breaking No4468 Mallard *backs off the turntable at Scarborough after working in from York on 9 July 1988. This was one of several runs commemorating the 50th anniversary of its 1938 world speed record. After withdrawal for preservation in 1963, the 1937-built Pacific reverted to its original condition, complete with wheel valances.*

Below: On 26 November 1937, the 100th Gresley Pacific to be built – A4 No4498 (BR No60007) – was fittingly named after its designer. Now owned and maintained by the A4 Locomotive Society, on 23 May 1959 Sir Nigel Gresley *set a postwar world record for steam traction of 112mph.*

LNER A4 Class 8P6F 4-6-2

Built: Doncaster works, 1935–38 (35 built)

Weight: 102 tons 19cwt (locomotive)
60 tons 7cwt (non-corridor tender)/64 tons 19cwt (corridor tender)*

Driving wheel diameter: 6ft 8in

Boiler pressure: 250lb/psi

Cylinders: (3) 18½in diameter x 26in stroke

Valve gear: Walschaerts (piston valves); Gresley-Holcroft conjugated gear to inside cylinder

Coal capacity: 9 tons*

Water capacity: 5,000 gallons

Tractive effort: 35,455lb (at 85% boiler pressure)

(coal capacity of corridor tenders originally 8 tons, giving a tender weight of 62 tons 8cwt. From 1937, capacity increased to 9 tons)*

LONDON & NORTH EASTERN RAILWAY

V2 Class 6MT 2-6-2

A quarter of a century's experience in locomotive design was distilled in the V2, Nigel Gresley's last major achievement. When the first of the class was outshopped from Doncaster in June 1936, Gresley was celebrating 25 years as Chief Mechanical Engineer, first of the Great Northern Railway and, after 1923, of the LNER. That year, his achievements were acknowledged with a knighthood.

During this period, Gresley had equipped the LNER with a fleet of modern, high-speed passenger engines and classes of six- and eight-coupled freight machines that handled the LNER's voluminous mineral traffic. However, rail freight in general was facing growing competition from road transport. One way that the LNER met this challenge was by introducing a fast, overnight Anglo-Scottish service that could handle anything from parcels to bulk loads. In many respects the forerunner of today's container train, the LNER's publicity department settled on the name 'Green Arrow' for the newcomer. However, it needed a special breed of locomotive to handle both the loads and the schedules. The A3 Pacifics would have been suitable, but were fully occupied with passenger duties.

In 1935, the LNER revealed that its Doncaster drawing office was working on a new design for 'heavy long-distance work'. A 4-6-0 wheel arrangement had been considered, but the vote had gone to a 2-6-2, or Prairie type. While 2-6-2 tender engines were commonplace in the United States, this was a novelty for Britain. Here, the 2-6-2 arrangement had been confined almost exclusively to tank locomotives.

While unusual, Gresley's 2-6-2 was not radically new. Essentially, it was a variation of the A3 Pacific (pages 106-107). Gresley's trademark 3-cylinder configuration was retained, along with conjugated gear to the valves of the middle cylinder. The boiler was a shortened version of that used on the A3 and, at 6ft 2in diameter, the driving wheels were six inches smaller. LNER standard six-wheel 4,200-gallon tenders were allotted to the class.

Initially, Doncaster built only five V2s, headed by the now-preserved No4771 (BR No60800). This was promptly named after the fast freight service for which it had been designed – *Green Arrow*. Successful trials with this quintet led to both Doncaster and Darlington works going into full production.

The V2s had the free-steaming qualities that the LNER's operating department required. Not only were they capable of working vacuum-braked freights at up to 60mph, they could deputize for Pacifics on express passenger schedules. In peak condition, a V2 all but matched them for sustained high-speed running. One was reliably timed at 93mph on the 'Yorkshire Pullman', while another attained 101.5mph on a test train.

These Gresley thoroughbreds had one drawback. They may have been 'do anything' engines, but they were far from 'go anywhere' ones. With a 22-ton axleloading, they

Left: Following the completion of its most recent (and privately-sponsored) overhaul, the National Collection's 1936-built V2 2-6-2 Green Arrow was repainted in British Railways lined green as No60800. Many commentators – while acknowledging the achievements of the A4 Pacifics – consider the mixed traffic V2s to be Sir Nigel Gresley's masterpieces.

Opposite: In perfect weather on 30 September 1989, LNER-liveried No4771 Green Arrow sparkles as it gallops past the dry stone walls of Ais Gill with a southbound 'Cumbrian Mountain Express' from Carlisle to Hellifield. Throughout their lives, the 3-cylinder V2s were regularly called upon to deputize for Pacifics on express passenger workings and seldom disappointed.

Above: A King's Cross engine prior to retirement in August 1962, in the summer of 1987 Green Arrow returned to London to work specials to Stratford-upon-Avon. It was captured backing down on to its train at Marylebone on 2 August.

LNER V2 Class 6MT 2-6-2

Built: Darlington and Doncaster works, 1936–44 (184 built)

Weight: 93 tons 2cwt (locomotive)
51 tons 0cwt (tender)

Driving wheel diameter: 6ft 2in

Boiler pressure: 220lb/psi

Cylinders: (3) 18½in diameter x 26in stroke

Valve gear: Walschaerts (with derived motion to middle cylinder) (piston valves)

Coal capacity: 7 tons 10cwt

Water capacity: 4,200 gallons

Tractive effort: 33,730lb (at 85% boiler pressure)

were limited to around 40 out of every 100 of the LNER's route miles. The V2s were barred, for example, from all the ex-Great Eastern main lines.

Whatever the V2s achieved before 1939 and after 1945 will always be eclipsed by their astonishing feats of haulage during World War II. Trains of 20-plus vehicles, loaded to 700 tons, proved within their compass. On at least one occasion, a single V2 hauled 26 coaches from Peterborough to London. Given this capacity for work, it was not surprising that construction was allowed to continue through the war years. When it ceased in 1944, the class numbered 184. They were the last Gresley-designed engines to be produced.

The V2s performed equally competently for British Railways, leaving their mark on the 'Waverley' route between Carlisle and Edinburgh, and on the ex-Great Central main line between London Marylebone and Sheffield. Their swansong came on the Edinburgh-Aberdeen run, working alongside the last of the LNER A2 and A4 Pacifics. For many, the V2 was Gresley's masterpiece. With the sole survivor, No60800 *Green Arrow*, currently approved to work main-line specials, it is still possible to sample that assessment, albeit on something less taxing than those 20-coach wartime hauls.

LONDON & NORTH EASTERN RAILWAY

K4 Class 5P6F 2-6-0

By the mid-1930s, train loadings over the LNER's West Highland line were stretching the abilities of the Gresley K2 2-6-0s and double-heading was commonplace. Something more powerful was needed, but the route was one that imposed strict limitations on axleloading and – because of its sharp curvature – wheelbase length. When his civil engineer ruled out both any eight-coupled design and the existing K3 Mogul, Nigel Gresley opted to build a locomotive tailored to the Glasgow-Crianlarich-Fort William-Mallaig run. A 2-6-0 wheel arrangement was chosen, with 5ft 2in coupled wheels to give the adhesion required to grapple with 300-ton loads on the grades.

The outcome was an amalgam of proven components. With a diameter of 5ft 6in and a barrel length of 11ft 1in, the boiler was a variant of that used by Gresley on four previous designs, the K2 Mogul, the D49 4-4-0 and the J38 and J39 0-6-0s. It was partnered by the firebox of the B17 'Sandringham' 4-6-0. The wheelbase was equivalent to that of the K3 2-6-0 and the newcomer additionally shared its predecessor's three cylinders, Walschaerts motion and leading pony truck design. As with other Gresley 3-cylinder machines, conjugated drive to the middle cylinder was employed. The cylinders and their associated 8in diameter piston valves were incorporated into a single 'monobloc' casting, which also formed the smokebox saddle. The prototype K4, No3441, left Darlington works for Eastfield depot in Glasgow in January 1937. After five weeks of crew training and being confined to goods work, it made its debut on a passenger train on 4 March.

The steam pressure on No3441 had been set at 180lb/psi, which resulted in a tractive effort of 32,940lb. It was soon apparent that this brought little improvement in average speeds over the existing K2 Mogul. Moreover, No3441 responded sluggishly when up against the gradients of the West Highland line. Gresley reacted by raising the steam pressure to 200lb/psi, which saw the tractive effort leap to a hefty 36,598lb. The K4 could now demonstrate its true capabilities, handling 300-ton trains and with maximum speeds around 60mph on level ground. However, as with all the Gresley 2-6-0s, it could be a rough ride at such speeds. Another advantage of the newcomer was that it used only marginally more coal in working 300-ton trains than the K2s did with considerably lighter loads.

The successful trials with No3441 led to five more K4s being ordered. Apart from the prototype, *Loch Long,* all were named after Highland chieftains and grandees. The K4s quickly endeared themselves to the Scottish crews and, apart from some heavily loaded summer trains, eliminated uneconomic double-heading over the West Highland. Sadly, performances declined – as with all Gresley 3-cylinder engines – with the significant reduction in maintenance standards during wartime. Despite this, the K4s retained their pre-eminence on the West Highland line until the arrival in 1947 of the first Thompson B1 4-6-0s. When, after nationalization, these were followed by an influx of LMSR Stanier 5MT 4-6-0s and new LNER K1 2-6-0s, the Gresley engines were confined increasingly to

Left: With the 'West Highlander' headboard mounted on the smokebox of a K4 2-6-0, and Gresley teak-bodied coaches, this could be a Scottish scene from the 1930s. However, this is Bewdley, on the Severn Valley Railway, and the 5.05pm departure for Kidderminster on 25 September 1993. No3442 The Great Marquess is the sole survivor of the six K4s, a design tailored to the demands of the Glasgow-Mallaig run. Outshopped from Darlington in July 1938, No3442 went straight to Eastfield depot in Glasgow. Its working life ended as it had begun, in Scotland, but on the east coast rather than the west, at Thornton Junction in Fife in October 1961.

Left: LNER lined black livery graced the first of the K4s, No3441 Loch Long, *when it entered traffic in January 1937. Footplate crews soon appreciated the practical advantages it offered over the K2 2-6-0, and a hike in boiler pressure rectified an initial sluggishness on gradients. That summer, No3441's performances merited an order for five more engines, although only one – No3442 – was completed in time for the 1938 summer peak. Nos3443-46 emerged from Darlington works – in lined apple green – in December 1938. Here, on 20 September 1997, the preserved example carries its post-1948 lined black livery.*

LNER K4 Class 5P6F 2-6-0

Built: Darlington works, 1937–38 (6 built)

Weight: 68 tons 8cwt (locomotive)
44 tons 4cwt (tender)

Driving wheel diameter: 5ft 2in

Boiler pressure: 200lb/psi

Cylinders: (3) 18½in diameter x 26in stroke

Valve gear: Walschaerts, with conjugated gear driving on to inside cylinder (piston valves)

Coal capacity: 5 tons 10cwt

Water capacity: 3,500 gallons

Tractive effort: 36,598lb (at 85% boiler pressure)

Right: Scotland's K4 No3442 The Great Marquess *approaches Bewdley, on the Severn Valley Railway, passing GWR 'Manor' 4-6-0 No7819* Hinton Manor *waiting to depart for Bridgnorth. Operating in Wales and Cornwall, the 'Manors' enjoyed similar Celtic connections.*

Above: Only five years separate K4 2-6-0 No3442 The Great Marquess *(left) and WD 'Austerity' 2-10-0 No600* Gordon *of 1943 yet, in design terms, they represent two different design schools. The change was imposed by war, but would have been necessary without that dramatic intervention.*

goods workings. One K4, No3445, had been rebuilt by Gresley's successor, Edward Thompson, in 1945 as a 2-cylinder machine, becoming the prototype for the K1 (pages 174-175).

During the 1950s, the K4s' sphere of operation enlarged and they began to appear at locations such as Edinburgh, Perth, Forfar, Ayr and Tweedmouth. In 1959, all were concentrated at Thornton Junction depot in Fife and withdrawn from there *en masse* in October 1961. However, the late Viscount Garnock promptly bought No61994 (LNER No3442) *The Great Marquess* from British Railways and had the engine overhauled to working order. Based at Leeds, No3442 undertook railtour work until forced into retirement by the ban imposed on steam working by BR in 1968. From 1972, the locomotive was stored on the Severn Valley Railway until, in 1980, another overhaul got underway. *The Great Marquess* was recommissioned in April 1989 and made a nostalgic return to the West Highland line that summer. It remains on the Severn Valley, unfortunately sidelined awaiting major repairs.

GREAT WESTERN RAILWAY

7800 'Manor' Class 5MT 4-6-0

Introduced in 1938, the 'Manors' were the smallest and lightest of the Great Western 4-6-0s. As such, they were able to venture into territory barred to the heavier 'Castles', 'Halls' and 'Granges'. Although a new type of boiler was produced for the class, the Swindon No14, elsewhere economy appears to have been paramount. The driving wheels and motion components were recovered from scrapped Churchward 4300 class 2-6-0s. The tenders, too, were second-hand, mostly built between 1905 and 1914.

With an axleloading of just 17 tons 5cwt, the 'Manors' came into the GWR's 'blue' category for route restrictions. This was a code to indicate which classes of locomotives were allowed where. Each category had a maximum axleweight and, in descending order, a designated colour – red, blue or yellow. (The lightest classes were left 'uncoloured'.) Discs of the appropriate colour were applied to each cabside. The larger 4-6-0s fell into the 'red' group, with the 'Kings' having a ranking all to themselves: 'Double Red'.

The first of the 'Manors', No7800 *Torquay Manor*, entered traffic in January 1938 and, by February the following year, 20 were in service. War forced the cancellation of an order for a further 20. The official GWR line on the class was that the 7800s were expected to work to existing schedules and with existing loadings, but with an all-round increase in efficiency. Unfortunately, for once, the 'make do and mend' policy prevalent at Swindon during the 1930s did not succeed. Unlike the 'Granges' of 1936, where the use of standard components and the

re-use of existing ones, had produced a masterpiece, the initial performance of the 'Manors' was comparatively mediocre. Were it not for the constraints of war, there is every reason to expect that Swindon would have recalled the engines for modification. Instead, the first examples were despatched to depots at Wolverhampton, Bristol, Gloucester, Shrewsbury, Westbury in Wiltshire and Neyland in South Wales.

However, the area with which the 'Manors' became synonymous was mid-Wales. Here they worked over the main lines of the erstwhile Cambrian Railway, which were off-limits to other 4-6-0 classes. This enduring association began in October 1938, when No7805 *Broome Manor* underwent clearance tests between Ruabon and Barmouth. The 'Manors' were also successfully employed in the West Country, where they were used for banking and piloting trains over the Devon banks between Newton Abbot and Plymouth. Their light axleloading allowed them across the Tamar, too, and on to the branch lines of Cornwall.

After nationalization, the newly created Western Region was authorized to build ten more of the class. Nos7820-29 were outshopped from Swindon in November and December 1950 with, curiously, no attempt to improve the steaming. True, with the new Standard classes on the drawing board, a British Railways edict permitted construction only of existing pre-nationalization designs. However, it is difficult to see how a 'Modified Manor' could have been classed a 'new design' and, as subsequent trials showed, the engines did not require too much work to

Left: Remarkably, almost one-third of the 'Manor' 4-6-0s live on in preservation and all nine have been in action since the class was officially extinguished in 1965. The first to be steamed in preservation was 1938-built No7808 Cookham Manor which was acquired by the Great Western Society as far back as 1966. During its 27-year working life, Cookham Manor operated all over the GW system, initially from Old Oak Common in London. No7808's last home was Gloucester. After enjoying main-line outings during the 1970s, the locomotive has been out-of-traffic at Didcot for many years.

correct their faults. Internal alterations to the blastpipe and an increase in air space in the firegrate, added to a new type of narrow chimney, noticeably improved the draughting. All were fitted with the new chimney in 1952 while, after trials on ten of the class, the other modifications became standard after 1954.

By 1959, 21 'Manors' were congregated in mid- and South Wales. Undoubtedly their most prestigious working was the 'Cambrian Coast Express', which they took over from a 'King' or 'Castle' at Shrewsbury and worked through to Aberystwyth. Others of the class operated in the Birmingham, Gloucester and Hereford areas, while the handful stationed at Reading frequently ventured on to the Southern Region line to Guildford and Redhill.

The first 'Manor' scrapped was No7809 *Childrey Manor*, withdrawn from Shrewsbury depot in April 1963 and cut up at Swindon. By May 1965, the numbers had been halved and the final two, No7808 *Cookham Manor* of Gloucester and No7829 *Ramsbury Manor* of Didcot were condemned in December 1965. However, no less than nine 'Manors' have survived, and all have added to their mileage figures in preservation, four of them on main-line railtours.

Left: No7828 Odney Manor *is one of ten 'Manors' built by BR, entering traffic in December 1950 at Neath, in South Wales. A nine-year stay at Shrewsbury began in November 1952, after which No7828 moved to Croes Newydd and, in March 1963, to Aberystwyth.* Odney Manor *returned to Shrewsbury in January 1965 and was withdrawn that October. It returned to steam in 1988 and has since seen action on a number of preserved lines including the East Lancashire Railway. On 27 April 1991, in the company of ex-Manchester Ship Canal 0-6-0T No32* Gothenburg, *No7828 strides away from Bury Bolton Street with a service to Rawtenstall.*

Above: Smart in its BR livery, the last of the Great Western-built 'Manors', No7819 Hinton Manor *was delivered to Carmarthen shed in February 1939. It remained a Welsh engine throughout its working life and returned to steam, on the Severn Valley Railway, in 1977.*

GWR 7800 'Manor' Class 5MT 4-6-0

Built: Swindon works, 1938–39/1950 (30 built)

Weight: 68 tons 18cwt (locomotive)
40 tons 0cwt (tender)

Driving wheel diameter: 5ft 8in

Boiler pressure: 225lb/psi

Cylinders: (2) 18in diameter x 30in stroke

Valve gear: Stephenson (piston valves)

Coal capacity: 6 tons 0cwt

Water capacity: 3,500 gallons

Tractive effort: 27,340lb
(at 85% boiler pressure)

LONDON MIDLAND & SCOTTISH RAILWAY

'Princess Coronation' Class 8P 4-6-2

The 5MT 4-6-0s and 8F 2-8-0s may have been the most numerous of his designs, but the enduring image of a Stanier locomotive remains a 'Coronation' class Pacific attacking Shap or Beattock bank. These magnificent machines were the pinnacle of 4-cylinder locomotive development in Britain and arguably the world. Ironically, though, the impetus for their construction came from the LMSR's east coast rival, the LNER.

In 1935, the LNER's high-speed streamlined services had set new standards for rail travel in Britain. The LMSR responded, belatedly, by introducing the 'Coronation Scot' service. It was inaugurated in July 1937, with locomotives specifically designed to maintain 6-hour London-Glasgow schedules on a regular basis.

Like the LNER's A4s, the new 'Princess Coronations' were streamlined. A bathtub-like shroud covered the locomotives, the first five of which were adorned with a blue-and-silver chevron-striped livery. This quintet, Nos6220-6224, was followed by a further five in a maroon-and-gilt colour scheme (Nos6225-6229). The intention was that these would work other expresses, principally to Scotland, but also to Merseyside. However, the next five Pacifics, Nos6230-6234, were non-streamlined, revealing the handsome and powerful profile that lurked beneath the 'bathtub'.

In February 1939, No6234 *Duchess of Abercorn*, demonstrated just how powerful. Many lessons had been learned from experience with the 'Princess Royals' (pages 126-127). The superheater now consisted of 40 elements; the boiler was vastly improved; and the cylinder layout was modified, with the inside cylinder valves operated by rocking shafts working off the outside valve spindle crossheads. The grate area was enlarged to an enormous 50sq ft and the driving wheel diameter increased by three inches to 6ft 9in.

On its test run between Glasgow and Crewe, with a 20-coach load amounting to 605 tons, *Duchess of Abercorn* recorded a cylinder horsepower of 3,330 – the highest of any British steam locomotive before or since. Moreover, the Pacific was climbing the 1 in 99 of Beattock bank at the time at a steady 63mph. The downside was that it was taking *two* firemen to satisfy the appetite of the fire.

The 'Coronations' were fast as well as strong. On a special run from Euston to Crewe in 1937, the doyen of the class, No6220 *Coronation*, set a new British speed record of 114mph. The reputation of the 'Coronation Scot' spread far-and-wide and, in 1939, an entire train was sent to tour the United States. With No6220 unavailable, No6229 assumed its guise and covered 3,120 miles touring 38 cities.

Left: For a period, No46229 Duchess of Hamilton, exchanged the maroon it had always worn in preservation for the postwar lined green it received in 1953. Here, it poses at Buckley Wells, on the East Lancashire Railway, on the morning of 24 February 1998, prior to working a photographers' charter. Outshopped from Crewe in September 1938, No46229 lost its streamlining in November 1947.

Opposite: No46229 Duchess of Hamilton starts away from Marylebone with a special working in the spring of 1985. Its first home had been among the Stanier Pacifics and 'Royal Scots' housed at Camden. However, by nationalization it was a Crewe North engine. October 1957 found No46229 back at Camden, and it was retired from Edge Hill, Liverpool, in February 1964.

LMSR 'Princess Coronation' Class 8P 4-6-2

Built: Crewe works, 1937–48 (38 built)

Weight: 105 tons 5cwt (108 tons 2cwt streamlined)
(locomotive)
56 tons 7cwt (tender)

Driving wheel diameter: 6ft 9in

Boiler pressure: 250lb/psi

Cylinders: (4) 16½in diameter
x 28in stroke

Valve gear: Walschaerts, with
rocking shafts to inside
cylinders (piston valves)

Coal capacity: 10 tons 0cwt

Water capacity: 4,000 gallons

Tractive effort: 40,000lb
(at 85% boiler pressure)

Below: 1938-built No6233 Duchess of Sutherland *was non-streamlined from the outset and allocated to Camden until January 1948. After a long period at Crewe North, No6233 ended at Edge Hill and was bought by Butlin's Holiday Camps. In 1970, the locomotive was entrusted to Norfolk's Bressingham Steam Museum. Now in the care of the Midland Railway Centre, No6233 is due to return to steam during 2000.*

Below: Brand-new, the second of the 'Coronations', No6221 Queen Elizabeth *sports the original, bewhiskered streamlined condition of the class at Polmadie (Glasgow) on 19 June 1937. No6221 was a Glasgow engine for most of its working life, ending its days at Carlisle Upperby in May 1963. It was scrapped at its birthplace of Crewe.*

The outbreak of war put paid not only to record-breaking, but to high-speed luxury expresses. However, the prodigious pulling power of the 'Coronation' Pacifics ensured their continued usefulness and further construction was allowed. Still with streamlined casings, Nos6235-6248 were delivered between 1939 and 1943, although the last four were painted an unprepossessing plain black. Nine more non-streamlined examples were constructed up to 1948. The final pair appeared under the aegis of Stanier's successor, George Ivatt, who made some modifications, fitting roller bearings and a 'Delta'-type trailing truck.

Over a four-year period, from 1945 until 1949, the streamlined casings were removed from all 38 Pacifics. In the ensuing years, they appeared in five colours: lined black, lined green, two shades of blue and, finally, lined maroon. Based at Camden (London), Crewe North, Edge Hill (Liverpool), Carlisle and Polmadie (Glasgow), the 'Coronations' worked on the West Coast until the early 1960s when they simply ran out of suitable work. All were withdrawn between 1962 and 1964, with No6256 *Sir William A. Stanier F.R.S.* the last to be condemned. Today, No46235 *City of Birmingham* resides, appropriately, in the Birmingham Museum of Science and Industry. Privately-owned No6233 *Duchess of Sutherland* is undergoing overhaul at the Midland Railway Centre in Derbyshire, and the National Railway Museum's No46229 *Duchess of Hamilton* has been the subject of a scheme to restore it to its original streamlined condition.

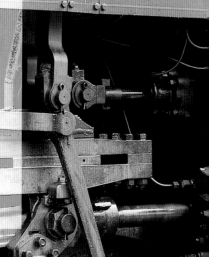

Setting Standards

1940–1960

SR 'Merchant Navy' Pacific

SR Q1 class • LNER B1 class

Ministry of Supply/WD 'Austerity' 2-10-0

Ministry of Supply/WD 'Austerity' saddletank

GWR 6959 'Modified Hall'

SR 'Battle of Britain', 'West Country' Pacifics

LMSR 2MT Mogul • LMSR 2MT Prairie tank

LMSR 4MT Mogul • GWR 1500/9400 pannier tanks

LNER A1 class Pacific • LNER A2 class Pacific

LNER K1 Mogul • BR Standard 'Britannia' Pacific

BR Standard 5MT 4-6-0 • BR Standard 4MT 4-6-0

BR Standard 4MT 2-6-4T • BR Standard 4MT Mogul

BR Standard 2MT Mogul • BR Standard 8P Pacific

BR Standard 9F 2-10-0

1940–1960

Setting Standards

World War II took a huge toll of Britain's railway network. Between September 1939 and the end of 1942, it suffered over 10,000 bombing attacks, yet even during the worst of the 'Blitz', services were never seriously interrupted. Over the same period, locomotives ran some 1,870 million miles and increased their time in traffic by 7,000,000 hours. Train loadings on passenger services doubled and there was a 32 per cent increase in traffic. All the while, a shortage of staff, especially skilled fitters, saw maintenance levels decline to an unprecedented low. As never before, the steam locomotive demonstrated its rugged durability and capacity for hard work.

Steam locomotive construction continued during wartime, although with the emphasis firmly on utility engines, such as the Thompson B1 4-6-0 of the LNER and the Great Western's 'Modified Hall'. One glorious exception to the rule was the Southern's 'Merchant Navy' Pacific. Despite being categorized as a mixed traffic type, few doubted that Oliver Bulleid's design was intended for high-speed running. In many respects, it was the most advanced of its type built in Britain up to that point, and one of the most complex. Simplicity of construction and ease of maintenance were not among Bulleid's priorities. They were, however, the guiding principles for Robert Riddles, who was given the job of ensuring there were sufficient locomotives to maintain supplies to the Allied forces after the invasion of Europe in 1944. Initially, the Stanier 8F 2-8-0 of the LMSR was chosen as standard, but when this proved too time-consuming and expensive to

Above: Seen in its original streamlined, or 'air-smoothed' condition, 'Merchant Navy' class Pacific No35015 Rotterdam Lloyd dashes through Weybridge, Surrey, with a southbound express in September 1952. Introduced in 1941, this Bulleid design was the most advanced express passenger type to be built during the 1940s.

build, Riddles produced designs for a 2-8-0 and a 2-10-0 that fully justified the epithet of 'Austerity'. Although intended to be almost 'disposable', over 700 of these engines remained in service in Britain for a further 20 years or more.

Less than three years after the war's end, on 1 January 1948, Britain's railways were nationalized. What form of motive power the new British Railways should concentrate on developing was one of the first choices facing the government-appointed Railway Executive. The United States had opted for diesels, but British experience of diesel traction was chiefly limited to shunters and railcars. There were just two main-line diesels at work, both built by the LMSR in 1947. Moreover, the fuel oil would have to be imported. In terms of running costs, electric traction was far more attractive but required the heavy long-term investment that the post-war British economy could not sustain. Steam traction was fuelled by indigenous coal, but British Railways' motive power inheritance was, to say the least, diverse. There were around 20,000 engines spread over more than 400 classes. Many dated back to the Victorian era and, after the demands of wartime, many were life-expired. However, construction was continuing of several existing classes, while deliveries of others, such as the LNER K1 2-6-0, did not begin until after nationalization.

Above: American influence in post-World War II British locomotive design was partly a result of experience with US Army Transportation Corps S160 2-8-0s – No3278 among them – that were shipped across the Atlantic prior to D-Day.

The decision was taken to remain faithful to steam while seeking ways to modernize and improve its efficiency. A team headed by Robert Riddles was given the task of designing a range of standard locomotive types that would embody the best features of pre-nationalization designs. They were expected to undertake a wide range of duties, and achieve high mileages between overhauls. Wherever feasible, components would be standardized across the range. Simplicity was paramount, as was availability: the usefulness of the new locomotives was not to be compromised by loading gauge constraints.

During 1948, comparative tests were undertaken throughout Britain between the most recent designs of the GWR, LMSR, LNER and SR. Most of the results were inconclusive, but if there was one 'star performer', it was the Southern's 'West Country' class Pacific. Unfortunately, 3-cylinder engines with 'air-smoothed' casing and chain-driven valve gear did not come into the 'simple' category.

In most respects, the most modern locomotives then being built were the 2-6-0s and 2-6-2 tanks designed by George Ivatt for the LMSR. They were already employing the rocker grates, hopper ashpans and self-cleaning smokeboxes that radically simplified the filthy chore of ash disposal and fire-cleaning. Ivatt's ideas, and much else of contemporary LMSR practice, found their way into the British Railways Standard classes. In planning the Standard designs, Riddles and his colleagues envisaged the locomotives remaining in service into the 1970s, by which time – as in France and Germany – major trunk routes would have been electrified. Over 20 years, the investment would have been repaid. That it was not has remained a matter of controversy.

It is undeniable that the Standards were a mixed bunch. At least two designs – the Class 6 'Clan' Pacific and Class 3 2-6-0 – were superfluous, as was clear from the construction of a mere ten and 20 engines respectively. Another seven were adaptations of LMSR designs, with the Class 4 2-6-4 tank and 4MT 2-6-0 and 4-6-0 perhaps the most successful. Of the remaining three, the 'Britannia' Pacifics were excellent machines, but the solitary Class 8 Pacific, *Duke of Gloucester*, was a case of what might have been. Errors in construction, which drastically inhibited the performance of what was unquestionably an immensely promising design, have only recently emerged.

The last, and most numerous of the BR Standards, the 9F 2-10-0, was also the best. It was only the third ten-coupled locomotive built in Britain, and a fitting coda for the country that gave steam traction to the world. Construction of what, to many, was the finest heavy freight locomotive ever designed in Britain, began in 1954. It concluded – 251 engines later – in 1960, a full five years after the political decision to phase out steam traction was taken.

Above: The first of British Railways' Standard Pacifics, No70000 Britannia *of 1951, stands alongside the last, the solitary 8P No71000* Duke of Gloucester *of 1954, at Carnforth. Only since preservation has the true potential of the* Duke *become evident.*

Some of the conclusions in the 1955 Modernization Plan were incontestable. Steam locomotives were labour-intensive in a postwar society that was experiencing a labour shortage. No number of gadgets could disguise the fact that, at root, maintaining and servicing steam locomotives was the kind of dirty and laborious work that few were now prepared to undertake. Steam traction, in some quarters, had also become deeply unfashionable: an anachronism in the jet age. Across the Channel, the French had taken the world speed record – and by some margin, as two electric locomotives both broke the 200mph barrier.

The difficulty in Britain was that, at government level, the urge to modernize was tempered by one to compromise. Unlike in France, large-scale electrification was not an option. The West Coast Main Line linking London with the West Midlands, Manchester and Liverpool was the only trunk route deemed worthy of electrification on the 25kvAC overhead system. Instead, there was a hasty influx of assorted diesel classes, many of them underpowered and unreliable and some, quite simply, disastrous.

However, there was to be no turning back. Just two years after the completion of the last of BR Standard locomotives, 9F 2-10-0 No92220 *Evening Star*, came the first withdrawals. Many of the 999 Standards enjoyed working lives of less than ten years as, area-by-area, steam traction was eliminated. Its final stronghold was in north-west England and the last working steam depots at Carnforth, Rose Grove (Burnley) and Lostock Hall, near Preston, became places of pilgrimage. In August 1968, 138 years after the Liverpool & Manchester Railway had hosted the first inter-city trains, it was fitting that these same cities bade farewell to some of the last scheduled steam-hauled services. 11 August 1968 should have been the day the fires went out for the last time but, as many of the illustrations here show, British steam – and the British enthusiasm for steam locomotives – was not so easily extinguished.

SOUTHERN RAILWAY

'Merchant Navy' Class 8P 4-6-2

Few locomotive designs have polarized opinion as did the first of Oliver Bulleid's Pacific designs for the Southern Railway, the 'Merchant Navy'. Like its designer, the 'MN' was a combination of the ingenious and the impractical. At its best, it was a wonderful machine, free-steaming, powerful and smooth-riding. At its worst, it was a running shed foreman's nightmare. It was a locomotive that demanded as much as it gave.

The emergence of the first of the 'MNs', No21C1, from Eastleigh works on 17 February 1941, must have excited all who witnessed it. The novelty began with the outer casing, officially described as 'air-smoothed' rather than streamlined. Then there were the unusual-looking wheels which were based on the American 'boxpok' design. They were lighter than the traditional spoked wheel, but also stronger and gave all-round support to the tyre. Another innovation was the use of electric lighting, not only for headcode lamps and tail lights but to illuminate the injectors, driving wheels, front bogie, trailing truck and mechanical lubricators.

These were among the visible products of Bulleid's radical thinking. The key to the design, though, was the boiler. With a working pressure of 280lb/psi – higher than any other British locomotive – and a superheat temperature of 400°C, it was the best steam-raiser ever developed for a British locomotive. The firebox, too, broke new ground in being of all-welded steel construction rather than the traditional riveted copper. This brought savings in cost and weight but the fabrication process pushed contemporary welding technology to its limit. Within seven years, all the first ten boilers had to have their fireboxes replaced. X-ray inspections were introduced to monitor the state of the welding in other boilers.

The most controversial aspect of the design, however, was Bulleid's unique variety of valve gear. In theory, the idea of chain-driven valve gear operating within a totally enclosed oil bath, isolated from contamination and therefore virtually maintenance-free, was a fitter's dream. In practice, though, corrosion came from water oozing into

Above: Sporting 'Golden Arrow' regalia, an immaculate No35028 Clan Line stands outside Marylebone depot, London, in March 1985. It was rostered to haul an evening special to High Wycombe and return. Built at Eastleigh in 1948, and rebuilt there in 1959, Clan Line was bought by the Merchant Navy Locomotive Preservation Society in 1967.

Left: No35027 Port Line is one of three of the 11 surviving 'Merchant Navies' to have worked in preservation. Withdrawn from Weymouth depot in September 1966, Port Line languished in a scrapyard until 1982. Since the completion of its restoration in 1988, it has been based on the Bluebell Railway, where it was photographed approaching Horsted Keynes.

SR 'Merchant Navy' Class 8P 4-6-2

Built: Eastleigh works, 1941–49 (30 built)

Weight: 94 tons 4cwt/97 tons 18cwt* (locomotive)
48 tons 10cwt/53 tons 10cwt* (tender)

Driving wheel diameter: 6ft 2in

Boiler pressure: 280lb/psi/250lb/psi*

Cylinders: (3) 18in diameter x 24in stroke

Valve gear: Bulleid chain-driven/Walschaerts*

Coal capacity: 5 tons

Water capacity: 5,100 gallons/6,000 gallons*

Tractive effort: 37,515lb/33,495lb*
(at 85% boiler pressure)

(after rebuilding)*

the oil bath, while leaking oil induced wheelslip and, on many occasions, fire in the boiler lagging.

Dwelling on the failings of the 'Merchant Navy', though, would paint a misleading picture. Much about Bulleid's design was outstanding. His ingenious method of balancing eliminated the perennial problem of hammer-blow on the track. The trailing truck gave the smoothest of rides and was adopted for the British Railways Standard classes. The Pacific was heavy on coal and water but, in performance terms, delivered everything Bulleid had promised.

Soon after the delivery of No21C1 (Bulleid preferred the Continental style of incorporating the engine's wheel arrangement within its number), the decision was taken to name the new class. With the U-boat war in the Atlantic at its height, the Southern decided to honour the merchant seamen and shipping lines involved.

Construction of the 30 'Merchant Navies' occupied seven years, with the last being built after nationalization in 1949. The engines' new owners, British Railways, took a

long, hard look at the record cards and they did not make for impressive reading. Rebuilding began in 1956, with No35018 *British India Line*, and was completed by October 1959. The principal visible alterations were the replacement of the chain-driven valve gear by the Walschaerts variety, the removal of the air-smoothed casing and the substitution of the stovepipe chimney for a more conventional casting. Much else besides was changed, but the engineer in charge of the work, R.G. Jarvis, always maintained that the rebuilt Pacifics were 'still 90 per cent Bulleid'.

In their new guise, the 'MNs' put in several years' memorable service and showed they had lost none of their capacity for fast running. The 100mph mark was exceeded on occasions. Withdrawals began in 1964, but seven soldiered on until the last month of Southern steam, July 1967. Eleven escaped scrapping, including No35029 *Ellerman Lines* which is now a sectioned exhibit at the National Railway Museum in York. Three others have been restored to working order.

SOUTHERN RAILWAY

Q1 Class 5F 0-6-0

World War II brought a huge increase in freight traffic to the English Channel ports but the locomotive fleet of the primarily passenger-carrying Southern Railway was ill-equipped to deal with it. Its most up-to-date freight locomotive was the unremarkable Q class 0-6-0 of 1938, Richard Maunsell's last design for the company. His successor, Oliver Bulleid, acknowledged that more powerful machines were required. He also knew that, on the Southern, weight restrictions would compromise the usefulness of any eight- or ten-coupled heavy freight engine. The challenge led him to produce what would be the last class of British 0-6-0, the extraordinary inside-cylinder Q1 of 1942.

Wartime shortages dictated that Bulleid needed to save on materials as well as weight in designing the Q1. This meant dispensing with almost every traditional embellishment of the British locomotive, such as wheel splashers and running boards. Further weight savings came from the use of 'boxpok' wheels, which were half the weight of the spoked variety, and from the use of a material known as Idaglass for the boiler lagging. Since this could not bear any weight, it was not wrapped around the boiler as normal but supported on the frames, so giving the Q1 its unorthodox appearance. The boiler barrel itself was in one piece, tapering from 5ft 9in diameter to 5ft 0in. It was fed by a firegrate of 27sq ft area, the largest of any British 0-6-0. Bulleid shaped the smokebox to give a larger volume than the conventional circular type and into that fitted a 5-nozzle multiple jet blastpipe. This terminated in a brutally plain 'bucket' chimney. Throughout, to save weight and cost, fabrications were used instead of castings. The result was a locomotive developing over 30,000lb tractive effort but weighing only 51 tons 5cwt – around 14 tons lighter than other classes of comparable weight and power. The Q1 had the distinction of being not only the last, but the most powerful British 0-6-0.

Construction of the 40 Q1s was divided between the workshops at Brighton (NosC1-C16, C37-C40) and Ashford, Kent (C17-C36). All were delivered during 1942. Bulleid intended the engines to have a limited lifespan but

SR Q1 Class 5F 0-6-0

Built: Ashford and Brighton works, 1942 (40 built)

Weight: 51 tons 5cwt (locomotive) 38 tons 0cwt (tender)

Driving wheel diameter: 5ft 1in

Boiler pressure: 230lb/psi

Cylinders: (2) 19in diameter x 26in stroke

Valve gear: Stephenson link (outside admission piston valves)

Coal capacity: 5 tons

Water capacity: 3,700 gallons

Tractive effort: 30,080lb (at 85% boiler pressure)

Left: Although designed for goods work, the Q1s were no strangers to passenger haulage, as here. With a tractive effort of 30,080lb, it was the most powerful of all British 0-6-0s yet Bulleid's weight-saving schemes produced an engine and tender together weighing around 14 tons less than a conventional design of similar size and power.

the class remained intact for 21 years and was widely used, both by the Southern and by British Railways. Their haulage capacity was tempered only by a limited braking capability when hauling loose-coupled freights.

In the main, the Q1s were confined to the Southern's South Western and Central sections, although for a time some were allocated to Tonbridge in Kent. Examples were based at Eastleigh in Hampshire, Three Bridges in Sussex and at Hither Green in south-east London. The largest contingents were to be found at Guildford, in Surrey, and at Feltham in south-west London. The depot there served a large marshalling yard and its stud of Q1 0-6-0s was mainly rostered to work the North Downs line between Reading and Redhill, and on cross-London inter-regional freights. These took the Q1s to Acton, Willesden and Cricklewood, and to the Eastern Region yard at Temple Mills, near Stratford.

The first Q1 to be withdrawn was No33028 in February 1963. It had a defective cylinder that was deemed not worth repairing. The final trio, Nos33006, 33020 and 33027, were retired from Guildford in January 1966. The doyen of the class, NoC1 (33001), was selected to join the National Collection and has been on long-term loan to the Bluebell Railway.

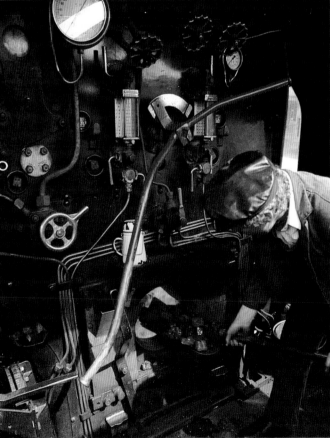

Left: Even today, the starkly functional appearance of Oliver Bulleid's wartime Q1 heavy freight 0-6-0 is startling. NoC1, pictured here at Sheffield Park on the Bluebell Railway, was the doyen of the class and enjoyed a working life of 22 years before being withdrawn from Guildford depot in 1964. It has been in the care of the Bluebell Railway since 1977.

Above: Firing the Q1, whose 27sq ft firegrate was the largest of any British 0-6-0. However, the boiler was a fine steam producer and, compared to other designs, firing was not onerous. Crews praised the Q1's haulage capabilities and the fair turn of speed its 5ft 1in wheels could deliver. The most prominent of the footplate controls is the red, double-handed regulator.

LONDON & NORTH EASTERN RAILWAY

B1 Class 5MT 4-6-0

The mixed traffic B1 4-6-0 was Edward Thompson's first new design for the LNER and unquestionably the most successful produced during his five-year reign. Thompson had taken over as chief mechanical engineer following the sudden death of Sir Nigel Gresley in 1941. Gresley had been planning to meet the LNER's need for a secondary passenger and fast freight locomotive with a production series of his 3-cylinder V4 2-6-2. Wisely, given the wartime conditions, Thompson abandoned the scheme in favour of something simpler and cheaper, both to build and maintain. However, the end product was straight out of the Gresley mould.

The prototype for the new B (later reclassified B1) class 4-6-0 was built at Darlington and entered service on 12 December 1942. It was the first 2-cylinder main-line locomotive constructed for the LNER since the Grouping, such had been Gresley's faith in the 3-cylinder layout. With cost savings a wartime priority, the LNER's draughtsmen went to great lengths to re-use existing patterns, jigs and tools to economize on materials and labour. Extensive use was made of welding instead of steel castings. The boiler was derived from the Diagram 100A type fitted to the B17 'Sandringham' 4-6-0s but with a larger grate area and an increase in boiler pressure to 225lb/psi.

The appearance of No8301 (subsequently renumbered No1000) coincided with a visit to Britain by the Prime Minister of South Africa, Field Marshal Jan Smuts. In his honour, the engine was named *Springbok*, the first of 40 to be named after breeds of antelope. The sixth to be built was named *Bongo* and this risible appellation soon became the nickname for the class. More illustriously, No1379 was named *Mayflower* after the ship that carried the Pilgrim Fathers to America. More mundanely, 18 other B1s took the names of LNER directors

Not that there were many B1s to be named during the war years. Constraints on production meant that the first ten were not completed until 1944. However, Thompson then placed substantial orders with two outside builders, Vulcan Foundry and the North British Locomotive Company of Glasgow. Between April 1946 and April 1952, NBL built 290 B1s. Over that period the cost of each rose from £14,893 to £16,190; Vulcan Foundry contributed 50 at £15,300 apiece. Orders for the B1s, which became Nos61000-61409 under British Railways auspices, totalled 410 but only 409 were ever in traffic. No61057 was written off after a collision in 1950 and never replaced.

As befits 'go anywhere' engines, the B1s operated throughout LNER territory. The first batch was distributed among depots on the former Great Eastern section: Ipswich, Norwich and Stratford, in London. They were an immediate success and were soon working the Liverpool Street-Harwich boat trains, the 'Hook Continental' and the 'Day Continental'. B1s were also a familiar sight on other top-link workings such as 'The East Anglian', 'The Broadsman' and 'The Fenman'. During the 1950s, over 70 B1s were stationed on ex-GE lines.

They enjoyed similar popularity on ex-Great Northern and Great Central territory, with engines based at Sheffield Darnall regularly rostered for the 'Master Cutler' and 'South Yorkshireman' expresses. Elsewhere, there were substantial allocations in Scotland, West Yorkshire and on Humberside. The first to be withdrawn, apart from the ill-fated No61057, was No61085 in November 1961. Officially, the class was rendered extinct in September 1967 but enthusiasts saved two from the scrapline: No1306, currently housed at the Nene Valley Railway near Peterborough, and the Thompson B1 Locomotive Trust's No1264. Based on the Great Central Railway in Leicestershire, this mercurial machine has not been without problems since its restoration in 1997. However, outstanding performances over the West Highland line in the summer of 1999 reinforced the view that the B1 was one of the most useful locomotives the LNER and BR possessed.

LNER B1 Class 5MT 4-6-0

Built: Darlington and Gorton works; North British Locomotive Company, Glasgow; Vulcan Foundry, Newton-le-Willows, Lancashire, 1942–52 (410 built)

Weight: 71 tons 3cwt (locomotive)
52 tons 0cwt (tender)

Driving wheel diameter: 6ft 2in

Boiler pressure: 225lb/psi

Cylinders: (2) 20in diameter x 26in stroke

Valve gear: Walschaerts (piston valves)

Coal capacity: 7.5 tons

Water capacity: 4,200 gallons

Tractive effort: 26,878lb (at 85% boiler pressure)

Above: The elder of the two surviving Thompson B1 4-6-0s is No1264, which was outshopped by the North British Locomotive Company of Glasgow on the eve of nationalization, in December 1947. The inscription 'Parkeston' on the bufferbeam refers to No1264's early years based at the Essex coast depot. Its final years were spent at Colwick, Nottingham.

Left: British Railways lined black livery suited the B1 4-6-0, unquestionably the most successful of Edward Thompson's designs. No61190, seen on shed at Holbeck, Leeds, on 28 June 1961, entered traffic in May 1947, based at Doncaster. For 15 years, between June 1950 and January 1965, it worked out of Immingham depot on Humberside.

WAR DEPARTMENT

'Austerity' Type 8F 2-10-0

As the tide of war turned in 1942, the Allies began planning the liberation of occupied Europe. Keeping the invasion forces supplied with munitions, vehicles, fuel and food would be vital. Railways would play an important role, but no reliance could be placed on the war-ravaged locomotive fleets of France, Belgium and The Netherlands. Britain and the United States therefore embarked on a huge programme of locomotive construction.

The brief was straightforward: these machines had to be quick and cheap to build, easy to maintain and able to run on whatever quality of fuel was available. In Britain, they were tagged 'Austerities'. They also had to cope with track hastily relaid after bombing or sabotage and this demanded a lighter-than-normal axleloading. Anticipating the varying conditions in which the locomotives would have to work, the firebox was designed for quick conversion from coal to oil-firing. Additionally, much tender-first running was expected and an inset bunker improved rearwards vision.

Britain contributed two types of locomotive: a 2-8-0 and a 2-10-0, both drawn up by a team headed by Robert Riddles. Although only 150 of the latter were built, they were unquestionably the finer engines. All the 2-10-0s were constructed by the North British Locomotive Company in Glasgow. The first appeared in December 1943 and the last in September 1945.

Many of the early engines saw service on two of Britain's railways, the LMSR and the LNER, before their military call-up. Between August and November 1944, they were ferried from Southampton to Dieppe to take up duties in France and Belgium. Some were sent on to the Middle East, principally Egypt and Syria. In February 1945, Major General D.J. McMullen, the Allies' Director of Transportation, wrote to Robert Riddles:

'Everyone loves the 2-10-0. It is quite the best freight engine ever turned out in Great Britain and does well even on Belgian "duff" which is more like porridge than coal!'

On 9 May 1945, the day after Germany's surrender, WD 2-10-0 No73755 became the 1,000th 'war locomotive' shipped to Europe.

The 'Austerities' continued to perform useful work in peacetime. Four remained in Syria, while 16 of the Egyptian contingent were transferred (at a cost of £12,500 each) to the Hellenic Railways of Greece. By far the largest number – 103 – congregated in The Netherlands where some continued working until the mid-1950s.

Given its restricted route availability, Britain's railways were less enthusiastic about adopting the long-wheelbase ten-coupled 'Austerity'. Its eight-coupled cousin was preferred. Unlike Germany or the United States, Britain had

Above: Pictured at Alresford, on the Mid-Hants Railway, WD 2-10-0 No601 Sturdee is surrounded by the kind of vehicles it would have encountered during its two years 'military service' in Egypt (1944–46). It then spent 28 years with Greece's Hellenic State Railways.

Above: Like No601 (left), WD No3672 was one of 16 2-10-0s shipped to Greece in January 1946, where it became Hellenic State Railways LB class No960. Along with its classmate, it returned to Britain in 1984 and both are now based on the North Yorkshire Moors Railway.

no tradition of using ten-coupled engines. The 0-10-0 wheel arrangement was only ever employed on two locomotives (the Midland Railway's Lickey Incline banker and the Great Eastern's 'Decapod') and the 2-10-0 was unknown. Nevertheless, British Railways did take 25 2-10-0s into stock, WD Nos73774-96/98-99 becoming BR Nos90750-74. Apart from rare loan spells, they spent their days on freight traffic in southern Scotland and were allocated principally to the depots at Carlisle Kingmoor, Motherwell and Grangemouth. All were retired between 1961 and 1962.

Happily, at least four of the WD 2-10-0s have survived. Several were retained by the Army and the last of those, No600 *Gordon* (WD No73651), can be seen on the Severn Valley Railway. Two engines repatriated from Greece have found homes on the North Yorkshire Moors Railway, No601 *Sturdee* (WD No73652) and No3672 *Dame Vera Lynn* (WD No73672). That historic 1,000th engine, No73755, is on display in Utrecht's transport museum, honouring the contribution made by its type to the revival of rail transport in postwar Holland.

Above: Close-up of the Walschaerts gear of NoWD600 Gordon. *Built by North British as WD No73651 in December 1943, it worked on the Longmoor Military Railway in Hampshire until 1969. Though now based on the Severn Valley Railway, the engine remains MoD property!*

WD 'Austerity' Type 8F 2-10-0

Built: North British Locomotive Company, Hyde Park works, Glasgow, 1943–45 (150 built)

Weight: 78 tons 17cwt (locomotive)
55 tons 10cwt (tender)

Driving wheel diameter: 4ft 8½in

Boiler pressure: 225lb/psi

Cylinders: (2) 19in diameter x 28in stroke

Valve gear: Walschaerts (10in diameter piston valves)

Coal capacity: 9 tons

Water capacity: 5,000 gallons

Tractive effort: 34,215lb (at 85% boiler pressure)

WAR DEPARTMENT

'Austerity' Saddletank 4F 0-6-0ST

Moving loaded 16-ton coal wagons around a colliery or power station; dragging iron-ore hoppers about a steelworks; even supplying an army with fuel and ammunition are tasks that call for a locomotive of rugged, no-frills simplicity, brute strength and dogged reliability. The Hunslet six-coupled saddletanks met all those requirements. They were the last steam locomotives to be built for Britain's industrial railways and many of the 73-or-so survivors are working on in preservation.

The type originated in the 1930s. There was an urgent need for a more powerful breed of locomotive to undertake shunting and transfer work within large industrial complexes such as steelworks. Companies approached the Hunslet Engine Company of Leeds, in West Yorkshire, for a new design to meet this requirement. Hunslet proposed a development of its successful saddletank design of 1923, but using 18-inch instead of 16-inch diameter cylinders. The idea was accepted and, in 1937, the first order was placed for this new class of

inside-cylinder heavy shunting engine. Hunslet listed it as the '50550' class and, had it not been for events two years later, the locomotives might have enjoyed only the relative anonymity of industrial usage.

World War II brought a new customer for the Hunslet saddletank – the British government. The Ministry of Supply, acting on behalf of the War Department, needed shunting locomotives for military use. The first choice was the proven Fowler 3F 0-6-0T of the LMSR but Edgar Alcock, Hunslet's chairman, argued for his more modern '50550'. It certainly met the performance target: a minimum of two years' work between overhauls, regardless of operating conditions, and the ability to start a 1,000 ton train on the level, or a train of 300 tons on a gradient of 1 in 50. Alcock won the day and in January 1943 the Leeds factory outshopped its first engine for the MoS. However, demand soon outstripped Hunslet's production of four to five engines a month. Construction was sub-contracted to six other builders with Hunslet

Above: Introduced in 1943, the Hunslet 'Austerity' saddletank became the mainstay of railway operations at many collieries, steelworks and other industrial concerns. Today, several preserved railways rely on them for motive power, among them Peak Rail in Derbyshire whose No68006 is pictured here awaiting departure from Darley Dale on 26 October 1997. The original No68006 (this locomotive is masquerading as it) was one of 75 saddletanks acquired by the LNER in 1946–47, becoming its J94 class and numbered 68006-80.

overseeing deliveries and acting as a central ordering point for components and materials. Over the next four years, 377 entered service.

Although the end of the war left many engines surplus to military requirements, new civilian roles awaited them. After No71486 had impressed during trials in November 1945, the LNER acquired 75, classifying them J94 and numbering them 8006 to 8080. All entered British Railways stock in 1948 and were used at locations such as Immingham and Hull docks, and at Ferme Park yard in London. Their most famous exploits, however, came on the tortuous curves and formidable gradients of the Cromford & High Peak branch in Derbyshire. The J94s proved themselves to be the masters of this moorland line until its closure in 1967.

The LNER was not the only customer for redundant saddletanks. The newly formed National Coal Board bought 47 and found them so useful that they promptly ordered a new batch from Hunslets. At one time, 234 were in NCB service. Further orders came from steel companies, and – surprisingly – from the Army. During the 1950s and 1960s, the '50550' was the most numerous

steam locomotive in industrial service in Britain and Hunslet continued construction up to 1964. The final two examples, bought by the NCB at £15,000 apiece, took the class total to 484.

The stock was gradually reduced, either through the introduction of diesels or the contraction of the coal and steel industries. Nevertheless, it was only in the 1980s that the last of the saddletanks was retired from colliery use. Over its 40 years' working life, the Hunslet design was little altered, although there were some significant modifications to postwar examples. These included the use of Giesl ejectors to make more productive use of the exhaust blast, automatic underfeed stokers, four-jet blastpipes, and copper fireboxes instead of steel. Some engines were fuelled by a gas system to obtain smokeless operation. Even the most rugged types can benefit from a little refinement!

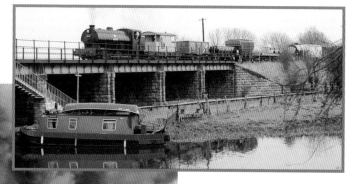

Above: On the kind of short-haul freight duty for which it was designed, the Nene Valley Railway's No68081 crosses the River Nene at Wansford. A Hunslet product of 1943, this saddletank became War Department No75006. It was sold into private ownership in 1952 and worked in open-cast collieries in Northumberland until 1968. It ended its days at Onllwyn, Glamorgan, before being privately preserved in 1976. After a five-year restoration, No68081 entered NVR service in 1984.

Above: 'Austerity' saddletank No3809, built by Hunslet in 1954, was one of its class fitted with the Austrian-developed Giesl ejector. Now based on the North Norfolk Railway, No3809 turns on the 'clag' as it storms away from Sheringham, having just slowed to collect the single line token from the signalman. It is at the head of an afternoon service to Holt on 3 September 1995.

WD 'Austerity' Saddletank 4F 0-6-0ST

Built: Hunslet Engine Company, Leeds; Hudswell Clarke & Co., Leeds; W.G. Bagnall, Stafford; Robert Stephenson & Hawthorn, Newcastle-upon-Tyne and Darlington; Vulcan Foundry, Newton-le-Willows, Lancashire; Andrew Barclay & Sons Co., Kilmarnock; Yorkshire Engine Company, Sheffield, 1943–64 (484 built)

Weight: 48 tons 5cwt

Driving wheel diameter: 4ft 3in

Boiler pressure: 170lb/psi

Cylinders: (2) 18in diameter x 26in stroke

Valve gear: Stephenson (slide valves)

Coal capacity: 2 tons 5cwt

Water capacity: 1,200 gallons

Tractive effort: 23,870lb
(at 85% boiler pressure)

GREAT WESTERN RAILWAY

6959 'Modified Hall' Class 5MT 4-6-0

Frederick William Hawksworth succeeded Charles Collett as chief mechanical engineer of the Great Western in 1941. He was 57. That it had taken such a talented individual so long to reach the top of the ladder (Hawksworth had joined the GWR in 1898, aged 15) was in part due to the reluctance of his predecessor to relinquish the post. However, it was also a reflection of a complacency and lack of initiative among the GW hierarchy. After being in the vanguard of locomotive development throughout the first three decades of the 20th century, Swindon had stagnated. Its pioneering ideas had been taken up and pursued by the likes of Gresley and Stanier.

Hawksworth had the experience, ability and vision to regain that lost initiative. Circumstances, unfortunately, would conspire against him. Several bold ideas were frustrated by wartime conditions and, after 1945, by the growth of corporate responsibility for motive power policy (in the shape of the government-appointed Railway Executive). He devised a 4-6-2 which, in theory, would have been the most powerful express passenger locomotive ever built in Britain. When its rejection coincided with the Southern's Oliver Bulleid gaining approval for his far more radical 'Merchant Navy' design, Hawksworth was understandably

angered. Throughout his eight years in charge on the GWR, Hawksworth generally had to settle for making his mark with the pragmatic rather than the prestigious.

Ostensibly, the first of his designs was an update, yet the construction of the 'Modified Halls' marked the most radical change in Swindon practice since the Churchward era. Hawksworth's use of plate frames throughout the design was a daring break with the Churchward gospel. The cylinders were cast separately from the smokebox saddle and bolted to the frames on each side. A stiffening brace was inserted between the frames and extended to form the smokebox saddle. The exhaust pipes leading from the cylinders to the blastpipe were incorporated into this assembly.

Additionally, Churchward's bar-frame bogie, which had been adapted for the original 'Hall' in 1924, was replaced by a plate-frame structure with individual springing. There were changes, too, above the running board. Hawksworth decided that the declining quality of coal reaching the Great Western's depots necessitated a higher degree of superheating. A larger three-row superheater and header regulator were fitted into the Swindon No1 boiler.

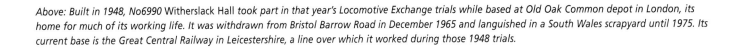

Above: Built in 1948, No6990 Witherslack Hall *took part in that year's Locomotive Exchange trials while based at Old Oak Common depot in London, its home for much of its working life. It was withdrawn from Bristol Barrow Road in December 1965 and languished in a South Wales scrapyard until 1975. Its current base is the Great Central Railway in Leicestershire, a line over which it worked during those 1948 trials.*

Improvements were subsequently made to the draughting on some engines, while others were fitted with hopper ashpans. Many of the later examples were attached to Hawksworth's simplifed design of straight-sided tender which gave the crew greater protection from the elements.

The first of the 'Modified Halls' was outshopped from Swindon in 1944. It carried plain black livery and was unnamed (it was to be another three years before all of the initial batch of 12 locomotives received names). In total, the class numbered 71 when construction ceased in 1950 and carried the numbers 6959-99 and 7900-29. The 6959 class 4-6-0s ran freely, steamed well, and were popular with both footplate and maintenance staff. After the unambitious designs of Collett's final years, they restored Swindon's reputation, and 14 soldiered on to the end of steam on BR's Western Region in 1965. Seven have been preserved.

Above: Posing by the coal stage at Didcot Railway Centre on 8 May 1995, No6998 Burton Agnes Hall *entered traffic in January 1949, allocated to Cardiff Canton shed. After spells at Shrewsbury and Fishguard, and in the West Midlands and London areas, on New Year's Day 1966, No6998 had the melancholy duty of hauling the last steam-hauled train on BR's Western Region, between Oxford and Banbury. It is now owned by the Didcot-based Great Western Society.*

Above: Sporting the 'Cornish Riviera Express' headboard is No6960 Raveningham Hall *which was sent new to Old Oak Common, London, in March 1944. It subsequently worked out of Reading and Oxford depots before withdrawal in June 1964. Acquired for preservation in 1972, No6960 was overhauled in time to represent the GWR at the Rail 150 cavalcade held at Shildon, County Durham, in 1975. Subsequently, No6960 spent some 20 years on the Severn Valley Railway, from whose Bridgnorth terminus it is seen departing with a train for Kidderminster.*

GWR 6959 'Modified Hall' Class 5MT 4-6-0

Built: Swindon works, 1944–50 (71 built)

Weight: 75 tons 16cwt (locomotive)
46 tons 14cwt (tender)

Driving wheel diameter: 6ft 0in

Boiler pressure: 225lb/psi

Cylinders: (2) 18½in diameter x 30in stroke

Valve gear: Stephenson (piston valves)

Coal capacity: 6 tons

Water capacity: 4,000 gallons

Tractive effort: 27,275lb (at 85% boiler pressure)

SOUTHERN RAILWAY

'WC'/'BB' Class Pacifics 7P5F 4-6-2

Essentially a scaled-down version of the 'Merchant Navy' of 1941, the first of Oliver Bulleid's 'light Pacifics' – No21C101 – was outshopped from Brighton works in May 1945. Over the following six years, it would be joined by a further 109 engines, with Brighton sharing construction with the ex-L&SWR works at Eastleigh. From possessing not a single Pacific-type locomotive, in ten years the Southern Railway assembled a fleet of 140. Whether the smallest of the 'big four' companies, whose longest run was from London to the north coast of Cornwall, needed quite so many express passenger engines is a question that remains open to debate.

As it had done so brilliantly with the 'King Arthurs', 'Lord Nelsons' and 'Schools', the Southern's astute publicity department saw an opportunity in the new arrivals. They were named after cities, towns and tourist spots in south-west England, beginning with Devon's cathedral city of Exeter, where No21C101 was named in a ceremony on 10 July 1945.

However, in November 1946, by which time 48 'West Countries' were in traffic, the naming policy changed. The class was beginning to be based on the Central and Eastern Sections and names were chosen which would be appreciated in the counties of Kent and Sussex: those of the aircraft, airfields, Royal Air Force squadrons and key personalities that had fought in the Battle of Britain only six years previously.

The 'WC' and 'BB' Pacifics, as their titles were abbreviated, shared many of the components and design features of their bigger brethren, the 'Merchant Navies'. These included the 'air-smoothed' casing and Bulleid's innovative, if problematic, chain-driven valve gear. The principal changes were aimed at saving weight in an attempt to broaden the new locomotives' route availability. They were successful, and the axleloading of just over 18 tons allowed the light Pacifics to work over almost all the Southern system.

Production of the new Pacifics continued at rates of between one and four a month up to December 1948, by which time 89 were in traffic. The following year saw just 11 built, including the first three from Eastleigh. Nine more engines emerged between February and May 1950, at

Seen accelerating away from Rothley with a Great Central service for Leicester North, rebuilt 'West Country' No34039 Boscastle *is a tribute to the perseverance of today's locomotive restorers.*

SR 'WC'/'BB' Class Pacifics 7P5F 4-6-2

Built: Brighton and Eastleigh works, 1945–51 (110 built)

Weight: 86 tons 0cwt (locomotive)
42 tons 12cwt/47 tons 15cwt/47 tons 18cwt (tender)
(weights varied with water capacity – see below)

Driving wheel diameter: 6ft 2in

Boiler pressure: 280lb/psi (later reduced to 250lb/psi)

Cylinders: (3) $16\frac{1}{8}$in diameter x 24in stroke

Valve gear: Bulleid (chain driven)/Walschaerts
(piston valves) (after rebuilding)

Coal capacity: 5 tons

Water capacity: 4,500/5,000/5,500 gallons
(according to size of tender)

Tractive effort: 27,720lb (at 85% boiler pressure)

which point construction was halted with just one more locomotive on order. There was speculation that it was undergoing a major re-design to overcome the failings of some of Bulleid's more suspect innovations. Although now working in the Republic of Ireland, Bulleid made his disapproval plain and No34110 *66 Squadron* emerged untouched from Brighton works in January 1951. The seed of change had been sown, however.

The fundamental drawback of mechanisms such as Bulleid's chain-driven gear was that they demanded a level of maintenance that, in the 1950s, was no longer justifiable or even, in some areas, available. In 1956, a scheme was drawn up to rebuild all 30 'Merchant Navies' along conventional lines and, the following year, the decision was taken to apply the same treatment to 60 of the light Pacifics. There were many detail alterations, but the fundamental changes were the subsitution of Walschaerts valve gear and the removal of the air-smoothed casing. In its place, large square smoke deflectors were fitted.

Whatever the failings of the original, few would dispute that, as a steam-raiser, the Bulleid boiler was unsurpassed. Even if their fuel consumption was on the high side, the Pacifics' performance level was outstanding, whether speeding to the resort towns of the West Country or storming the banks at the head of boat trains for the Channel ports. Electrification, first of the Kent coast routes and then of the Bournemouth line, spelt the end for the Bulleids, although 21 light Pacifics remained on the books until the last day of Southern steam in July 1967.

Incredibly, no less than 20 'West Countries' and 'Battle of Britains' eluded the cutter's torch, nine of them in unrebuilt condition. Altogether, nine have been restored to working order including No34027 *Taw Valley* and No34092 *City of Wells* which have been responsible for some stirring main-line runs in recent years.

Above: Brighton-built in March 1950, 'West Country' No34105 Swanage *retained its original streamlined, or 'air-smoothed' casing. Based at Bournemouth almost until its withdrawal in October 1964, No34105 was subsequently preserved and returned to working order on the Mid-Hants Railway.*

Right: Bulleid Pacifics in tandem as rebuilt 'Merchant Navy' No35005 Canadian Pacific *pilots 'West Country' No34101* Hartland *through Swithland on the Great Central Railway. The latter is the sole survivor from only six Bulleid 'light Pacifics' built at Eastleigh, entering traffic in February 1950. It was withdrawn in July 1966.*

LONDON MIDLAND & SCOTTISH RAILWAY

2MT Class Mogul 2-6-0

In the aftermath of World War II, the LMSR took stock of its locomotive fleet and its likely future requirements. It concluded that all its locomotive needs could be met by just 11 types. The colossal restocking of the Stanier era had left Britain's largest railway company well supplied with express passenger, secondary passenger, mixed traffic and heavy freight loocmotives. All that was missing were lightweight designs to replace the large numbers of elderly engines that the weight-restricted secondary and branch lines still relied upon.

In 1946, the LMSR's chief mechanical engineer, George Ivatt, drew up schemes for a 2-6-0 tender locomotive and 2-6-2 tank in the class 2 power category. The proposed maximum axleloading of just 13 tons 11cwt would impose very few restrictions on route availability. Evident throughout was Ivatt's insistence on simple, easy maintenance and efficient operation. Most of the components – including the Swindon-style taper boiler with separate dome and top feed – were standardized between the two designs.

Likely operating conditions were thoroughly assessed, as were ways of reducing the laborious tasks of engine preparation and disposal. Crews enjoyed the provision of rocking grates, self-emptying ashpans, self-cleaning smokeboxes and side-window cabs. The enclosed tender cab and inset bunker took the discomfort and difficulty out of working tender- and bunker-first. (This was bound to be a regular occurrence given the absence of turntables on many secondary lines.) In all practical aspects, right down to the ladder at the rear that gave quick, safe access to the water filler cap, the Ivatt Class 2 Mogul and its tank

equivalent were the most modern small engines produced for a British railway for decades.

Initially, however, the 2-6-0 tender design did not deliver the expected performance. The finger of blame pointed at the draughting and a number of experiments were conducted with blastpipe diameters and chimney types, both at Derby and Swindon. The problem solved, the Ivatt Mogul was able to show what an economical machine it was. It also rode well and was capable of rapid acceleration and a fair turn of speed.

By nationalization in 1948, only 20 Moguls had been delivered but the newly formed British Railways continued construction for a further five years. By the end of 1953, 128 were in service, with just over half the class being constructed at Crewe. In 1947, No6417 had the honour of becoming the last locomotive built there under LMS auspices. However, their activities were not confined to LMS territory. Eighteen engines from a batch constructed at Darlington went to the Eastern (five) and North Eastern (13) Regions and the final 25 were allocated the Western. These were also built at the ex-Great Western works at Swindon which, showing characteristic independence, dispensed with the prescribed lined black livery and turned its quota out in lined green. And very smart they looked, as the now-preserved No46521 of the Severn Valley Railway testifies.

The first Ivatt 2-6-0 to be withdrawn was No46407, in1961, but 39 lasted until 1967. Seven have been preserved and three of those have been restored to working order. All three have also worked main-line specials in recent years.

Above: Built in 1953, No46521 was one of 25 Ivatt Moguls built at Swindon and it spent its working life in central Wales. During a loan spell on the Gloucestershire Warwickshire Railway in 1993, No46521 departs Winchcombe with an afternoon train for Toddington.

Above: In its inauthentic, but undeniably smart, crimson lake livery, Crewe-built No46441 displays some of the key features of the design: the tender, with its inset bunker and cab; the Belpaire firebox, taper boiler and top feed; and the Walschaerts valve gear.

LMSR 2MT Class Mogul 2-6-0

Built: Crewe, Darlington and
Swindon works, 1946–53
(128 built)

Weight: 47 tons 2cwt (locomotive)
37 tons 3cwt (tender)

Driving wheel diameter: 5ft 0in

Boiler pressure: 200lb/psi

Cylinders: (2) 16in* diameter x
24in stroke

Valve gear: Walschaerts
(piston valves)

Coal capacity: 4 tons

Water capacity: 3,000 gallons

Tractive effort: 17,410/18,510lb*
(at 85% boiler pressure)

(from No46465, the cylinder
diameter was increased to
16½in with a resulting
increase in tractive effort)*

Above: No46443 is one of seven Ivatt 2MT 2-6-0s in preservation and, like No46521 (opposite), is based on the Severn Valley Railway. It is seen pulling into Bewdley with a Kidderminster-Bridgnorth service on 13 June 1993. No46443 spent most of its working life at Derby but was a Newton Heath (Manchester) engine upon withdrawal in March 1967.

LONDON MIDLAND & SCOTTISH RAILWAY

2MT Class Prairie Tank 2-6-2T

The Ivatt 2MT 2-6-2T of 1946 has been described as Britain's best branch-line locomotive. This accolade stemmed, in part, from a shrewd move by its designer, George Ivatt. Before the locomotive went into production, Ivatt had a full-size mock-up built and invited comments from both footplate crews and maintenance staff. This enabled worthwhile improvements to be incorporated at the drawing-board stage

As any side-by-side comparison would reveal, the undoubted inspiration for the Ivatt tank was Churchward's GWR 4500/4575 class Prairie of 1906. The Ivatt, though, took full advantage of new technology developed over the ensuing 40 years. Like its tender engine equivalent (previous page), it was equipped with the latest in labour-saving devices. Although 2 tons 5cwt heavier than the Churchward engine, better weight distribution gave the Ivatt an axleloading 2 tons 6cwt lighter, just 13 tons 5cwt.

In many key respects, the 2MT 2-6-2T and 2-6-0 were identical. They had the same boiler pressure, coupled wheel diameter and grate area (17½sq ft), and shared a tube heating surface of 924½sq ft. The superheater surfaces both added up to 134sq ft, while the firebox contributed 101sq ft. Another feature in common was the improvement in draughting obtained after evaluation on the Swindon test bed.

Though designed for the LMSR, only ten of the Ivatt tanks wore the company's livery. The remainder were constructed for British Railways, and the 130-strong class became Nos41200-41329. No41272 had the distinction of being the 7,000th locomotive built at Crewe works, and sported commemorative plaques. It was also one of 50 engines (Nos41210-29, 41270-89 and 41320-29) fitted with vacuum control gear for push-pull operation. Vacuum-controlled auxiliary regulator valves were fitted in each steampipe leading from the superheater header to the cylinders. These were operated mechanically by linkage from a diaphragm-type vacuum cylinder. The driver was able to operate these valves from a compartment at the front of the train. His fireman remained on the locomotive but communication between the two crewmen was maintained through a system of bell codes.

The usefulness of the Ivatt tanks is confirmed by the range of their operations. As well as being located throughout former LMSR territory, they could be found in north Wales, Devon, Somerset and in south-east England. The first deliveries replaced ageing L&NWR 2-4-2 and 0-6-2 tanks, as well as Midland 0-4-4 tanks, on branch-line work. Bletchley engines were used on the Newport Pagnell branch and between Leighton Buzzard and Dunstable. Bedford's allocation was employed on the line

Above: One of four surviving Ivatt Prairie tanks, No41312 was built at Crewe in May 1952 and spent its 15-year British Railways career on the Southern Region being based at Faversham, Ashford (Kent), Barnstaple, Brighton, Bournemouth – from where it worked the last steam-hauled service over the Lymington branch in April 1967 – and Nine Elms (London). It can now be found at work on the Mid-Hants Railway.

LMSR 2MT Class Prairie Tank 2-6-2T

Built: Crewe and Derby works, 1946–52 (130 built)

Weight: 63tons 5cwt /65tons 4cwt*

Driving wheel diameter: 5ft 0in

Boiler pressure: 200lb/psi

Cylinders: 16in/16½in* diameter x 24in stroke

Valve gear: Walschaerts (piston valves)

Coal capacity: 3 tons

Water capacity: 1,350 gallons

Tractive effort: 17,410lb/18,510lb*
  (at 85% boiler pressure)

(from No41290 on, cylinder diameter increased
  by ½in with consequent increase in weight and
  tractive effort)*

Above: Since 1949-built No41241 spent several years working out of Bath depot, this scene, in the company of 'West Country' Pacific No34092 City of Wells, could easily be from its Somerset and Dorset days. Instead, the pair were pictured in June 1983 at Haworth, on the Keighley & Worth Valley Railway.

Above: Front-end details of the Ivatt 2-6-2T No41241 including the boiler top feed, steampipe, lubricator and sandbox filler cap. The 10G shedplate on the smokebox door indicates a Skipton, North Yorkshire, engine.

to Hitchin, while Watford locomotives worked to St Albans (Abbey) and from Harrow and Wealdstone to Stanmore. Neasden's 2-6-2Ts replaced ex-Great Central Class C13 4-4-2 tanks on the Chesham branch. Rugby engines hauled locals to Leamington Spa and Coventry, as well as working the Weedon-Leamington branch. Bristol Barrow Road's stud made regular appearances on the ex-Midland joint line between Bath Green Park and Mangotsfield. Others were employed on Somerset and Dorset services between Highbridge and Burnham-on-Sea. In north Wales, the allocations at Bangor and Llandudno Junction travelled widely, including over the Blaenau Ffestiniog branch.

Electrification had long been the priority on the Southern Region which meant that the Ivatt engines, by a considerable margin, became its most modern passenger tanks. They were often called upon to undertake duties rostered for class 4 power and acquitted themselves remarkably well. The Southern distributed its allocation far-and-wide, from Faversham in Kent to Barnstaple in Devon. They were also based at Plymouth, Eastleigh and Stewarts Lane in London. A few ended their days on pilot and empty stock workings at London's Waterloo terminus.

The last of the Ivatt tanks was withdrawn by British Railways in 1967, but four have survived. Two of those have been restored to working order: No41241 on the Keighley & Worth Valley Railway and No41312 on the Mid-Hants Railway. The other pair, Nos41298 and 41313 are destined one day to work on the Isle of Wight Steam Railway.

LONDON MIDLAND & SCOTTISH RAILWAY

4MT Class Mogul 2-6-0

If ever a British engine looked all-American it was the Ivatt 4MT Mogul. To those accustomed to the traditional clean lines and well-hidden plumbing of the UK product, it was a culture shock to rival that delivered by Bulleid's Southern Railway Q1 0-6-0 of five years earlier. George Ivatt, the chief mechanical engineer of the LMSR, undoubtedly became acquainted with current American practice during World War II. In the period leading up to the D-Day landings of June 1944, large numbers of the US Army Transportation Corps S160 2-8-0s were used on Britain's railways. They then took up their intended role of supplying the liberating armies in Europe but left a lasting impression in some quarters.

Characteristic features of the S160, and of American design in general, found their way into Ivatt's last contribution to the restocking of the LMS's locomotive fleet, the 4MT 2-6-0. The prototype which emerged from the ex-Lancashire & Yorkshire Railway workshops at Horwich, near Bolton, in 1947 was utterly devoid of frills. The emphasis was on economy, both in construction and running costs. Ivatt had produced the machine postwar austerity demanded. It had an axleloading low enough to work on secondary routes, and the power to better the performance of the elderly 0-6-0s that it would replace.

Though produced for the London Midland & Scottish, only three were built in time to wear LMSR colours before nationalization on 1 January 1948. Construction continued, however, with the ex-LNER works at Doncaster and Darlington joining Horwich to produce, by 1952, a total of 162. British Railways numbered them 43000 to 43161. Besides such startlingly distinctive (for Britain) features as the fully exposed driving wheels, high running boards, very visible pipework, absence of front drop-plate and high-pitched cab, the early examples also sported an enormous double chimney. This was a consequence of its twin exhaust outlets being angled outwards in opposite directions, so requiring an unusually long casting. The effect of this device on the draughting, and therefore the combustion and steam-raising properties of the design, was unfortunately dire.

Trials were conducted using a singularly ugly stovepipe chimney before the specification was altered to a straightforward single blastpipe and chimney. Existing locomotives were modified to suit and further improvements in the draughting were achieved by the ex-Great Western team at Swindon. After the modifications, the full potential of Ivatt's design, which had an excellent boiler, could finally be realized.

When required, the Ivatt 4MTs displayed a fair turn of speed. Usually, though, they were found on unspectacular secondary duties. Their allocations extended beyond London Midland territory into the Eastern and North Eastern regions, and ten found their way to Scotland. Their reputations were made, though, in East Anglia and the northern Pennines. The Midland & Great Northern Joint line that meandered through northern Cambridgeshire and Norfolk became home to 34, while another group had the task of battling both the gradients and the climate on the trans-Pennine Stainforth route between Darlington and Tebay. In contrast, the 4MTs regularly worked the boat trains which ran from London's St Pancras to the port of Tilbury on the Thames estuary.

Alongside ease-of-access, Ivatt's quest to lighten the maintenance burden also saw the fitting of rocker grates, self-cleaning smokeboxes and hopper ashpans. All were features which became compulsory on the later British Railways Standard designs.

The Ivatt 4MT 2-6-0 did much useful, if unspectacular, work. Its role was as plainly functional as its looks. The first withdrawals took place in 1963 but four of the class hung on until the end of British Railways steam working in 1968. One has survived into preservation, No43106, on the Severn Valley Railway (where it is affectionately known as 'The Flying Pig'!).

Above: Undergoing cleaning in Bridgnorth yard on the Severn Valley Railway is the sole survivor from the once 162-strong Ivatt 4MT Moguls, No43106. Ease of maintenance was a key aspect of the design, hence the high running plate fully exposing wheels and motion, and the plentiful exterior pipework. Darlington-built in 1951, No43106 arrived on the SVR straight out of British Railways service in 1968.

LMSR 4MT Class Mogul 2-6-0

Built: Darlington, Doncaster and Horwich works, 1947–52 (162 built)

Weight: 59 tons 2cwt (locomotive)
40 tons 6cwt (tender)

Driving wheel diameter: 5ft 3in

Boiler pressure: 225lb/psi

Cylinders: (2) 17½in diameter x 26in stroke

Valve gear: Walschaerts (piston valves)

Coal capacity: 4 tons 0cwt

Water capacity: 3,500 gallons

Tractive effort: 24,170lb (at 85% boiler pressure)

Above: No43106 crosses the Severn at Victoria Bridge near Arley with an afternoon Bridgnorth-Bewdley service in September 1982. The bridge was built by John Fowler in 1861. At this time, No43106 was one of the locomotives approved for main-line running.

Below: No43106 spent the first five years of its life allocated to South Lynn depot in Norfolk and worked over the ex-Midland & Great Northern Joint Railway system linking Peterborough, March, King's Lynn, Cromer and Yarmouth. Working in tandem with the SVR's set of ex-LNER Gresley teak coaches, therefore, is wholly appropriate.

1500/9400 Class Panniers 4F 0-6-0PT

The 9400 and 1500 classes were the last shunting engines built for the Great Western Railway and, like the majority of their predecessors, they were pannier tanks. The 9400 was essentially an update of the 5700 class of 1929. That, in its turn, was based on a design from the Victorian era. In 1946, over 800 of the 5700s were in service, yet the running department put in a request for yet more shunters. The first response of the GWR's chief mechanical engineer, F.W. Hawksworth, was simply to restart the 5700 production line. The story goes that this was overruled by the GWR chairman, Sir James Milne. He thought it was time the public saw empty stock workings into and out of London's Paddington Station being handled by something a little less antique-looking!

While the prototype, No9400, displayed some updated features when it appeared in 1947, it was not a radical departure from GW tradition. The brass safety valve bonnet and copper-capped chimney were still there, as were the inside cylinders and Stephenson valve gear. Nine more appeared from Swindon in the same year, the last engines to be built by the Great Western Railway.

Without question, the 9400s did prove useful engines but as shunters they began with one significant drawback. The increased cab width over the 5700 meant that the regulator and brake valve controls were less accessible to the driver while looking out of the cab during shunting operations. Complaints were lodged and modifications made, including the fitting of a second, pivoted handle to the brake valve.

Another flaw in the design was less easy to correct. Fitting the coned and domeless Swindon Standard No10 boiler brought the weight of the 9400 up to 55 tons 6cwt, six tons heavier than the 5700. This forced the civil engineer severely to restrict where the 9400 could go – not ideal in an engine intended to work in all manner of goods yards and carriage sidings. Having got their new shunters, the operating people – who would have been happy with a repeat order of 5700 tanks – now found they were limited in where they could use them.

In traffic, the 9400s demonstrated how Churchward's setting of the Stephenson valve gear was ideal in arduous low-speed conditions. This was most evident on the Lickey incline between Bristol and Birmingham where a number acted as banking engines. The sight of three, or even four, of these pannier tanks pushing a heavy freight up the grade for all they were worth was a memorable sight.

GWR 9400 and 1500 Class 4F 0-6-0PTs

Built: (9400) Swindon works; Robert Stephenson & Hawthorn, Newcastle-upon-Tyne and Darlington; Bagnall Engine Company, Stafford; Yorkshire Engine Company, Sheffield,1947–49 (210 built) (1500) Swindon works, 1949 (10 built)

Weight: (9400) 55 tons 6cwt (1500) 58 tons 4cwt

Driving wheel diameter: 4ft 7½in

Boiler pressure: 200lb/psi

Cylinders: (2) 17½in diameter x 24in stroke

Valve gear: (9400) Stephenson (1500) Walschaerts

Coal capacity: 3 tons 10cwt

Water capacity: (9400) 1,300 gallons (1500) 1,350 gallons

Tractive effort: 22,515lb (at 85% boiler pressure)

Right: Displaying its outside Walschaerts gear – the only class of GWR pannier so fitted – No1501 awaits its next duty at Kidderminster, on the Severn Valley Railway. When new, No1501 was allocated to Old Oak Common, London, and in December 1950 began a 10-year stay at Southall depot. Withdrawn by BR in 1961, No1501 was sold into colliery service, entering the ranks of preserved locomotives in 1970.

Above: 9400 class pannier No9466 was built by Robert Stephenson & Hawthorn at its Newcastle-upon-Tyne plant in 1952, one of a batch of 30 engines. The locomotive was briefly based at Gloucester before swapping cathedral cities and moving to Worcester where it remained for eight years. After spells at St Philip's Marsh, Bristol, and Tondu, South Wales, No9466 was withdrawn from Cardiff (Radyr) in June 1964. It is pictured here on the main demonstration line at Didcot Railway Centre, piloting a Class 35 'Hymek' diesel hydraulic, a not uncommon occurrence during the epidemic of diesel failures during the 1960s!

Left: Since being restored to working order in 1985, No9466 has travelled widely from its home of the Buckinghamshire Railway Centre. There have been several appearances at London Underground's 'Steam on the Met' event. Here, in its usual immaculate condition, No9466 pilots ailing LNER Thompson B1 4-6-0 No1264 on the approach to Amersham with an afternoon train from Harrow-on-the-Hill on 24 May 1998.

Hawksworth's other shunting locomotive displayed an American influence. There was a marked resemblance between the 1500 pannier tank of 1949 and the US Army 'switchers' seen in Britain during World War II. The 1500 was promoted as a '24-hour' engine. To achieve this, it would not need to leave its post for routine attention such as oiling round. That meant the use of outside cylinders and valve gear, since inside cylinder engines had to be positioned over a pit for even basic maintenance. In other respects – cylinder dimensions, wheel diameter, boiler type and the extensive use of welding in its manufacture – the 1500 mirrored its predecessor, the 9400. Yet, despite its 'austerity' look (running boards were omitted, for example), it was even heavier.

The 1500 had an exceptionally short wheelbase of only 12ft 10in. This enabled it to negotiate, albeit at slow speed, curves with a radius as tight as three chains. Unfortunately, this advantage was offset by the effect of the overhang at each end: anything above a moderate speed and the 1500 could become worryingly unsteady. Only ten were built and they were principally employed in the London area. Eventually, several of the class ended up in colliery service, including the only survivor, No1501. Two of the 9400s have survived: the doyen of the class, No9400, is part of the National Collection, while the privately-owned No9466 has become one of the stars of the preservation world, renowned equally for its reliability and never-less-than immaculate turn-out.

LONDON & NORTH EASTERN RAILWAY

A1 Class Pacific 8P6F 4-6-2

Edward Thompson's rebuilding of the first of the Gresley Pacifics, No4470 *Great Northern*, in 1945 had more to do with personality than practicality. It was Thompson's way of demonstrating that the Gresley era had well and truly ended. The rebuild was to be the basis of a new class of 4-6-2s that, judging from the prototype, would have been uninspiring performers. However, knowing that Thompson was approaching retirement, the drawing office at Doncaster appears deliberately to have prolonged the planning for the new Pacific. This gave Thompson's successor, Arthur Peppercorn, time to make significant changes. Far from being uninspired, the revamped design was one of the finest of British express locomotives. Its classification – A1 – was a fitting description.

Not all of Thompson's work was discarded. His scheme for the steam circuit was sound, as was the fitting of a large firegrate. At 50sq ft, it was 20 per cent bigger than that of the Gresley A4 and generated ample power even from poor quality coal. In most other respects the A1

resembled its predecessor, the A2 Pacific of 1947. The principal difference was in the driving wheel diameter which, at 6ft 8in, was 6in greater than that of the A2. The arrangement of cylinders and valve gear was the same and the boilers were interchangeable. However, unlike the A2, all the Peppercorn A1s were equipped with double chimneys and blastpipes.

The A1 had the distinction of being the last pre-nationalization express passenger design. However, by the time the first of the class, No60114, emerged from Doncaster in August 1948, the British Railways era was eight months old. Doncaster shared the construction with Darlington works, which contributed 23, and all 49 A1s were completed by the end of 1949.

Initially, the A1s were distributed the length of the East Coast Main Line, from Edinburgh to London. 'Top Shed' – King's Cross – was home to eight. Four were based at Grantham, five at Doncaster and six at York. Two Tyneside depots shared 16, with four at Heaton and 12 at Gateshead.

Above: Peppercorn A1 Pacific No60130 Kestrel *races through Sandy, Bedfordshire, at the head of an up express for Kings Cross on 7 August 1961. Outshopped from Darlington in September 1948,* Kestrel *went new to Doncaster and enjoyed spells at Kings Cross and Grantham before ending its days based in the Leeds area. It was withdrawn in October 1965.*

Above left: No60162 Saint Johnstoun *awaits its next duty on shed at Holbeck, Leeds, on 20 July 1962. This was the last of A1s to be built, emerging from Doncaster works in December 1949. Retirement came in October 1963 after a career spent based in Edinburgh, first at Haymarket and, briefly from September 1963, at St Margaret's.*

Left: Seen in the yard at Holbeck on 4 December 1964 is the first of the Peppercorn A1s, No60114 W.P. Allen. *Built in August 1948, No60114 spent almost two years at Kings Cross before reallocation to Copley Hill, Leeds, and – in February 1953 – to Grantham. Its last years, from September 1957 until withdrawal in December 1964, were spent at its birthplace of Doncaster.*

Above: On 7 August 1961, the 3.40pm from Kings Cross to Leeds and Bradford was entrusted to A1 Pacific No60148 Aboyeur, at the time a Copley Hill engine. Darlington-built in May 1949, Aboyeur was on the books of Kings Cross and Grantham sheds before settling down for a nine-year spell at Copley Hill in August 1955. Apart from a month spent at Gateshead, Aboyeur spent its remaining days in the Leeds area, being withdrawn from Ardsley in June 1965.

LNER A1 Class Pacific 8P6F 4-6-2

Built: Darlington and Doncaster works, 1948–49 (49 built)

Weight: 104 tons 2cwt (locomotive) 60 tons 7cwt (tender)

Driving wheel diameter: 6ft 8in

Boiler pressure: 250lb/psi

Cylinders: (3) 19in diameter x 26in stroke

Valve gear: Walschaerts (piston valves)

Coal capacity: 9 tons 0cwt

Water capacity: 5,000 gallons

Tractive effort: 37,397lb (at 85% boiler pressure)

Five were allocated to Haymarket, Edinburgh, and a further five went to Copley Hill, Leeds.

Above all, though, the A1s were renowned for their reliability. By 1961, the class had accumulated 48 million miles, equivalent to 202 miles each calendar day. These were statistics unmatched by any other steam locomotives on British Railways. Some of the best performances were put in by Nos60153-57 which, in a move to increase mileages between general repairs, were fitted with roller bearing axleboxes. Between 1949 and 1961, this quintet totalled 4.8 million miles, with an average mileage between works overhauls of 120,000. In a single year, No60156 *Great Central* of King's Cross ran 96,000 miles.

If there was a drawback to the Peppercorn A1, it was its riding. There were wide variations between individual class members, with some very rough indeed. The cause, apart from the inevitable axlebox wear, lay in the leading bogie. This was the same as that fitted to Thompson's B1 4-6-0 but no adjustments were made at the design stage to tailor it for the heavier A1. Changes to the loading of the bogie side control springs usually brought the riding up to a level comparable with other express passenger types.

By the summer of 1966, all 49 had gone for scrap. The last to be withdrawn was No60145 *Saint Mungo* of York, after a working life of just 17 years. However, their reputations endured and, in the early 1990s, the A1 Steam Locomotive Trust was formed to construct what would have been the fiftieth member of the class. When complete, No60163 *Tornado* will be the first main-line steam locomotive built in Britain since 1960. With sponsorship and help from companies as diverse as Rolls-Royce and British Steel, the project is steadily progressing. Fittingly, the A1 is to be assembled at Darlington and approval is being sought for 90mph main-line running.

LONDON & NORTH EASTERN RAILWAY

A2 Class Pacific 8P7F 4-6-2

Arthur Peppercorn's brief tenure in charge of the LNER's locomotive affairs produced three locomotive designs which, although derivative, were distinguished developments of the originals. One was a small-wheeled 2-6-0 based on the Gresley K4 (see pages 174-175), while the others were Pacifics. Classified A1 (pages 170-171) and A2, both built on the work of Peppercorn's predecessor, Edward Thompson. However, the performance of the Peppercorn engines was in sharp contrast to the unreliable Thompson designs on which they drew and in the A2 Peppercorn delivered – in terms of tractive effort – the most powerful express passenger locomotive ever to work in Britain.

Whether out of wartime expediency or envy of the stature attained by his predecessor, Sir Nigel Gresley, Edward Thompson took over as the LNER's chief mechanical engineer in 1941 determined to impose his own ideas.

Right: Peppercorn A2 Pacific No60532
Blue Peter undergoes a major overhaul
at ICI Wilton, Teesside, in August 1991.
Its Kylchap double blastpipe is
illuminated within the smokebox.

Early victims of Thompson's 'new broom' were Gresley's magnificent P2 2-8-2s, which were rebuilt as Pacifics and re-classified A2/2. Thompson then ordered that the final four Gresley V2 2-6-2s under construction were also turned out as Pacifics, the A2/1s (but retaining their V2 boilers). He followed these with a series of brand-new 4-6-2s, classified A2/3.

In all three categories – rebuilds, conversions and new engines – Thompson dispensed with one fundamental of the Gresley 3-cylinder format: the conjugated drive to the centre cylinder. Instead, all three cylinders had separate sets of Walschaerts gear, with the inside cylinder driving

The sole survivor of the Peppercorn A2s, No60532 Blue Peter, *stands outside the trainshed at Bo'ness on 24 October 1993. The A2 was taking part in a Bo'ness and Kinneil Railway gala weekend.*

Above: One of the Gresley features discarded by Edward Thompson but shrewdly reintroduced by his successor, Arthur Peppercorn, was the v-fronted cab. The simple act of angling the spectacle glasses reduced reflections from the footplate at night.

on to the leading coupled axle. The outside cylinders drove on to the second of the three driving axles. This was one innovation that Peppercorn retained when he took over in 1946. Several of Thompson's quirkier notions, however, were abandoned and certain Gresley features reintroduced, including the 'banjo' dome and the V-fronted cab.

The first of the Peppercorn A2s, No525 *A.H. Peppercorn*, was outshopped from Doncaster in December 1947, on the eve of nationalization. The modernity of the design was immediately apparent. A rocking grate, hopper ashpan and self-cleaning smokebox were all incorporated and, following the example of Bulleid's Southern Railway Pacifics, electric lighting. The first two A2s were turned out in LNER apple green livery, and this colour was also applied to the next 13 engines, delivered between January and August 1948. Repainting in British Railways brunswick green began the following year.

The A2s immediately displayed their qualities. They were fast, free-steaming and powerful. However, this did not preclude Doncaster from fitting five of the class – including the now-preserved No60532 *Blue Peter* – with Kylchap double blastpipes and chimneys. This device was the brainchild of the brilliant French engineer, Chapelon, and his Finnish counterpart, Kylala. On the A2s, it swiftly proved its worth with significant improvements in steaming capability and fuel economy.

Initially, the A2s were based at depots the length of the East Coast Main Line, ranging from New England (Peterborough) in the south to Edinburgh's Haymarket. In 1949, five were put to work on the Edinburgh-Dundee-Aberdeen route and proved the ideal engines for its stiff gradients and sharp curvature. The A2s also worked to

LNER A2 Class Pacific 8P7F 4-6-2

Built: Doncaster works, 1947–48 (15 built)

Weight: 101 tons 6cwt (locomotive)
60 tons 7cwt (tender)

Driving wheel diameter: 6ft 2in

Boiler pressure: 250lb/psi

Cylinders: (3) 19in diameter x 26in stroke

Valve gear: Walschaerts (divided drive)
(10in diameter piston valves)

Coal capacity: 9 tons

Water capacity: 5,000 gallons

Tractive effort: 40,430lb (at 85% boiler pressure)

Perth, Glasgow, Carlisle, Newcastle-upon-Tyne and, occasionally, more southerly outposts. In 1963, Nos60525, 60530 and 60535 surprisingly crossed the traditional LNER-LMSR divide and were allocated to a Glasgow depot, Polmadie. They replaced Stanier 'Coronation' Pacifics over the ex-Caledonian Railway route to Carlisle.

The swansong of the A2s, though, came in eastern Scotland with many memorable performances over the Aberdeen road during the early 1960s. However, it was on Stoke bank in Lincolnshire, location of *Mallard*'s 1938 world speed record, that No60526 *Sugar Palm* attained a speed of 101mph. That record for the A2s came in 1961; the following year, the first of the class was scrapped. The last three – Nos60528 *Tudor Minstrel*, No60530 *Sayajirao* and No60532 *Blue Peter* – were retired in June 1966.

LONDON & NORTH EASTERN RAILWAY

K1 Class Mogul 5P6F 2-6-0

Among the locomotives of Sir Nigel Gresley rebuilt by his successor, Edward Thompson, was one of the 3-cylinder K4 2-6-0s of 1937, No3445 *MacCailin Mor* (see pages 138–139). These engines were very much 'horses for courses': only six were built and they all worked on the West Highland line between Glasgow and Mallaig. The K4s were strong machines but, as with all the Gresley 3-cylinder designs, their performance suffered with declining maintenance standards. That was the situation Thompson faced in 1945, after war had taken its toll of his staff and his resources.

Thompson entrusted the rebuilding of No3445 as a 2-cylinder Mogul to his principal assistant, Arthur Peppercorn, who must have been impressed by the outcome. When he replaced Thompson as chief mechanical engineer, Peppercorn made the rebuild the basis for a new class of 2-cylinder 2-6-0s, the K1. Several modifications were made, however. The running boards were redesigned to improve access to the cylinder steam chests and there were changes to the leading pony truck, the cylinder linings and the boiler. The new engines were also longer and received bigger tenders, holding 4,200 gallons of water instead of the 3,500 gallons of the K4.

An order for 70 of the new mixed traffic 2-6-0s was placed with the North British Locomotive Company of Glasgow. They were the last steam locomotives built to an LNER design, although all were delivered under British Railways auspices. Numbered 62001-70, they entered service between May 1949 and March 1950.

LNER K1 Class Mogul 5P6F 2-6-0

Built: North British Locomotive Company, Glasgow, 1949–50 (70 built)

Weight: 66 tons 17cwt (locomotive) 52 tons 4cwt (tender)

Driving wheel diameter: 5ft 2in

Boiler pressure: 225lb/psi

Cylinders: (2) 20in diameter x 26in stroke

Valve gear: Walschaerts (piston valves)

Coal capacity: 7 tons 10cwt

Water capacity: 4,200 gallons

Tractive effort: 32,080lb (at 85% boiler pressure)

Above: Peppercorn K1 2-6-0 No2005 gets into its stride on the 1 in 37 climb out of Grosmont with a North Yorkshire Moors Railway morning service for Pickering in August 1991. The NYMR has been home to this last of the K1s since 1974. Built by the North British Locomotive Company in 1949, No2005 has been in the care of the North Eastern Locomotive Preservation Group since 1972.

Left: As with the Gresley K4, from which the design was derived, the Peppercorn K1 became a familiar sight on the West Highland line. Fittingly, therefore, the preserved No2005 has put in several seasons' work between Fort William and Mallaig. In July 1987, with the mountains of Bealach Breac and Seann Chruach as a backdrop, No2005 heads for Mallaig, passing the isolated chapel near Polnish, a distinctive landmark along the route.

Above: Reflections on the valve gear and motion of the K1, illustrating how the LNER apple green livery was extended to wheels, spokes, tyres and counterweights. Walschaerts gear drives on to 5ft 2in diameter coupled wheels.

The Peppercorn K1s proved to be useful and versatile engines. They worked extensively over ex-LNER territory but were chiefly associated with north-east England and, following in the footsteps of their predecessors, the K4s, the West Highland route. Like so many post-nationalization classes, the K1s had lamentably brief lives. All were withdrawn between 1962 and 1967, but the last to be retired managed to escape the cutting torch – but only just. In an ironic twist it was acquired as a source of a spare boiler for, of all things, the solitary preserved K4, No3442 *The Great Marquess*. In 1972, however, the K1 was donated, still with its boiler, to the North Yorkshire Moors Railway-based North Eastern Locomotive Preservation Group.

By 1975, the K1 had been restored to main-line running order and made an appearance at the Stockton & Darlington Railway 150th anniversary celebrations at Shildon, County Durham. Since then, NELPG has endeavoured to keep the locomotive on the main line (apart from when compulsory overhauls fall due). Recalling memories of the K1s in Scotland, it has enjoyed several memorable seasons on the summer Fort William-Mallaig service. Most of its time in preservation has been in LNER apple green livery; strictly incorrect for a locomotive built in 1949, but undeniably handsome. Recently, however, the K1 has appeared in BR lined black as No62005. In this guise, in May 1999, it broke new ground by working steam specials over London's Metropolitan Line.

BRITISH RAILWAYS

'Britannia' Class Pacific 7P6F 4-6-2

After the nationalization of Britain's railways in 1948, a team was set up to design a series of modern, versatile 'Standard' locomotive classes. The team, headed by Robert Riddles, first arranged a series of exchange trials to compare the best that the old 'Big Four' companies could offer. It was a fascinating exercise but, at heart, Riddles must have known which among existing designs came closest to meeting the requirement for simplicity, economy and ease of maintenance. They were the locomotives of his old employers, the London Midland & Scottish Railway – or at least those produced since 1932, when William Stanier took over as chief mechanical engineer. Every one of the Standard designs owed a debt to LMS practice, including the first to appear, the Class 7 'Britannia' Pacific.

Emphasizing the LMSR influence, the 'Britannia' was designed in the Derby drawing office and all 55 engines were built at Crewe. The first, No70000 Britannia, was

unveiled in January 1951 and set the pattern for naming the class after great Britons: poets and playwrights rubbed smoke deflectors with an assortment of historical figures. Despite this pedigree, there were teething troubles. In October 1951, all 25 in service were temporarily withdrawn after the driving wheels were observed shifting on their axles!

The first of the British Railways regions to sample what the new Standards had to offer was the Eastern. It urgently needed more powerful locomotives for the London to Norwich run and they were enthusiastically welcomed. They brought class 7 power to a line that had never enjoyed anything greater than a class 5, and they did not disappoint. Initially, the first 14 engines were divided between the depots at Stratford, in east London, and Norwich. Then three crossed the Thames to the Southern Region. One was No70004 William Shakespeare which, when new, was displayed at the 1951 Festival of Britain.

Above: Between June 1951 and June 1958, No70014 Iron Duke was allocated to Stewarts Lane, London (shedcode 73A), to work the 'Golden Arrow' boat train. It was then transferred to the London Midland Region, ending its days at Carlisle Kingmoor. Withdrawal came in 1967.

BR 'Britannia' Pacific Class 7P6F 4-6-2

Built: Crewe works, 1951–54 (55 built)

Weight: 94 tons 0cwt (locomotive)
   BR1 49 tons 3cwt/BR1A 52 tons 10cwt
   BR1D 54 tons 10cwt (tenders)

Driving wheel diameter: 6ft 2in

Boiler pressure: 250lb/psi

Cylinders: (2) 20in diameter x 28in stroke

Valve gear: Walschaerts (piston valves)

Coal capacity: 7 tons (BR1, BR1A tenders)
   9 tons (BR1D tender)

Water capacity: 4,250 gallons (BR1)/5,000 gallons
   (BR1A)/4,725 gallons (BR1D)

Tractive effort: 32,150lb (at 85% boiler pressure)

Above: Pictured heading eastwards out of Salisbury, the first of the British Railways Pacifics, No70000 Britannia was privately preserved in 1969 and, after overhaul, recommissioned by its designer, R.A. Riddles, in May 1978. During the 1990s, it performed regularly on the main line.

Above: Front-end detail of the single-chimney 'Britannia', with the chime whistle prominent at the rear of the smokebox. Within its 6-feet diameter boiler, Britannia houses almost a mile of tubes, flues and superheater elements.

This celebrity status continued as its new owners maintained it in sparkling condition to work the prestige 'Golden Arrow' boat train, a duty it shared for a time with classmate No70014 *Iron Duke*.

All this was in sharp contrast to the reception the 'Britannias' received on the Western Region. Around 15 spent time there – they were even given the names of legendary Great Western locomotives – but only one depot managed to get the best out of them. Cardiff Canton succeeded where Plymouth Laira and London's Old Oak Common failed. The 'Britannias' became star performers on the 'Red Dragon' and 'Capitals United' expresses. Another famous named train regularly rostered for 'Britannia' haulage was the 'Irish Mail', using engines based at Holyhead. These were part of the London Midland contingent which started at 12 locomotives and, by 1967, embraced all 55 of the class.

The pace of construction slowed after 1952 , with the last 17 'Britannias' being delivered over a 21-month period between January 1953 and September 1954. The final five became the first to be allocated to a Scottish depot, Glasgow's Polmadie. To mark the fact, they were named after firths, the Scottish term for river estuaries. They were mainly employed on expresses to Liverpool and Manchester.

Displaced by diesels from the Eastern and Western Regions, by 1966 the 'Britannia' Pacifics were concentrated on the London Midland Region. The days of working prestige expresses were over; now they were relegated to freight and parcels workings around north-west England. All but seven ended their days at Carlisle's Kingmoor depot. Two that did not were the only ones to survive: the first to be built, No70000 *Britannia* (withdrawn from Newton Heath, Manchester, in May 1966) and the last to be retired, No70013 *Oliver Cromwell*. Based at Carnforth, it was used on the specials that marked the end of steam on British Railways in August 1968. Today, No70013 is a static exhibit at Bressingham Steam Museum in Norfolk.

Standard Class 5 5MT 4-6-0

There were those who questioned the inclusion of a 4-6-0 of power class 5 among the 12 British Railways Standard designs. Even as the programme was being drawn up by Robert Riddles and his team, construction of the equivalent Stanier 'Black 5' of the LMSR was continuing (the class would eventually total 842). Additionally, British Railways' stock contained over 400 ex-LNER B1s and more than 300 'Halls' and 'Modified Halls' of Great Western origin. Surely, the argument ran, these added up to more than enough mixed traffic 4-6-0s?

Evidently BR's operating authorities thought otherwise. Moreover, the inclusion of a 5MT 4-6-0 in the Standard scheme allowed the incorporation of worthwhile improvements over its pre-nationalization predecessors, particularly to the benefit of footplate crews. Doncaster was appointed parent design office but the bulk of the construction (130 engines) was undertaken at Derby. Doncaster contributed the remaining 42.

With neither the resources nor the time for experimentation, as with all the Standards, the Class 5 4-6-0 owed much to proven – mostly LMSR – practice. A doctrine of ease of operation and simplicity of maintenance had been established under Sir William Stanier and nurtured by his successors, Fairburn and Ivatt. Unsurprisingly, therefore, the Type 3B boiler employed on the 5MT 4-6-0 was near-identical to that carried on the Stanier equivalent. Additionally, there was only a half-inch difference in cylinder diameter. Among noteworthy changes, the most visible were a two-inch increase in driving wheel diameter, to 6ft 2in, and the higher running plate.

The first of the 4-6-0s, No73000, was outshopped from Derby in April 1951 and 30 were in service by January 1952. There then followed an 18-month gap before deliveries resumed. Doncaster Works began production of the 5MT in August 1955, with No73100. By February 1956, it had built 25, with the remaining 17 of its quota being delivered between December 1956 and May 1957. The following month, No73154 concluded the Derby order.

The 5MT was one of several Standard steam classes still under construction when, in 1955, the Modernization Plan for British Railways was unveiled. Despite the huge investment being made in the Standards, the Plan nevertheless called for the complete replacement of steam traction. In the main, these replacements would be diesel locomotives and multiple units, all fuelled by imported oil. To many railway workers, including Robert Riddles, the policy was short-sighted. The future, he believed, lay in electrification and his new main-line steam locomotives would serve Britain's railways adequately until that electrification was completed. To make his point, Riddles instigated some modest experiments to demonstrate how

Above: One of five preserved Class 5MT 4-6-0s, No73096 was built at Derby in 1955 and withdrawn from Patricroft in November 1967. Pictured bringing a southbound demonstration goods through Medstead and Four Marks, it returned to service on the Mid-Hants Railway in 1993.

the efficiency of the steam locomotive could be improved. One was the use of Caprotti rotary cam poppet valve gear, which was fitted to 30 of the Derby-built 5MT 4-6-0s, Nos73125-54. The Caprotti gear gave excellent steam distribution and, if driven well, these engines were easily capable of sustained speeds of over 80mph.

Sadly, the outcome of these experiments had no impact on policy. The working lives of the 5MT 4-6-0s spanned 17 years, but they remained a complete class of 172 for just seven of those. The first to be withdrawn was No73027 of Swindon depot in February 1964 but the final two, No73050 and 73069, lasted until the very end of standard gauge steam on British Railways, in August 1968.

Five of the class have survived, including one of the Caprotti-fitted engines, No73129. It is being restored, as is No73156. Another, No73050, awaits overhaul, but two can be seen in action: No73082 *Camelot* on the Bluebell Railway and No73096 on the Mid-Hants Railway.

Above: Resplendent in lined green, No73096 comes off shed at Ropley on the Mid-Hants Railway. Its working life included spells at Shrewsbury, Gloucester, Oxley (Wolverhampton), Nuneaton and Croes Newydd (Wrexham) as well as two stays at Patricroft. In recent years, it has made a triumphant return to main-line working.

BR Standard Class 5 5MT 4-6-0

Built: Derby and Doncaster works, 1951–57 (172 built)

Weight: 76 tons 4cwt (locomotive)
49 tons 3cwt (Types BR1, BR1H); 51 tons 5cwt (BR1B); 52 tons 10cwt (BR1G) 53 tons 5cwt (BR1C); 55 tons 5cwt (BR1F) (tenders)

Driving wheel diameter: 6ft 2in

Boiler pressure: 225lb/psi

Cylinders: (2) 28in diameter x 19in stroke

Valve gear: Walschaerts (piston valves)*

Coal capacity: see table below

Water capacity: see table below

Tractive effort: 26,120lb (at 85% boiler pressure)

(* engines Nos73125-54 fitted with British Caprotti rotary cam poppet valve gear)

Tender types

BR1: 4,250 gallons/7 tons, Nos73000-73049

BR1G: 5,000 gallons/7 tons, Nos73050-73052

BR1H: 4,250 gallons/7 tons, Nos73053-73064

BR1C: 4,725 gallons/9 tons, Nos73065-73079; 73090-99; 73135-73144

BR1F: 5,625 gallons/7 tons, Nos73110-73119

BR1B: 4,725 gallons/7 tons, Nos73080-73089; 73100-73109; 73120-73134;73145-73171

Left: Fresh from overhaul at Derby works on 16 August 1962, 5MT 4-6-0 No73131 awaits return to its home depot of Patricroft (26F). Built at Derby in 1956, this was one of 30 of the class equipped with Caprotti rotary cam poppet valve gear (the cam box can be glimpsed above the cylinder). No73131 remained a Patricroft engine up to retirement in January 1968.

BRITISH RAILWAYS

Standard Class 4 4MT 4-6-0

As with the majority of BR Standard designs, the Class 4MT 4-6-0 drew heavily on postwar LMSR practice. Apart from the barrel being nine inches longer, the boiler and firebox were copies of those fitted to the Fairburn 2-6-4 tanks of 1945. In terms of its role, however, the Standard 4 had greater affinity with the Great Western 7800 'Manor' class 4-6-0 of 1938. They were similar in power and equally versatile. Like the 'Manor', the 4MT had a low axleloading – just 17.25 tons – which gave it a wide route availability. However, unlike the 'Manors', it fitted comfortably within BR's L1 loading gauge and could operate over many lines from which the GW engines were barred.

The parent office for the design of the 4MT 4-6-0 was Brighton but the job of constructing the 80-strong class went to Swindon. The process occupied six years, during which time British Railways unveiled the modernization plan that spelled the end for steam traction. Considering that announcement, some questioned the need to continue building the Standards, especially moderately powered 4-6-0s and 2-6-0s which BR possessed in abundance. In the event, less then a handful of orders were cancelled, although these included a final batch of the 4MT 4-6-0s destined for the Eastern Region, Nos75080-89.

The 80 engines that were built were shared between the London Midland, Southern and Western Regions. The LMR and WR received Nos75000-64, all of which were attached to either BR2 or BR2A 3,500 gallon inset tenders. There was, however, a 'local difficulty' on the Southern: the absence of track water troughs. Its 15-strong allocation, Nos75065-79, therefore received high-sided BR1B tenders with a 4,725-gallon capacity. The Southern's engines were also among those that received double chimneys. Trials at Swindon had shown that these raised steaming capacity appreciably.

Like the larger Standard designs, the 4MT 4-6-0s were equipped with rocker grates, hopper ashpans and self-cleaning smokeboxes. End-of-run disposal of a steam locomotive was never a pleasant task, but these devices at

BR Standard Class 4 4MT 4-6-0

Built: Swindon works, 1951–57 (80 built)

Weight: 67 tons 18cwt (locomotive)
50 tons 5cwt (BR1B tender);
42 tons 3cwt (BR2, BR2A tenders)

Driving wheel diameter: 5ft 8in

Boiler pressure: 225lb/psi

Cylinders: (2) 18in diameter x 28in stroke

Valve gear: Walschaerts (piston valves)

Coal capacity: 7 tons (BR1B tender); 6 tons
(BR2, BR2A tenders)

Water capacity: 4,725 gallons (BR1B tender);
3,500 gallons (BR2, BR2A tenders)

Tractive effort: 25,515lb (at 85% boiler pressure)

Right: Like many surviving BR Standard locomotives, Class 4 4-6-0 No75027 has now spent much longer in preservation than it did working for British Railways. The Bluebell Railway's No75027 was built at Swindon in 1954 and first allocated to Laira (Plymouth). In the ensuing 14 years it saw service around Oxford, on the Somerset & Dorset route, in central Wales and in the Liverpool area. Retained to work ballast trains on the Grassington branch, it was withdrawn from Carnforth in August 1968.

least made it easier, quicker and cleaner. In contrast to the Pacifics and the 5MT 4-6-0, however, the 4MT was fitted with plain rather than roller bearings. No doubt the extra cost was considered unjustifiable in a second-string locomotive.

The 4MT 4-6-0s were widely used on secondary and cross-country routes. Perhaps their most famous, and most photographed, exploits came on the ex-Cambrian line through mid-Wales connecting Shrewsbury with Machynlleth, Aberystwyth and Pwllheli. Here they worked in tandem with their cousins, the GW 'Manors'. The Southern engines were usefully employed on semi-fasts, especially out of London's Waterloo. These services had frequent stops and called for locomotives with good acceleration and 'sprinting' ability. The 4MT 4-6-0 fitted the bill admirably. Other engines found their way to the Somerset and Dorset line from Bath to Bournemouth, while a handful ended their days banking trains up Shap and Beattock banks on the West Coast Main Line. They also undertook steam's last rites on the picturesque Grassington branch, which ran from Skipton into the heart of the Yorkshire Dales. A quintet of 4MT 4-6-0s based at Skipton and, subsequently, Carnforth, hauled ballast trains along the line from Rylstone quarry.

The largely unspectacular careers of the 4MT 4-6-0s ended between 1964 and 1968. The first withdrawal was No75067, from Eastleigh, in October 1964. The Carnforth five, however, lasted to the end: Nos75009, 75019, 75020, 75027 and 75048 were all retired in August 1968. Of those, No75027 became one of six surviving 4MT 4-6-0s, two of which, Nos75014 and 75069, have seen action on the main line. Two others, Nos75029 and 75078, have worked regularly in preservation and only No75079 has yet to be restored.

Above: No75078 went new in 1956 to Exmouth Junction depot, Exeter, and spent the remainder of its BR career on the Southern Region before withdrawal in July 1966. After six years on the scrapline, No75078 joined the fleet of the Keighley & Worth Valley Railway, entering service in 1977. On a summer's day in July 1983, it crosses Mytholmes Viaduct with a train for Oxenhope.

Below: Harnessed to a 4,725-gallon tender for service on the Southern Region (which was devoid of water troughs), No75069 entered service at Dover in September 1955. It was retired in September 1966 but taken to the Severn Valley Railway for restoration in 1973.

BRITISH RAILWAYS

Standard Class 4 Tank 4MT 2-6-4T

The Class 4MT tank, the third most numerous of the BR Standards after the 9F 2-10-0 and the 5MT 4-6-0, entered traffic in 1951. It was designed at the one-time London, Brighton & South Coast Railway workshops in Brighton (and, in the main, constructed there), but the pedigree was pure LMS. The 2-cylinder 2-6-4 tanks of Stanier and Fairburn provided a well-proven starting point. However, departures from the LMS blueprint were needed to bring the newcomer into line with BR's 'universal' L1 loading gauge. Born from painful experience of a legacy of incompatibility, this laid down the limits of height and width for all the BR Standard classes. The distinctive curves of the cabsides, bunker and sidetanks of the 4MT tank were not a last flourish on the part of a Brighton draughtsman hankering after the stylish days of Stroudley. They were simply a means of keeping within the L1 dictates, but nevertheless made for a handsome-looking locomotive.

Although Brighton took overall responsibility for the design, detail work – as with the majority of the Standard types – was farmed out to other BR workshops. Swindon,

Derby and Doncaster all made contributions. The last two also constructed a proportion of the 155-strong class, Derby turning out 15 and Doncaster ten. The rest were Brighton-built. They were numbered in the series 80000-80154.

The Class 4MTs were regarded as the tank engine equivalents of the Class 4 4-6-0 tender engines (Nos75000-75079) and shared the same boiler type (BR5). Most of the motion components – the rods, links and guides – were duplicated between the two classes, although the tanks differed in one respect. They were equipped with two slidebars to support the crosshead.

In the original distribution plan for the Standards, the Class 4MT tanks were mainly to have been divided between the Scottish, Southern and London Midland Regions. Initially, the North Eastern Region was given just three and the Eastern and Western none at all. Eventually, though, the Eastern became home to some 40 engines and they became the mainstay of commuter services on the London, Tilbury & Southend line. Working out of the

Right: Bunker-first Standard 4MT tank No80079 drifts into Arley at the head of a Severn Valley Railway service for Bridgnorth. Built at Brighton in March 1954, No80079 spent eight years in the less sylvan setting of the London, Tilbury and Southend line, based at Plaistow (London) and, from December 1956, Tilbury depots. After the LT&SR electrification, it departed for the Western Region, ending its BR career at Croes Newydd (Wrexham) in July 1965. No80079 – which continues to be a popular main-line performer – has been a SVR engine since 1971.

depots at Plaistow, in east London, Tilbury and Shoeburyness, they put in excellent work on these demanding duties up to the completion of electrification in 1961.

The 4MT tanks became a familiar sight elsewhere in London. They operated out of Euston on fast suburban services to Bletchley; from St Pancras to Bedford; and from Marylebone to destinations in the Chiltern district. They even returned to Brighton territory, working services over the non-electrified outer suburban lines. In their later years, they handled parcels and empty stock workings out of Waterloo.

The brisk acceleration of the Standard 4 tanks, and their fair turn of speed, made them ideal for hauling tightly-timed suburban services, as they proved in and around Glasgow as well as London. They also established their usefulness on branch line workings in the West Country and on the ex-Cambrian Railway routes in Wales. Here, the Western Region mainly inherited locomotives displaced from the Tilbury line.

On the North Eastern Region, they could be seen working the coast line from Whitby to Scarborough, and

the class made a brief appearance on the Somerset & Dorset. Their versatility made them popular locomotives, something which has extended into preservation. With 15 survivors, the 4MT tank is numerically the largest of the preserved BR Standards. Eight have been, or are in service and three have been approved for main-line working. The restoration of two more approaches completion. One of British Railways success stories looks set continue.

BR Standard Class 4 Tank 4MT 2-6-4T

Built: Brighton, Derby and Doncaster works, 1951–57 (155 built)

Weight: 86 tons 13cwt

Driving wheel diameter: 5ft 8in

Boiler pressure: 225lb/psi

Cylinders: (2)18in diameter x 28in stroke

Valve gear: Walschaerts (piston valves)

Coal capacity: 3 tons 10cwt

Water capacity: 2,000 gallons

Tractive effort: 25,515lb (at 85% boiler pressure)

Opposite: Two generations of Brighton-built locomotives are prepared for service at Sheffield Park on the Bluebell Railway. Standard 4MT 2-6-4T No80064 (Brighton, 1953) dwarfs an earlier breed of fast suburban tank locomotive, Stroudley A1X 0-6-0T No55 Stepney (Brighton, 1875). No80064 was first allocated to Watford Junction for Euston commuter services and then spent the years 1959–62 on the Southern Region.

Above: North Yorkshire Moors Railway's No80135 erupts from the tunnel mouth at Grosmont at the head of a train for Pickering in July 1981. Brighton-built in 1956, No80135 is another survivor from the ex-LT&SR allocation of Standard tanks, ending its BR career at Shrewsbury in July 1965. It arrived on the NYMR in April 1973, where it was restored in an undeniably smart, but wholly inaccurate, lined green livery.

BRITISH RAILWAYS

Standard Class 4 4MT 2-6-0

The utilitarian 2-6-0 produced by George Ivatt for the LMS in 1947 (pages 166-167) provided the starting point for this BR Standard equivalent. However, as a comparison will show, a little more in the way of frills was sanctioned for the BR version. For example, a fallplate now linked the raised footplating to the front bufferbeam, substantially improving the frontal aspect. In other respects – cylinder size, wheelbase, boiler pressure – the Standard and the Ivatt were identical and fulfilled very much the same roles. The chimney, cab, boiler and other lesser components, though, were off the Standard menu.

Design work was undertaken at Doncaster, which was also responsible for building 70 of the 115-strong class. The last in the series, No76114, was also the final steam locomotive to be constructed at the 'Plant', as Doncaster works was known. It was the last of a line that included Stirling's Singles, Ivatt's Atlantics and Gresley's Pacifics. The remaining Standard Moguls were products of the ex-Lancashire & Yorkshire works at Horwich.

With its 5ft 3in diameter driving wheels, this sixth of the BR Standard designs was clearly biased towards freight working. An axleloading of only 16 tons 15cwt meant its route availability was virtually unrestricted. Batches were allocated to every BR region bar the Western (although several were to end their days at WR depots). When new,

35 were sent to the Scottish Region, where they worked over the bleakly dramatic Waverley route between Carlisle and Hawick. Others appeared on the 'coast road' from Dumfries to Stranraer. The Scottish examples were mainly concentrated in Ayrshire and around Glasgow: at one time Corkerhill depot was home to ten of the class. Five, though, found their way to Aberdeen (where they were regulars over the Elgin line) and three to Thornton, in Fife.

The Southern's Moguls (originally 37 of them) also became concentrated in one area, around Eastleigh, Southampton and Bournemouth. They were used on cross-country services between Portsmouth, Salisbury and

Above: Authentically coupled to a rake of BR maroon Mark 1 coaches, Class 4MT 2-6-0 No76079 strides away from Bolton Street tunnel with an East Lancashire Railway service for Rawtenstall on 27 April 1991.

Right: Viewed from the footbridge, 4MT 2-6-0 No76017 pulls into Ropley with a Mid-Hants Railway Alresford to Alton service in September 1989. Built at Horwich works in June 1953, No76017 spent its entire BR career on the Southern Region, first at Eastleigh and, from March 1960 until withdrawal in July 1965, Salisbury. It came to the MHR in 1974.

Cardiff, Reading to Redhill, Brighton to Bournemouth and over the Swanage branch. Their most celebrated duty was the London Waterloo to Lymington boat train. However, this had nothing to do with the engines' capabilities; it was simply that, among tender locomotives, only a 2-6-0 (or 4-4-0) could fit on to the turntable at Brockenhurst!

At first, the North Eastern region scattered its 13-strong allocation far-and-wide: Darlington, Gateshead, Hull, Sunderland and York. Later, all were concentrated at either Kirkby Stephen or West Auckland to work over the Stainmore route whose viaducts were not only spectacular but had severe weight restrictions. Like their smaller cousins, the Class 2MT 2-6-0s (pages 186-187), the 4MT Moguls were ideal for this line. They worked coal trains as well as passenger services and were a regular choice for excursions from Tyneside to the Lancashire coast resorts.

Apart from a pair allocated to Leicester, most of the London Midland Region's batch of 15 spent their working lives in the Liverpool, Manchester and Preston areas. The Eastern Region divided its 15 between two London depots. Five went to Stratford, on the ex-Great Eastern

section, and the remainder to the one-time Great Central depot at Neasden. Made redundant by dieselization, the Stratford engines were transferred to the Southern and arrived at Brighton. The Neasden locomotives also departed the capital, in this case for Chester and ex-Cambrian Railway territory.

In 1964, Eastleigh's No76028 became the first of the Standard 4MT 2-6-0s to be withdrawn. Three years later, No76084 of Springs Branch, Wigan, was the last. However, it had the good fortune to become one of four of the class to be spared the cutter's torch. However, of this complement only classmates Nos76017 and 76079 have seen service in preservation.

BR Standard Class 4 4MT 2-6-0

Built: Doncaster and Horwich works, 1952–57 (115 built)

Weight: 59 tons 15cwt (locomotive)
42 tons 3cwt (Type BR2A tender);
50 tons 5cwt (Type BR1B tender*)

Driving wheel diameter: 5ft 3in

Boiler pressure: 225lb/psi

Cylinders: (2) 17½in diameter x 26in stroke

Valve gear: Walschaerts (piston valves)

Coal capacity: 6 tons (Type BR2A tender); 7 tons (Type BR1B tender)

Water capacity: 3,500 gallons (Type BR2A tender); 4,725 gallons (Type BR1B tender)

Tractive effort: 24,170lb (at 85% boiler pressure)

(* Type BR1B high-sided tenders attached to engines working on the Southern Region)

BRITISH RAILWAYS

Standard Class 2 2MT 2-6-0

'Marvellous little engines' was the verdict of one railwayman on these smallest of the BR Standard tender locomotives. He was G.C. Bird, and for a period in 1953 he was relief shedmaster at Kirkby Stephen in Cumbria. Given the depot's engines worked the northern trans-Pennine line between Darlington, Tebay and Penrith, it was a well-earned tribute. Often in appalling weather, they daily faced the climb to the 1,370ft Stainmore summit. However, not all the duties allotted to the Class 2MT Moguls were quite so arduous. Although only 65-strong, the class was widely distributed, with examples allocated to every region except the Southern.

The Western Region received the first ten, Nos78000-09, and despatched them to Oswestry in Shropshire. From here, they worked over the ex-Cambrian Railway routes in central Wales. The North Eastern Region based nine at West Auckland, while there were smaller contingents at places as diverse as Sheffield, Rhyl, Chester, Motherwell and Liverpool. It is unlikely that any of the 999 BR Standards ventured further north than No78052 which, for a short time in 1957, worked the Dornoch branch off the main line between Inverness and Wick.

The BR Standard 2MT 2-6-0 was almost identical to an earlier 'go-anywhere' design, the LMSR's Ivatt Mogul of 1946 (pages 162-163). The differences were mainly in the substitution of BR fittings for the LMSR variety, with the taller and wider chimney casting of the BR engine being the most noticeable. Also distinctive were the upper cab side sheets which were sharply angled to come within loading gauge constraints. Like the Ivatt, the BR design had a tender cab to enhance crew protection and visibility when running tender-first. The tender itself was BR Type 3, the smallest in the standard range.

Darlington works was responsible for building the entire fleet of 65 locomotives and, for a time, construction of the LMSR and BR designs overlapped. The last, No78064, was completed in 1956 but the class remained intact for just seven years. Coincidentally, the first to be withdrawn – No78015 in November 1963 – was also a Darlington-based engine.

Like its LMSR counterpart, the Standard Mogul was arranged for a low axleloading, just 13 tons 15cwt. This allowed it to operate on most lightly laid routes and secondary main lines. Bizarrely, some of the class had a speedometer fitted. It seemed superfluous given that few, if any, of their workings would have come into the high-speed category!

Among crews, the 2MT 2-6-0 gained a reputation for being very sure-footed. Some maintained, however, that the engines did not always steam well. The loudest complaint, though, was about the draughty and dirty footplates. This was surprising given the efforts of Robert Riddles and his team to optimize working conditions in the Standards' cab layouts.

The BR Standard 2MT Mogul was officially rendered extinct in May 1967 with the withdrawal of No78062 from Bolton depot. Four were saved from the scrapline but only the Keighley & Worth Valley Railway's No78022 has been restored to working order. Of the remaining three, No78019 is undergoing restoration on the Severn Valley Railway while No78018 has returned to its birthplace of Darlington for similar treatment. No78059 is on the Bluebell Railway where, in the absence of a suitable tender, the decision was taken to rebuild it as one of the tank engine equivalents of the 2MT 2-6-0, the 84000 series.

Above: On loan to the Bluebell Railway, 2MT 2-6-0 No78022 climbs away from Sheffield Park with a train for Kingscote on the afternoon of 19 October 1997. More-or-less identical to the LMSR Ivatt 2MT Mogul, this was the smallest of the Standard tender engines.

Left: Running plate (driver's side) of the 2MT 2-6-0 showing the mechanical lubricator, lubrication runs, sandbox and boiler feed pipe. This design had the normal slide type of regulator valve in the dome, but the rodding to the cab was external.

BR Standard Class 2 2MT 2-6-0

Built: Darlington works, 1952–56
(65 built)

Weight: 49 tons 5cwt (locomotive)
36 tons 17cwt (tender)

Driving wheel diameter: 5ft 0in

Boiler pressure: 200lb/psi

Cylinders: (2) 16½in diameter
x 24in stroke

Valve gear: Walschaerts (piston valves)

Coal capacity: 4 tons

Water capacity: 3,000 gallons

Tractive effort: 18,513lb
(at 85% boiler pressure)

Above: The Standard 4 Loco Preservation Society completed the restoration of 2MT Mogul No78022, seen here running round at Keighley, in October 1992, since when the locomotive has been a valuable member of the Keighley & Worth Valley Railway fleet. No78022 entered service at Sheffield Millhouses in May 1954 and spent 12 years working on the Eastern and London Midland Regions, being retired from Lostock Hall, Preston, in 1966.

Standard Class 8 8P 4-6-2

In one sense, the solitary British Railways Class 8 Pacific was built by accident. Certainly, the continued existence of this maverick owes much to chance. During the formulation of the BR Standard range, Robert Riddles had argued for the inclusion of an express passenger locomotive in this power class. The proposal was rejected, however, on grounds of cost. Then, in 1952, Stanier 4-6-2 No46202 *Princess Anne* was wrecked beyond repair in the appalling crash at Harrow and Wealdstone. There was now a gap in the Pacific roster for the West Coast Main Line. Riddles' suggestion to fill it by building a prototype for the stillborn Standard Class 8 was accepted.

Riddles' first scheme was for an enlarged version of the 2-cylinder Class 7 'Britannia' Pacific. Unfortunately, the size of cylinder required would infringe loading gauge limits. To obtain the power output he wanted, Riddles reluctantly had to opt for a 3-cylinder layout. There were notable precedents for this, principally the Gresley Pacifics of the LNER, but Riddles did not want a repeat of the problems associated with the Gresley conjugated valve gear. The Italian-British Caprotti rotary cam poppet valve gear offered a reliable alternative. It also solved the problem of obtaining effective steam distribution to the inside cylinder and was free of the wear that affected conventional motion parts.

L.T. Daniels of the British Caprotti company optimized the valve gear and recommended marrying it to a Kylchap exhaust system. This remarkable device, developed by the French engineer André Chapelon and his Finnish counterpart M.M. Kylala, had demonstrated its capabilities on express locomotives both sides of the English Channel. To the dismay of both Daniels and Riddles, an orthodox Swindon-type double chimney and blastpipe had already been fabricated. In vain, Daniels argued that it would prove incapable of coping with the fierce exhaust generated by the Caprotti gear; the choke area was simply too small.

Above: The solitary BR Class 8 Pacific No71000 Duke of Gloucester *stands on the turntable at Didcot Railway Centre, its home for much of the 1990s, during which the Duke was an exciting main-line performer. Its performances were in sharp contrast to the 'maverick' reputation it acquired during eight years' service with British Railways.*

Opposite: Floodlighting highlights the detail of the British Caprotti rotary cam poppet valve gear fitted to 3-cylinder Pacific Duke of Gloucester, as the exhaust from its double chimney drifts into the night sky. The Duke was paraded for nocturnal photography in the yard at Buckley Wells on the East Lancashire Railway – its present home – on 24 February 1996.

BR Standard Class 8 8P 4-6-2

Built: Crewe works, 1954 (1 built)

Weight: 101 tons 5cwt (locomotive)
53 tons 14cwt (tender)

Driving wheel diameter: 6ft 2in

Boiler pressure: 250lb/psi

Cylinders: (3) 18in diameter x 28in stroke

Valve gear: British Caprotti rotary cam poppet valve gear

Coal capacity: 10 tons 0cwt

Water capacity: 4,325 gallons (with Type BR1J tender, fitted with coal pusher. No71000 was harnessed for a time to a 4,725-gallon BR1E tender)

Tractive effort: 39,080lb (at 85% boiler pressure)

The fitting of the Swindon chimney was the first, and most damaging, of a number of miscalculations that would compromise the performance of the Class 8 Pacific. Others only came to light much later. The ashpan was wrongly dimensioned and the damper door spaces had been drastically undersized, severely limiting the amount of air reaching the fire at high outputs. It was no wonder the locomotive was criticized for its poor draughting and unhealthy appetite for coal and water. The price of a good run with No71000 was usually an empty tender. What, in theory, should have been a high-performance machine gained a reputation as erratic, unpredictable and difficult to fire. It was no surprise that its working life, spent based at Crewe North depot, was limited to eight years.

Upon withdrawal in 1962, No71000 was at first retained for the National Collection. It was then decided that only the cylinder assembly and valve gear were of interest. After these were removed the remains were despatched for scrap, and if ever a locomotive looked beyond restoration it was surely No71000 *Duke of Gloucester*. However, undeterred by the enormity of the

task, the Duke of Gloucester Locomotive Trust was formed. The decaying hulk was acquired in 1974 and rebuilding completed in the autumn of 1986. The opportunity was taken to put right the errors that had blighted the locomotive during its British Railways days and, at long last, the vital Kylchap exhaust was fitted. Further work was then undertaken to bring the *Duke* up to the standard required for main-line running. No71000 made its main-line debut in April 1990, producing a series of spectacular performances. Those who recalled the enigmatic *Duke* of BR days were astonished by the transformation.

Since 1990, further enhancement of the performance of *Duke of Gloucester* has removed any remaining doubt that a full complement of Standard Class 8 Pacifics would have numbered not only among the finest British express passenger locomotives, but the world's.

BRITISH RAILWAYS

Standard Class 9 9F 2-10-0

The 9F was easily the most successful of the Standard classes. While the other 11 designs came in for varying degrees of criticism, the 9F was an undisputed trtiumph from the start. For the country that gave steam traction to the world to go out on anything less would have been unforgivable. Yet viewed in economic terms, the 9Fs – at over £33,000 each – were a waste of money. The Modernization Plan of 1955 had announced the end of steam traction. Nevertheless, over 200 locomotives were built in the aftermath of a decision that, in a relatively short time, would render them obsolete. However, the belated introduction of the 9Fs owed nothing to production delays; it was solely an administrative judgement.

When the post-nationalization plan for new locomotive construction was drawn up, the most pressing need was deemed to be for mixed traffic engines. Heavy freight appeared well catered for by the influx of surplus War Department 2-8-0s. Moreover, every railway company – the Southern apart – had its quota of eight-coupled engines. The fleet totalled over 2,000.

Others, though, looked beyond the arithmetic. L.P. Parker, motive power officer of the Eastern Region, argued that a powerful, fast freight engine could work key round trips, such as the Midlands to London coal trains, within the footplate crew's eight-hour shift. The savings could be substantial. When the 9Fs finally arrived, he proved his point.

The BR Standard heavy freight locomotive was to have been a 2-8-2 but, encouraged by the success of his ten-coupled design for the War Department, Robert Riddles held out for a 2-10-0 configuration. It posed some problems for his drawing office team. For example, with a 21ft 8in coupled wheelbase, and no sideplay permitted in the coupled axles, negotiating tight curves could have proved problematic. The solution was to omit the flanges from the centre pair of driving wheels, allowing the 9F to round curves of 400ft radius (300ft when moving slowly). This, and a low axleloading of 15 tons 10cwt, saw the class subject to few restrictions.

As if to demonstrate the point, the first 9Fs to emerge from Crewe went to South Wales to take over the iron ore traffic from Newport docks to the steelworks at Ebbw Vale. In north-east England, they were given another iron ore working: the arduous climb from Tyne Dock to the steelworks at Consett, County Durham. Trains weighing 787 tons had to be hauled up gradients as demanding as 1 in 35. Unsurprisingly, the 9F proved the master of these trains. It was, after all, the kind of task it was designed for.

The surprise came when first the Western Region, and then the Eastern, began to use them on passenger trains.

Right: Among nine of the once 251-strong 9F 2-10-0s to have been preserved is No92203 which was built at Swindon in April 1959 and, after seven years on the Western Region, transferred to Birkenhead in September 1966. Retired in November 1967, the locomotive was bought by the artist, David Shepherd. It has visited a number of preserved railways including, here, the Mid-Hants.

Inset right: Cab interior (driver's side) of the Bluebell Railway's Crewe-built 9F 2-10-0 No92240. To the left of the vertical water gauge glass are the dials of the steam chest pressure gauge (upper) and the vacuum brake gauge (lower).

Above: In March 1960 British Railways took delivery of its last steam locomotive, 9F 2-10-0 No92220. To mark the event, the locomotive was painted in a lined green livery and named Evening Star. *Upon retirement in 1965, it became part of the National Collection. It is pictured here at Minehead, on the West Somerset Railway, on 15 June 1989.*

The 5-feet diameter drivers proved no obstacle to fast running and reports of speeds between 80 and 90mph were commonplace. Wear-and-tear on the running gear eventually put paid to the fun, but not before the 9Fs had left their mark on the fabled Somerset and Dorset route.

Construction of the 9Fs ceased in March 1960, with the delivery of No92220 from Swindon Works. As the final steam locomotive to be built for British Railways, it was honoured with the name *Evening Star*. Just four years later, the first examples were scrapped despite having at least two decades' work left in them. The last withdrawals came in 1967.

During their lifetime, the 9Fs were subject to a number of experiments and modifications, the most successful of which was the fitting of double chimneys. In sharp contrast, the building of ten engines (Nos92020-29) with the Italian-designed Crosti boiler – a response to an edict to reduce coal consumption – was disastrous. Mixed results were obtained from incorporating a Giesl ejector in No92250, and from installing American-designed Berkley mechanical stokers in Nos92165-67. They all tended to prove that Riddles and his team had got the 9F right at the outset. The 9F was the ideal locomotive for its time; regrettably, that time was all too short.

BR Standard Class 9 9F 2-10-0

Built: Crewe and Swindon works, 1954–60 (251 built)

Weight: 86 tons 14cwt (locomotive)
50 tons 5cwt (Type BR1B); 53 tons 5cwt (BR1C);
55 tons 5cwt (BR1F); 52 tons 10cwt (BR1G);
52 tons 7cwt (BR1K) (tenders)

Driving wheel diameter: 5ft 0in

Boiler pressure: 250lb/psi

Cylinders: (2) 20in diameter x 28in stroke

Valve gear: Walschaerts (piston valves)

Coal capacity: See table below

Water capacity: See table below

Tractive effort: 39,670lb (at 85% boiler pressure)

Tender types

BR1B: 4,725 gallons/7 tons Nos92020-29; 92060-66; 92097-99

BR1C: 4,725 gallons/9 tons Nos92015-19; 92045-59; 92077-86; 92100-39; 92150-64;

BR1F: 5,625 gallons/7 tons Nos92010-14; 92030-44; 92067-76; 92087-96; 92140-49; 92168-92202

BR1G: 5,000 gallons/7 tons Nos92000-09; 92203-50

BR1K: 4,325 gallons/9 tons Nos92165-67 (mechanical stokers)